Velvet on Iron

The Golden Rule should be, and as the world grows in morality, it will be the guiding rule of conduct among nations as
among individuals.

Theodore Roosevelt, *Annual Message* to Congress, 1904

Men secure peace by using their power justly and by
making it clear that they will not allow others to wrong
them.

Thucydides

Velvet on Iron
The Diplomacy of
Theodore Roosevelt

Frederick W. Marks III

UNIVERSITY OF NEBRASKA PRESS • LINCOLN AND LONDON

The publication of this book was assisted by a grant from The Andrew W. Mellon Foundation.

Portions of Chapter 3 are taken from Frederick W. Marks III, "Morality as a Drive Wheel in the Diplomacy of Theodore Roosevelt," *Diplomatic History* 2 (Winter 1978): 43–62.

Library of Congress Cataloging in Publication Data

Marks, Frederick W.
  Velvet on iron.

  Bibliography: p. 213.
  1. United States—Foreign relations—1901–1909.
2. Roosevelt, Theodore, Pres. U. S., 1858–1919.
3. Presidents—United States—Biography. I. Title.
E756.M37   973.91'1'0924 [B]   79–1216
ISBN 0-8032-3057-5

Manufactured in the United States of America

082100

For My Parents

Contents

Preface

FEW presidents have compiled a more striking record in the conduct of foreign relations than Theodore Roosevelt. Beginning with his controversial response to the Panamanian revolt and ending with his dispatch of sixteen battleships around the world, he stirred recurrent controversy and never let go of the headlines. At the same time, he kept the United States at peace during a period of nearly eight years and ensured that whenever American marines landed in strength on foreign soil, they did so by invitation rather than by force. A partial list of his ventures, solely in the area of peace keeping, would include mediation of disputes in Latin America, Europe, and Asia, as well as effective action on behalf of international arbitration and a world court. One of two presidents to win the Nobel Peace Prize, he also articulated a well-defined philosophy, of which the idea that nations are bound by the same moral code as individuals and the slogan "Speak softly and carry a big stick" comprise but a small part.

Such a record has naturally attracted the attention of a good many historians. No scholar, however, has undertaken to evaluate Roosevelt's diplomatic career in its entirety. There has been no sustained effort to define his style as a statesman, no attempt to reveal the degree to which his thought and action may have been a product of his time. The reputation he gained in the eyes of the world has never been the subject of scholarly analysis, nor has anyone grappled with the thorny subject of his credibility outside the context of a single diplomatic crisis. It is for this reason that the following essays were written. Interpretive in nature, they include no more than a small portion of the detail that would appear in a traditional narrative history. Their aim is rather to erect a conceptual framework capable of accommodating the full range of Roosevelt's record while revealing its underlying strategy and technique. Emphasis is placed upon his use of power as a bargaining counter, the consistent parallels between his handling of domestic problems and his approach to foreign policy, and the way in which he was influenced in both areas by a personal conception of morality. A separate chapter might well have been devoted to the subject of tact, since this was a key element in his performance and one which has received relatively little attention. It is discussed piecemeal, though, because it seems better understood in relation to other personal qualities.

The research for this study owes much to manuscript collections and government archives in Canada, Great Britain, the two Germanys, and the United States. Everywhere one goes it is apparent that much source material has vanished over the years, leaving gaps in the record so striking that they actually tell a story of their own, as will be seen in chapter two. I shall not attempt to acknowledge my debt to all the careful scholars who have preceded me. Suffice to say that the path has been smoothed and the burden greatly eased by such men as Howard Beale, Thomas Bailey, Raymond Esthus, William Harbaugh, and especially Elting Morison and John M. Blum, whose brilliant eight-volume edition of Roosevelt's letters proved invaluable from the start. Neither will I outline the difference between my own view of T.R. and that developed by others; this will become clear enough in the course of the book.

I would simply suggest that while interpretation, by definition, proceeds at its own risk, Roosevelt presents the historian with a special challenge in this regard not only because he was the product of an age whose values differed markedly from our own, but also because he succeeded in keeping so much of his diplomatic maneuvering off the record. He penned some fifteen thousand letters and published over thirty books; yet he conveyed most of his confidential messages by word of mouth and went to considerable length to ensure the discretion of his listeners. His reserve is particularly evident in situations involving a military demonstration, and he resorted to a show of force more often than most other chief executives. This, in turn, has led to an array of scholarly interpretation running from left to right over a confusingly broad spectrum. To take just one example, the world cruise of the battlefleet has been variously described as a "practice cruise," a "search for prestige," a warning to Japan, and an effort to educate public opinion on the need for a larger navy—each of these possibilities being advanced as the primary motive for Roosevelt's action. Nor is this unusual. Any investigation of Rooseveltian tactics opens the door to one unsolved mystery after another, pointing always to the need for a broader analysis of his underlying thought.

Finally, it should be said that although T.R. was not one to light a lamp and put it under a bushel, his first reaction, when asked to comment on his seven and a half years in office, was that he had enjoyed himself immensely! Never under any illusion as to the ephemeral nature of popularity, he took success in stride and cheerfully relinquished the reins of power when he could easily have won another term. With all of his preaching and penchant for capturing the limelight, there was a boyish self-deprecating quality about the man which saved him from hubris and makes it all the more incumbent upon historians to record his full claim to recognition. Too often, he has been dismissed as a colorful character, full of fire and fury, who managed by some combination of good luck and good advice to contain the force of a bellicose personality. Too often, we have been intent on the outward appearance of the Rough Rider to the neglect of his fundamental caution and cleverness. If the following essays succeed in laying bare some of his less obvious traits while at the same time revealing the complexity of his approach to international relations, they will have served a useful purpose.

Acknowledgments

A GREAT many persons have shepherded me along the
path of my research. Among these, I should particularly like to mention the following: Lady Williams-Ellis of
Llanfrothen, Wales, for sharing with me the memory of her
illustrious father, John St. Loe Strachey; Frau Dr. Maria
Keipert and Herr Dr. Bernhard Gëhling for their thoughtful
easing of my access to records of the Auswärtiges Amt in
Bonn; Frau Gerlinde Grahn and Frau Gisela Mokry for similar kindness and patient help in the Zentrales Staatsarchiv,
Potsdam.

Mr. C. A. Seaton of the *Spectator* furnished helpful advice; Mr. Michael Doran of the Courtauld Institute, London,
trusted me in a valuable but uncatalogued collection of Arthur Lee Papers; the staff of the American Embassy in East
Berlin provided efficient assistance at a crucial moment;
and Milton O. Gustafson, Chief of the Diplomatic Branch of
the National Archives' Civil Archives Division, allowed me
to inspect record stacks not normally open to the public.
Wallace Finley Dailey speeded my search of the Theodore
Roosevelt Collection at Harvard, while Professor John
Gable placed his energetic command of Rooseveltiana at my
disposal. Nor can I forget the helpfulness and courtesy of
staff members who assisted me at Princeton's Firestone
Library.

Permission to quote from various collections in the British Royal Archives was granted by The Librarian, Windsor
Castle. I have also quoted from the Theodore Roosevelt Collection at Harvard University by permission of both the

Houghton Library and the Theodore Roosevelt Association; from the Laurier Papers, Pope Papers, and Minto Papers by permission of the Public Archives of Canada.

I should like to acknowledge a special intellectual debt to Professors Bradford Perkins of the University of Michigan and Walter O. Forster of Purdue University. Their enthusiasm for Theodore Roosevelt proved more contagious than they may ever have realized at the time. Students who signed up for History 496, particularly Mr. Christopher Dukas, acted as the perfect conductor for my own restless enthusiasm, to say nothing of their imaginative questions and answers. My wife, Sylvia Ann, has assisted me during some of the most exciting as well as trying moments of research and writing. She buoys my spirit, inspires me to persevere, and generally keeps the sun shining. Finally, to my parents, for whom this essay was written, I owe all that I am as well as everything I hope to become.

Velvet on Iron

CHAPTER 1

Roosevelt in Context

W HILE no two periods of history are entirely comparable, the gap between 1900 and the present yawns especially wide. A ride on the Staten Island Ferry cost the same in 1975 as it did in Roosevelt's day, but there exists no such constancy in the realm of ideas. When Secretary of State Hay termed the war with Spain a "splendid little war," he presupposed a concept of war and a definition of honor curiously unfamiliar to the modern world. Likewise, when President McKinley claimed to have fallen on his knees and prayed for heavenly guidance in his decision to hold the Philippines, he was attuned to a set of values now unintelligible to anyone but a trained historian.

This first chapter is intended to raise the curtain and set the stage for an understanding of Roosevelt within the context of his time. His diplomacy, too often judged by the light of current standards, deserves to be measured against such yardsticks as tact, vision, and the ability to strike a sober balance between power and policy. Even this will not suffice, however—nor is it really possible—without due allowance for the intellectual climate of the time. However unique T.R. may have been as a personality, he was also the product of an age. As such, he inherited a well-defined attitude on questions ranging from ethics and individual responsibility to race and imperialism. To cite just one example, his ability to reconcile ardent nationalism with the steady pursuit of cosmopolitan goals was an accurate reflection of the public mood, which combined patriotic fervor with an equally broad concern for international peace and

1

progress. Similarly, many of the changes in America's relationship with the outside world after 1900 were an extension
of trends already under way.

Prominent among these trends was a gradual thaw in
relations with Great Britain. Following Lee's surrender at
Appomattox, the British yielded to one American demand
after another. Having agreed to pay a liberal indemnity for
wartime aid to the Confederacy, they came to regard Canada as indefensible against American attack and decided to
transfer their garrisons at Esquimalt and Halifax to other
parts of the world. No sooner had they acquiesced in President Cleveland's demand for an arbitrated settlement of the
Venezuela–British Guiana boundary dispute than they proceeded to show a marked preference for the English-speaking side of the Spanish-American War, going so far as to
welcome their victorious offspring to the imperial club. As
Bradford Perkins has shown in his graphic account of the
period, British tars cheered American sailors on their way to
Manila, and when the dust of battle had settled over Santiago, the streets of London were decked with stars and
stripes. Vestiges of hostility and suspicion remained on
both sides of the Atlantic. But England was beginning to
view American friendship as a distinct advantage, if not an
absolute necessity. As she did so, she bowed to the abrogation of the Clayton-Bulwer Treaty, which, for half a century,
had barred the way to American control of an isthmian
canal. She also courted McKinley and Roosevelt for an outright alliance and seemed to demonstrate her sincerity by
withdrawing units of the Royal Navy from their command
posts in the Caribbean.[1]

Roosevelt, who counted some of his closest friends and
favorite writers among the British, contributed handsomely
to the spirit of rapprochement. He liquidated virtually every
object of discord between the two countries and would probably have sought a more formal tie had he not feared the
veto power of German and Irish-American voters. In an age
when President McKinley could benefit from the publication of a pamphlet entitled "How McKinley is Hated in

England" and when the House of Representatives could
block the naming of an undersecretary of state because the
title sounded too British, it is hardly surprising that T.R.
concealed his pro-British feelings and did his best to mute
the adulatory tone adopted by such admirers as Edward
VII and Lord Bryce. He could only have been relieved when
John St. Loe Strachey, the influential editor of the London-
based *Spectator,* treated his accession to the presidency
with cautious restraint; for, as Strachey himself explained
in a letter to the White House, he knew what harm could be
done in the United States by anything which might seem to
"ticket a man as a friend to England."[2]

But even if there had been no hyphenate vote and Roosevelt had not believed, as he did, that the British responded better to reserve than to "gushing," he would have
been wise to soft-pedal his desire for Anglo-American partnership in deference to the heavy residue of isolationist sentiment in Congress.[3] Most Americans could not yet envision
their country as a significant force outside the Western
Hemisphere, much less committed to an entangling alliance.
Both protocols by which the Senate endorsed declarations
of the Hague Peace Conference included phrases reaffirming
the idea of separation between Europe and the New World.
Henry White's signature on the Algeciras settlement won
Senate approval only with an amendment denying American responsibility for the future of North Africa.[4] The decision to take the Philippines was upheld in Congress by the
thinnest of margins; and the war with Spain was preceded
by a unique congressional self-denial regarding the annexation of Cuba. Thus, while the country drew ever closer to
Britain and Roosevelt contributed all he could to the general
trend, he was prevented from carrying it to its logical conclusion by the twin restraints of tradition and politics.

Closely related to this development, and in a sense the
natural outgrowth of it, was a deterioration in Russian-
American friendship. Despite ideological differences, the
two countries had always found common ground in their
mutual fear of the Royal Navy, a fact eloquently demon-

strated at the darkest moment of the Civil War when units
of the Russian fleet made a welcome appearance in New
York and San Francisco.[5] By 1900, however, the situation
had come full circle. The common friends were now England
and the United States, the common enemy Russian imperialism. Czarist penetration of Persia, Afghanistan, and the
Balkans affected England alone; but Russian ambition in
China threw British and Americans together in a joint
defense of the Open Door policy. At the same time, American acquisition of the Philippines increased the national
stake in China while providing an imperial base from which
to support it.

The year 1898 was extremely important, not only because the Philippine adventure established the United
States as a potential antagonist of Russia, but also because
it threw her into conflict with still another former friend,
Japan. For several generations, Washington had assumed a
strong position in bringing Western culture to Nippon.
American agronomists, bankers, and educators poured into
Tokyo. But, as the strength of this stalwart land began to
mount and it adjusted to the modern mode of life, it experienced a renewal of pride in its native culture. In 1895, a
decisive victory over China gave the Japanese an inkling of
their potential military strength and brought them face to
face with the unwillingness of the West to allow them an
equal place in the imperial sun. The United States did not
join the concert of powers which set out to block Japanese
territorial growth, but American entry into the Philippine
archipelago, followed by a declaration of opposition to the
dismemberment of China, brought the interests of the two
countries into pointed conflict.

Although mutual fear of Russian aggrandizement drew
Tokyo and Washington together in much the same way that
it inspired the Anglo-Japanese Alliance of 1902, it was not
enough to reconcile Japan to America's westward march.
American leaders, motivated by long-range military and
commercial ambition, regarded Pearl Harbor as a vital step-
pingstone to world power as well as the key to hemispheric

security, while the Japanese coveted it for its large Oriental population and valuable strategic position.[6] Furthermore, Washington had to decide whether to build a fleet powerful enough to humble Japan or be content to gamble on Tokyo's grudging tolerance of the American presence in Manila. Roosevelt chose the former, and, by 1907, mutual suspicion and fear germinated to produce a full-blown war scare which caused him to mobilize the bulk of his battlefleet and send it en masse to the Pacific.

One other power whose relationship with the United States changed dramatically in this period was Germany. German-American relations were generally harmonious in the years before and after the Civil War. Millions of German immigrants had come to New York in the wake of the European revolutions of 1848, and a formidable German-American voting bloc had sprung into existence. The German language became an important subject in school, and by the 1870s and 1880s no nation was as influential in American university circles as the land of Bismarck. American students and professors flocked to Heidelberg and Göttingen, where they were introduced to such academic innovations as the Ph.D. degree and the graduate seminar. For seven years, all operas at New York City's Metropolitan Opera House were sung in German, while American social and political reformers looked to Berlin for inspiration in the campaign for industrial justice.[7]

Only the prospect of an isthmian canal threatened this idyllic calm. One can trace the rise of the modern American navy to the time when Congress first awoke to the danger of a European-controlled canal in the Western Hemisphere (1881–1883). From this time forward, the United States became increasingly sensitive on the subject of the Monroe Doctrine as well as increasingly able to put the Doctrine into effect. During the same period, Bismarck's policy of relying almost entirely on the army for German defense was superseded by the movement for overseas colonies, naval bases, and a fleet comparable to any afloat. It is significant that the German decision to launch an ambitious naval pro-

gram came the very same year that the United States acquired Pacific and Caribbean colonies for the peripheral
defense of an isthmian canal. The two countries were thus
placed on a collision course, for Germany was as anxious to
establish a commanding position within range of the new
canal as she was to join the worldwide race for colonies.

The situation became crystal clear in 1898, when a powerful German squadron steamed into Manila Bay, ready to
claim any portion of the Philippines not acquired by the
United States. President McKinley preempted the entire
island chain. Germany, not to be denied, purchased several
groups of Spanish islands in the South Pacific which placed
her squarely athwart American sea lanes running from
Hawaii to Manila. She also concluded a long campaign for
control of the Samoan Islands by agreeing in 1899 to settle
for all the territory except the island of Tutuila which, with
its fine harbor at Pago Pago, went to the United States. By
this time Bismarck had characterized the Monroe Doctrine
as "an extraordinary piece of insolence," and State Secretary of the Navy Admiral Alfred von Tirpitz was making no
secret of his desire for naval stations in the Western Hemisphere. What Tirpitz had in mind, specifically, was a base on
the coast of Brazil, where three hundred thousand German
nationals had already settled; he wanted another one on the
Galápagos Islands or Curaçao, and he believed that Germany should aim at all Dutch possessions in the Caribbean,
including St. Eustacius and Dutch Guiana.[8]

In the years 1901–1909, the kaiser established a permanent naval squadron in the Caribbean and South Atlantic.
He threatened openly to occupy Venezuelan ports and
ordered soundings off the coast of Marguerita and Santo
Domingo. The Dominican Republic offered Germany an anchorage at Samana Bay, and Captain Christmas made an
abortive but nonetheless disturbing effort to capture the
trade of St. John with the aim of eventual transfer to Germany. Ill feeling mounted when Germany appeared to block
an American bid for the Danish Virgin Islands. The upper

house of the Danish parliament defeated a motion to sell these unprofitable satellites by a bare margin of one vote when two bedridden members, aged ninety and eighty-seven, were brought 150 miles to Copenhagen so that they could cast their deciding nays with the assistance of a prompter.[9]

As time passed, Germany enhanced her commercial presence in Latin America to become the chief source of Mexican arms as well as the principal creditor of Colombia and Venezuela. As such, she was naturally suspected of engineering Colombia's rejection of the Hay-Herrán Treaty, which would have granted the United States the right to build a canal at Panama. She seemed anxious to acquire the assets of the old French canal company in order to build a "Suez" of her own. Not only did Bogotá's regular minister to the United States maintain "close and frequent association" with German agents and refuse to sign a canal treaty; he left his post in the company of a prominent German industrialist. In addition, Roosevelt had firsthand information that an agent of the Wilhelmstrasse was buying votes in the Colombian senate.[10]

The General Board of the navy regarded Germany, as late as 1906, as the foremost threat to American interests in the Atlantic as well as the Pacific. Admiral Dewey, who had become outspokenly anti-German after a brush with Admiral Diedrich's squadron in Manila, went so far as to predict in 1899 that the next war would be with Germany. Nor were naval officers the only ones to single out the Reich as a signal threat in the years 1901–1907. Henry Adams foresaw grave danger in a German victory over Britain or France, and Secretary of War Elihu Root predicted in 1900 that Germany was about to challenge the Monroe Doctrine. John Hay harbored a similar suspicion. Even Roosevelt expressed misgivings, though he tended to be less of an alarmist than Hay or Adams.[11] He hoped to see an effective makeweight to German power in the formation of an Anglo-French entente, just as he regarded a stalemate between

Russia and Japan as the best insurance against an attack on the Philippines or an assault on American commerce in the Far East.

American magazine editors contributed to the Teutophobia by taking offense at "Prussianism" and describing the German eagle as "greedy." Germany, it was said, sought aggrandizement "with no regard to right." Could the Monroe Doctrine be thought safe when the kaiser was preaching a "doctrine of force" and proclaiming that the future of Germany was "on the seas"? There was speculation on the meaning of the Pan-German movement as well as on German plans to absorb the Low Countries for absolute control of the Rhine. By 1905, the *North American Review* was anticipating Wilson's wartime rhetoric by linking "autocracy" with war. And in 1906, when a German swindler donned an imperial military uniform and gulled the mayor of Koepenik into giving him the keys to the town treasury, the incident was thought "possible only in Germany . . . the civil authorities are accustomed to bend the knee in all matters of militarism and blindly obey the commands of the king's coat."[12]

Historians have been inclined to discount the significance of the German threat due to a lack of documentary evidence in the surviving records of the German Foreign Office. Yet the absence of such material must be weighed against a considerable body of circumstantial evidence to the contrary.[13] Furthermore, German records were deliberately destroyed after World War I for political reasons, and there is a notable passage in the published memoirs of Chancellor Bernhard von Bülow which runs as follows:

On February 15, 1902, Prince Henry embarked at Bremerhaven . . . for New York [on a good-will tour]. Before his departure I sent him a long communication in which, among other matters, I explained that . . . the Prince was not to touch upon the Boer War on his own initiative [in conversation with American leaders]. . . . Nor was the Prince to speak on his own initiative of conditions in Central and South America, and *on no account to let any German aspirations in regard to these countries come to light.* If the Americans displayed uneasiness on the subject of German plans to gain a foothold in these regions, the Prince could assuage all such fears by pointing to the peacefulness of our policy and the many other urgent tasks that demanded our attention elsewhere in the world, while dismissing the thoughts of military conquest as quite absurd.[14] (Italics added.)

Needless to say, England contributed to the American fear of Germany since she shared it wholeheartedly. In 1903, there appeared an anonymous pamphlet entitled *German Ambitions as They Affect Britain and the United States*. This was published in London and coincided with the first serious alarm caused by German warships coming off the ways on the Baltic. Kiel, which served as the kaiser's most important naval base, was plainly inadequate to satisfy national ambition, just as some years later the Kiel Canal, with its shallow draft, could not accommodate the newest German dreadnoughts in their passage from the Baltic to the North Sea. The day seemed to be dawning when a new Napoleon would seize Holland and Belgium to launch an invasion of England from the channel ports.[15] The population of Germany stood at an impressive seventy million as compared with only forty million for France and an equal number for Britain. Germany was also about to challenge British control of the Persian Gulf through the construction of a Eurasian railway.

But even if German designs on Latin America and the Caribbean had been a myth, Americans perceived the threat to be eminently real at the time. And it is only in this context that one can comprehend the full meaning of Roosevelt's corollary to the Monroe Doctrine or his intervention in such places as Santo Domingo. Fear of Germany was so fundamental that it continued to shape American policy under the pacific aegis of Woodrow Wilson. Much as Wilson abhorred the prospect of bloodshed, he authorized a preemptive strike against Haiti and made it clear to Denmark that if she did not sell the Virgin Islands to the United States, he would rather seize them outright at the start of a European war than risk their falling into the hands of Germany. One

did not have to be Admiral Mahan to know that Charlotte
Amalie (St. Thomas) was the keystone of the West Indian
arch.[16] Only after World War I and Germany's demise as an
imperial power did Americans begin to look upon the Roosevelt Corollary as a needless psychological burden. But by
this time, they had acquired the Danish islands and were
beginning to assume the position of a world colossus. By
this time, too, the leading nations of Europe had agreed to
prefer arbitration to force as a means of collecting unpaid
debts. The idea of colonial conquest had lost its legitimacy,
and the Western Hemisphere seemed secure from outside
intervention.

Such, then, were some of the elements of international
relations as they were likely to affect the United States
when Roosevelt acceded to the presidency. Turning now to a
few of the intellectual currents which helped shape the mind
of the young president, one is struck, first of all, by a rather
pervasive sense of absolutism. Walter Houghton suggests
that "of all Victorian attitudes," dogmatism is "the hardest
for us to take . . . the imperious pronouncement of debatable
doctrines with little or no argument, the bland statement of
possibilities as certainties and theories as facts . . . in a
word, the voice of the Victorian prophet laying down the
law." Macaulay was accused of "oracular arrogance."
Thomas Arnold gave the impression of being stridently
didactic, and the list could be lengthened to include John
Ruskin, Herbert Spencer, and Theodore Roosevelt, among
others.[17]

An integral part of this spirit was the tendency to define
issues in terms of right and wrong. Roosevelt's use of the
word "wrong-doing" in his corollary to the Monroe Doctrine
(referring to situations which might warrant American intervention in Latin America), his allusion to Colombian
leaders as "homicidal corruptionists," indeed, his general
approach to the broad spectrum of issues can best be understood within the framework of Victorian values. This is not
to say that he held an irrevocable opinion on every question.
On the contrary, he believed most public issues to be pru-

dential rather than moral in nature, and he changed his
mind over the years on a variety of major topics. Still, there
is something about the self-assured Roosevelt that, to the
modern mind, smacks of Tennyson's alleged response to
a lady who came to him one day for an opinion on some
sketches that she had done. His terse comment: "Very bad:
don't do any more."[18]

Beneath the moral stance was a considerable residue of
old-line religious faith. The word "God" appeared repeatedly in leading books and magazines. Ex-President Cleveland, speaking at the installation of Woodrow Wilson as
president of Princeton, represented school tradition as
stressing "Christian faith" as well as "manliness" and
learning. Protestant church membership increased 75 percent in the two decades from 1885 to 1905. Likewise, the
Review of Reviews, with a monthly section entitled "Books
on Religion" or "Theological Discussion," introduced its
readers to eight new books dedicated to a religious theme in
one two-month period during 1902. Among the titles were
*Christian Apologetic, Study of the Gospels, Bible Charac-
ters,* and *The Ten Commandments.* Equally common were
such articles as "God's Highest Thought" (*Outlook*), "A
Jew on the Originality of Jesus" (*Review of Reviews*), and
"The Rock of the Church" (*North American Review*). Most
striking of all was the Sears, Roebuck catalogue for 1906,
which listed seventy-five different kinds of bibles.[19]

The social gospel of Walter Rauschenbusch and Charles
Kingsley, however much it may have eschewed theological
dogma, sounded typically didactic. Ministering to the down-
trodden became a mission demanding the spare time of professional men and intellectuals as well as the politician.
Gladstone, not content with his role as British statesman,
felt the need to involve himself personally in the reform of
prostitutes. Tennyson, who longed to "do good work," experienced severe pangs of conscience in the passive role of
poet. "Alas for me!" he once exclaimed to his friend Hallam,
"I have more of the Beautiful than the Good."[20] His poem,
"The Palace of Art," treats this very dilemma of the artist

torn between his role as social reformer and his instinct to create what is aesthetically pleasing.

At the same time, there existed a unique code of conduct known as "gentlemanly behavior." Like the social gospel, it conveyed a militant message, but it applied more to the level of the individual. Thackeray, in a lecture on George IV, informed his listeners that to be a gentleman was "to have lofty aims, to lead a pure life . . . and through evil or good to maintain truth always." The critic Matthew Arnold stressed respect for truth as well as love of goodness; and Kenelm Digby, when he published his five-volume defense of medieval chivalry, recalled an ancient code of behavior which placed compassion for the unfortunate alongside the practice of chastity.[21] The word "Christian" was often attached to the word "gentleman"—Roosevelt, for example, spoke of Admiral Mahan as a "Christian gentleman"—but it was generally sufficient to be regarded simply as a gentleman.[22]

In a classic description of what a boy of seventeen should have read, the librarian H. L. Elmendorf set down nearly all of the components of gentlemanly behavior. The lad should be exposed, first of all, to Robert Louis Stevenson's essay "Gentlemen," even though this was a subject about which he had probably "heard quite enough already." Here he would learn how General Grant showed magnanimity at Appomattox by allowing Confederate officers to keep their sidearms. He would also gain a vivid impression of "kindly living," "quick tact," and "gentle consideration of others." Included among the traditional favorites on Elmendorf's list were *Gulliver's Travels*, *Pilgrim's Progress*, and *Robinson Crusoe*. But the seventeen-year-old was expected to be equally well acquainted with "the history and customs of chivalry," because "everything in the ideals of the knight appeals to the nature of the manly boy"—"hardihood, manly activity, daring, self-sacrifice, respect, and gentle deference for woman, the righting of wrongs, the succor of the oppressed." The youth should be well versed in mythology, hero stories, and the Bible as literature. It would be instructive for him to read Howard Pyle's *Men of Iron*, Scott's *Ivanhoe*, and Macaulay's "Lays of Ancient Rome." Finally, he could turn to Aesop's *Fables* and Kipling's *Jungle Stories* for their lessons in the power of kindness, the "nobility of obedience," and the "strength of the weak."[23]

Newspapers were reporting "valiant deeds" in the war with Spain. British troops in China were said to have behaved like "gallant gentlemen." Occasionally, one encountered a reference to the practice of dueling, which still figured prominently on the Continent as an expedient for the defense of one's honor. The Bellegarde-Kapp duel in Henry James's *The American* was entirely characteristic, with Valentin de Bellegarde telling his American friend that "one's honor . . . only knows it is hurt; it doesn't ask when, or how, or where," Roosevelt himself was challenged in an indirect sort of way by the Marquis de Mores, although nothing came of it. Increasingly, the duelist aimed less to maim or kill than simply to force an admission of defeat from his opponent. Several organizations sought to eliminate the practice altogether. In Germany, the Anti-Dueling League was about to bring out a journal called the *Anti-Dueling League Review*, and Alfonso de Bourbon et Autriche-Este had just formed the International League Against Dueling.[24] Nevertheless, the affair of honor continued to find powerful support in custom and practice.

To move from dueling to the field of American foreign relations, there are no better exemplars of the gentlemanly breed than Theodore Roosevelt and his two secretaries of state, John Hay and Elihu Root. Hay, in particular, possessed all the attributes normally associated with a "fine gentleman." Urbane, cultured, and refined, he also exemplified the moral traits of courage and honesty. And just as he insisted on courtesy as an indispensable means of fostering Anglo-American rapprochement, he considered the congressional clamor for unilateral abrogation of the Clayton-Bulwer Treaty dishonorable as well as ill-mannered: "Every man must be the guardian of his own honor," he insisted, and "[mine] will not permit me to take part in such an act."[25]

Roosevelt, for his part, defined America's responsibility to its overseas empire in terms of noblesse oblige and held doggedly to the idea that a nation is bound by the same moral code as the individual. This meant that the United States must be no more willing to accept insult from abroad than to give it. It meant that Prime Minister Laurier of Canada and President Marroquín of Colombia were expected to honor their unwritten commitments, since a gentleman's word was his bond. The president lectured Russian diplomats on their proclivity for telling lies in the same manner that he concluded a "gentlemen's agreement" with Japan to deal with the sensitive issue of immigration. Such a formula had never been used before to formalize an understanding between nations, nor has it been employed since. But it suited the man as well as the age. Concerned about the form of negotiation as well as the substance, Roosevelt once remarked to his friend Arthur Lee that "a good deal of the fuss and feathers connected with traditional diplomacy does not come easily to Americans. But on the whole, I think I prefer the European idea to that which is cherished by a large section of my fellow countrymen—that shirt sleeves and bad manners are inseparable from true democracy."[26]

One reason why the code of the gentleman impinged so markedly upon foreign relations in 1900 was that diplomacy could still be regarded as something of a personal matter, often between members of the same family. Edward VII of England was the uncle, by blood or marriage, of the German kaiser, the Russian czar, and the Spanish queen, as well as the brother-in-law of the king of Greece.[27] In addition, public opinion exerted only the feeblest kind of restraint in a world of emperors, kings, and dictators. Few of the world's people kept abreast of current events, few were educated beyond the rudimentary level. Great changes were soon to come in such countries as Russia and China, but the time was not yet ripe. To speak, therefore, of a man like José Marroquín of Colombia as if he were beholden to public opinion is to set aside the context of history. President Marroquín controlled the press of his country as absolutely as he did its soldiery. He was in a position to shape whatever "opinion" there was to be; and Roosevelt, as will be seen, was under no illusion when he held him responsible for the rejection of the Hay-Herrán Treaty.

The personal world of rulers was, of course, paralleled by many other worlds of a similar kind. With the process of corporate management and the committee system still in their infancy, a family name might still be synonymous with an entire area of enterprise. Carnegie, Morgan, and other titans of the business world vied in power with the lords of the press; and each, within his sphere, exercised an influence comparable to that of Czar Alexander or Japan's Meiji Son of Heaven.[28] In an age of heroes, Enrico Caruso dominated the stage of the Metropolitan Opera; Commodore Dewey braved mine and cannon to smash the Spanish fleet at Manila; and the novels of Horatio Alger graced the bookshelf of every home.[29] Roosevelt wrestled with graft and corruption, overcame physical handicaps, and arrested outlaws. He plunged cold steel into the hide of a cougar. Eventually, he would deliver an hour-long campaign speech in Milwaukee with an assassin's bullet lodged deep in his chest.[30]

Related to the cult of the hero was a mounting interest in competitive sport. Roosevelt's preaching and practice of hard physical exertion may appear strange to a generation which has the automobile for its constant companion. His advocacy of the "strenuous life" and his exhortation to "hit the line hard" may smack of militarism to the reader of today. In fact, however, the entire country was caught up in a new world of sport and sportsmanship. Men were expected to prove their virility by engaging in rigorous exercise, and those who demurred were sure to invite ridicule in the form of some word specially coined to shame the man of ease—"sissy," "pussyfoot," "cold feet," "stuffed shirt," and "mollycoddle," to name but a few. Women were expected to abandon the traditional feminine affectation of delicacy. An attractive girl now was one who could romp with her man and ride horseback. Bicycling became fashionable for both sexes, and a special "female frame" was invented. Special racquets, golf clubs, even rowing oars, followed in swift succession. *Woman's Home Companion* featured a regular column on "Physical Culture for Women." Music exuded a muscular energy in the rhythm of Sousa's marches, ragtime, the high-kicking beat of the cakewalk, and "Ta-ra-ra-boom-der-e." Such magazines as *Harper's Weekly* and *Life* instituted regular sports departments. Then, too, there was Bernarr Macfadden, who achieved instant success with a new publication entitled *Physical Culture,* proclaiming as its motto "Weakness is a crime."

Equally telling was the fact that *Puck* published a "phrenological" chart of Uncle Sam showing a cranium with room for nothing but baseball, golf, bicycling, and the like. The English could not have failed to notice that Americans won nine out of fourteen contests in the Olympics of 1896, or that American boxers so dominated their sport after 1892 that the world championship became synonymous with the championship of the United States. Physical training took a regular place in the American school curriculum alongside the stock-in-trade of academia, while football and wrestling matches ascended in importance to the intercollegiate level. Basketball was invented in 1891; Dartmouth College initiated a winter carnival for skiers and skaters; and the Boy Scout organization, with its stress on camping and exercise, came to the United States from England.[31]

It was not accidental that Thomas Carlyle, one of the chief prophets of the age, had extolled Cromwell and Frederick the Great as exemplars of a life in which man was made to fight. Other cultural leaders who admired forceful and dynamic personalities included Robert Browning, who developed a fascination for the character of Hercules; Goethe, who popularized the idea of *Sturm und Drang;* Darwin and Marx, who hailed violent struggle as a beneficent principle of life; and Spencer, who applied the Darwinian model of competition to the condition of man. Within a space of thirty years, Creasy's *Fifteen Decisive Battles of the World* went through thirty-one editions, and Englishmen joined lustily in the slogan "We don't want to fight, but by jingo if we do, we've got the men, we've got the guns and we've got the money, too."[32]

In retrospect, two texts by the British author Thomas Hughes, both published close to the time of Roosevelt's birth, afford an excellent illustration of the overriding concern with physical combat and competition. *Tom Brown's School Days* appeared in 1857, followed within a few years by its sequel, *Tom Brown at Oxford.* The Browns were squires of England who had fought in every battle from Agincourt to Waterloo and who went on "fighting to a green old age." Tom's stated ambition at Rugby was to be "A 1 at cricket and football and all the other games. . . . I want to leave behind me . . . the name of a fellow who never bullied a little boy, or turned his back on a big one." It would be hard to find a statement more typical of Roosevelt or to come any closer to a basic tenet of his philosophy than Brown's insistence that "fighting, rightly understood, is the business, the real, highest, honestest business of every son of man"; or again, that "I am dead [set] against crying peace when there is no peace." T.R., who envisioned life as a never-ending *battle* to "do good work," had one basic complaint against pacifists: that in the name of peace, they would sit idly by while thousands of innocent Armenians and Cubans were put to the sword.[33]

Just as Charles Kingsley, the leading "Brown" in England, boasted of hunters and fighters in his family line and described himself as "a strong, daring, sporting, wild man-of-the-woods," so too did the foremost "Brown" in America cultivate the image of hunter and fighter. Roosevelt enhanced his reputation by leading troops into battle and was frequently observed on his way to the woods with rifle or chopping axe in hand. Just as Kingsley found in Shakespeare's sonnets an admission of weakness on the part of

the author, T.R. judged Henry James effeminate for his expatriate flight to England and his Olympian detachment
from the heat of everyday existence.[34]

No doubt Roosevelt was unique in the intensity with
which he sought physical vigor. One teatime guest at the
White House had the delightful experience of glimpsing a
grinning president in the full dress of a fencer. Nor was this
out of the ordinary. He drove himself so relentlessly that he
could walk or row up to twenty miles a day. One pictures
him climbing the Matterhorn on his honeymoon or remaining in the saddle for eighteen hours at a stretch. On
one memorable occasion, he finished the last forty-five
minutes of a fox hunt, hurdles and all, with a broken arm.
He wrestled with professional sparring partners in the Governor's Mansion, shifted to the less dangerous sport of boxing in the White House, and gave this up when it cost him a
portion of his eyesight—but only to take up jujitsu!

Every student of the Roosevelt saga knows that there
was good reason for such a frenetic pace. T.R. began life as a
frail and asthmatic child, believing that only through steady
application of will power to the task of body building would
he ever acquire the stamina necessary to play a normal role
in the affairs of men. What is less well known is that this
represented the conventional wisdom of the day. We are
told, for example, that when Sir John Morley beheld the
French Renan looking sickly and pale, he instantly urged a
regimen of exercise and fresh air. Henry White, one of the
ablest men in the American diplomatic service, spent several years in the out-of-doors to overcome a youthful tendency toward tuberculosis. Nor should one overlook the
case of Jules Jusserand, French ambassador to the United
States. This suave envoy and accomplished critic of medieval literature liked to recall how, as a youngster, he had
swum in the coldest possible water, gone without an over-
coat until he spat blood, and placed a board between his
mattress and sheets. Later in life, he was immensely pleased
that he could climb the blocks of a pyramid ahead of his
Egyptian guide.[35]

Not only did people believe in strenuous exercise; they paid attention to physical details which today sound superficial. It mattered then how men and women carried themselves, how they dressed, how tall or muscular they might happen to be. If the president remarked that a particular chap belonged "to the viking age," or if he was impressed with Oliver Wendell Holmes for having absorbed three bullets during the Civil War, such impressions were not unusual. The scholarly Jusserand once marveled at "a gigantic white-bearded Scot," and the editors of the *North American Review* approved the new king of Italy, at least in part, because he could "sit for hours in the saddle without feeling fatigued."[36]

In the sphere of foreign policy, this preoccupation with the physical contributed to the spirit of imperialism. What better way to remain fit than to engage in some colonial endeavor which demanded the highest level of toughness and self-discipline? The alternative to bodily vigor in this case might well mean annihilation at the hands of a superior number of native tribesmen. Excellence at sport allowed one to mix with the natives and popularize the culture of the mother country while, at the same time, keeping one's distance. Was it not said that when Gurkha met Gurkha in a contest of sportsmanship, all were "three parts Englishmen"? There were many who believed, along with Roosevelt, that the national fiber would be strengthened by shouldering the burden of empire, although he was unique in having his words on the subject translated into many foreign languages. In *The Strenuous Life,* he warned Americans against a life of safety and security. Trumpets of martial duty were beckoning them to the manly fray. They must not "sit huddled" within their borders or avow themselves "merely an assemblage of well-to-do hucksters who care nothing for what happens beyond." With the frontier movement at an end in the United States, they must build an isthmian canal and "grasp the points of vantage," for herein lay the path of honor and the means of maintaining the fighting edge. If the country did not go forward, "some stronger, manlier" power would step in and do the work instead.[37]

The Roosevelt who lived to hear Wilson sound the death knell of imperialism was born in a world of gunboat diplomacy where the use of force for the collection of debts was axiomatic. It was a world fast being carved into sections of rival empire. During the 1850s, France pushed into North Africa and Southeast Asia. Britain established herself at Hong Kong and penetrated to the heart of the Chinese economy. Russia took advantage of China's catastrophic Taiping Rebellion to lop off huge appendages of the Mandarin empire. By the last decades of the century, a great struggle was underway for the remaining uncolonized areas of the world, with nearly all of Africa falling into one colonial lap or another. Britain maintained the lead, with France close behind, Germany third, and the cross-channel competition especially keen. Indeed, had it not been for Anglo-French rivalry in the Pacific, there might have been no further room for the United States to expand in 1898.

Plainly, it was not a question of *whether* to rule, but rather of *who* would rule. The *North American Review* spoke favorably of a German-British-American condominium of Latin America because it was generally assumed that imperialism had proven to be a force for world peace.[38] According to the *Suddentsche Monatshefte* of Munich, if one were to "look at the map of Europe during the Middle Ages and see all the blood and agony and oppression and follow the many wars," one would "find that centralized power makes for peace and that the story of peace is the story of the concentration of sovereignty." To be sure, most observers distinguished between various forms of imperialism. Roosevelt deemed the breakup of the Turkish and Austro-Hungarian empires as much in the interest of world peace as the establishment of benevolent colonial rule in less developed parts of the world. He realized full well that the colonial record contained many a dark page and that imperialism represented but a temporary stage in the development of civilization. Yet he was impressed, as were his contemporaries, by the many cases in which it had proven to be an efficient method of bringing order out of chaos.[39]

There was France's achievement in Algeria, where an organized piracy of centuries had at last been extinguished. Prior to 1830, when the fleur-de-lis first began to wave over North Africa, the United States had paid annual tribute to pirate kings for the "privilege" of plying Mediterranean sea lanes. Not only had this humiliating practice been obviated, but the natives of North Africa were experiencing an immense benefit in agricultural yield, tax collection, sanitation, and roads. On a similar order was the work England was doing in the Sudan, where she had put an end to the dreadful Mahdi massacres. And the same was said about Russian conquest of the khanates of Central Asia.[40] When the British entered Malaya, local chieftains had been engaged in such devastating internecine strife over such a long period of time that they actually welcomed foreign intervention. Thereafter, it could be said that:

The total revenue of 1875 . . . was 409,394 dollars; in 1896 it amounted to 8,434,083.

The value of total imports and exports was in 1876, as far as could be ascertained, a million and a half dollars; in 1896 it just touched fifty millions.

In 1874, beyond an occasional native path or elephant track through the jungle, no road existed; now a network of well graded and macadamised roads traverse these states. In addition, railway works have been carried on, and are being rapidly extended, and last year's revenue from these was a little over 300,000 dollars.

Irrigation works have made good progress.

In civil administration the establishment of judicial and police tribunals, schools, hospitals, as well as a police station and gaols, all the needs of civilization, have been provided; nor has culture in the formation of museums and libraries, been wholly neglected.[41]

Such an account of imperialism, strange as it may sound to the modern ear, was standard fare in the early 1900s. The American record in Cuba, the German record in Kiaochow,

the Japanese feats in Korea appeared in too positive a light
to allow much doubt that the system as a whole operated to
everyone's advantage.

Nor was Malaya the only area where native leadership
invited imperial rule. Many people, wracked by riot and
anarchy, were ready to accept the imposition of order by an
outside power at the cost of nominal independence. The municipal council of Panama requested American supervision
of national elections in 1906, and many American officials
predicted that Cuba would seek annexation in view of the
fact that one of her major parties was on record as favoring
it. One of the best examples in the Western Hemisphere of a
native invitation to imperialism is the Dominican Republic,
which offered itself as a protectorate to both the United
States and Germany in 1849, to Spain in 1861, to the United
States again in 1877, to Germany again in 1898, and to the
United States for a third time in 1903.[42] Although Congress
balked at Roosevelt's decision to take charge of Dominican
customs in 1906, such action could hardly be construed as
irregular by the then-current standard. It had been authorized by international judges and welcomed by a helpless
Santo Domingo.[43] According to one observer:

Marauding bands roamed over the country; the capital was be-
seiged; the house of the American diplomatic representative was
repeatedly pierced by shells; American naval vessels were fired
upon, and one non-commissioned officer was killed, as the American diplomatic representative declared, deliberately; an American
merchant steamer . . . was fired upon . . . the unfortified town of
San Pedro de Macoris inhabited largely by foreigners, was taken
and retaken three times, and twice bombarded; American sugar
estates were preyed upon . . . the American railway, running from
Puerto Plata to Santiago . . . was seized . . . the tracks torn up and
a station burned.[44]

Even under normal circumstances, the Dominican Republic
had not been in the habit of collecting its own customs. The
job had been entrusted to a Dutch firm by the name of
Westendorp and Company. Westendorp was given certifi-

cates known as *pagares* which authorized a direct levy on specified merchants at the harbor docks. For years, the proceeds of this collection were turned over to the creditors of the Dominican government. In 1893, Westendorp was replaced by an American firm, the Santo Domingo Improvement Company. But the process remained basically the same.[45]

If, at a distance of eighty years, it is hard to imagine a time when the constructive side of imperialism drew so much favorable attention, it is equally difficult to understand the powerful patriotic sentiment that gripped Roosevelt's generation. By present-day standards, it appears hardly distinguishable from chauvinism. Viewed in its proper context, however, it turns out to be something of a rather different sort. Until the end of the nineteenth century, the United States had been despised by kings, patronized by intellectuals, and feared by few. Mexico, in 1846, expected to pluck the feathers of the American eagle the moment it crossed the Rio Grande. As late as 1891, the United States Navy could not face the prospect of doing battle with a disputatious Chile without misgivings. By 1900, however, the United States had not only fielded some of the largest armies known to man. She had become the world's leading producer of wheat, iron, coal, and steel. Three-quarters of the world's cotton grew to maturity in the land of Dixie, and American manufactured goods were worth three times as much as those produced in England.

The country exported more than it imported and was moving rapidly toward a similar balance in the area of foreign investment. Singer Sewing Machine opened its first plant in Glasgow in 1867. The Diamond Match Company exported an automatic dipping process to England in 1896 which captured 50 percent of the British market in five years. J. P. Morgan sought to acquire England's entire trans-Atlantic shipping business, and he might well have done so had Parliament not come to the assistance of Cunard. Britain approached the United States for its first loan at the turn of the century. Ford Motor Company opened its London office in 1908, and soon absorbed a third of the automobile market.

Predictably, the approach of American hegemony aroused suspicion and fear across the Atlantic, as well as the usual adulation accorded a potential winner. British journalist William T. Stead concluded that the United States exerted such irresistible force in social, political, and economic matters that the best future for his country lay in a form of reunion with the colonial offspring. At the same time, there was much talk in Europe and Latin America of the "American danger."[46] Germans fretted over American "arrogance" as well as the "danger" of American trusts. In one instance, Yankees were said to be acquiring the Bremen and Hamburg Lines; in another, it was rumored that financiers in the United States were about to gain control of the Canadian Pacific and Grand Trunk railroads.[47]

Americans, who now outnumbered the population of every European power except Russia, awaited the imminent triumph of democracy over aristocracy. They had no idea that a communist revolution would someday change the rules of the political game so radically that it would no longer be a contest between the many and the few, but rather between two forms of government both claiming to be popular. For the men of 1900, the future seemed cloudless. America, long a leader in the cause of women's suffrage, female education, peace organization, and political reform, would continue to point the way to progress. And while some observers, Roosevelt included, sensed the limitations of American democracy as a universal panacea, this did not lessen their pride in events of the past as well as the probable shape of things to come.[48]

Brooks Adams published *American Economic Supremacy* in 1899, about the same time that Andrew Carnegie came out with *Triumphant Democracy*. Although these titles speak for themselves, the graphic cover of Carnegie's book showed two pyramids, one representing democracy and standing squarely on its base, the other, symbolizing monarchy, turned upside down. Carnegie, known to some as the "Star-Spangled Scotchman," urged the British to join a Re-United States of America, noting that a majority of the English-speaking people were now republican and that the United States possessed sufficient wealth to purchase all of England, Ireland, and Scotland, along with the entire British national debt. A proud State Department under the leadership of "Jingo Jim" Blaine had already abandoned the use of such "British" terms as "gracious" and "gratefully" in its official correspondence. It no longer "ventured to hope" but rather "expected," when addressing a demand to Downing Street, and it elevated its first class envoys to the rank of ambassador. As if to swell the tide of nationalism still further, the Washington Monument was completed in 1893, and John Philip Sousa reached the crest of his popularity with such marches as "Semper Fidelis," "High School Cadets," and "Stars and Stripes Forever." Successful athletes representing the United States in overseas competition saluted "the good old American flag." They thrilled to the sound of the band as it crashed into "The Star-Spangled Banner." Indeed, it was said of the thousands of Americans present at Athens's Olympic Stadium in 1906 that they wanted nothing more than "to allow the eagle to scream." They were proud of "the natural ability of an American when placed in a position with responsibility on his shoulders," and they rejoiced that the games had been "a glorious event for Uncle Sam."[49]

To this could be added many other signs of the time: the "Pledge of Allegiance," the first appearance of multivolume histories of the United States, and a spate of spread-eagled rhetoric. In 1896, the year after Secretary of State Richard Olney fired his "twenty-inch" blast at England for her alleged aggression against Venezuela, Senator Roger Q. Mills proclaimed grandly in the national capital that "God was the author of the Monroe Doctrine." Two years later, Albert J. Beveridge delivered his celebrated "March of the Flag" speech, quoted so often it has lost its original air of earnest entreaty: "Have we no mission to perform? . . . [Are we] merely to rot in our own selfishness, as men and nations must, who take cowardice for their companion and self for their Deity—as China has, as India has, as Egypt has? . . . Fellow Americans, we are God's chosen people. . . . We cannot retreat from any soil where Providence has unfurled our banner."[50]

Only within such a context can one begin to gauge the true meaning of Roosevelt's language. Only in this setting can one imagine how the polished John Hay could boast that "the greatest destiny the world ever knew is ours."[51] To the average American of 1900, this was not chauvinism. It was a statement of fact.

Equally interesting is the realization that this same sentiment formed part of a *Weltanschauung* more international, in some respects, than anything before or since. The United States in the years 1901–1909, with all its bumptious insularity, reached out to the world with impressive zest. Roosevelt accelerated the trend toward world involvement, setting the compass and giving the example. But he himself was carried along by the momentum of a cosmopolitan age. Anyone privileged enough to scan the guest list for Edward VII's coronation would have realized in an instant the broadening influence of empire. London and other capitals of western Europe had become nerve centers for receiving and transmitting messages in virtually every tongue. This was a time when the Christian missionary movement, heavily based in America, brought news from all corners of the earth and, because it enjoyed unusual freedom of movement, held out great hope for the future of democracy and Christianity. With universal peace and world government seemingly near at hand, public-spirited men conceived a wide array of cultural and scientific projects designed to knit the people of the globe more closely together. The Russian linguist Zamenhof had only to devise an international language in 1887, and overnight Esperanto clubs flourished in every major city. Ambitious engineering projects based on a similar ideal were being pressed to completion, among them the laying of the Pacific cable and the digging of the

Simplon Tunnel between Italy and Switzerland. There was serious talk of tunneling the English Channel and the Bering Strait, while in the Western Hemisphere the goal was a transcontinental railway to link Canada with Chile.

Americans reflected this cosmopolitan spirit in a variety of ways. First, they went abroad in unprecedented numbers. Nellie Bly of the *New York World* set a record in 1889 when she circled the globe in less than the eighty days taken by Jules Verne's fictional hero, Phileas Fogg. By 1900, *International* magazine could report more than a hundred thousand people leaving the United States annually to take their leisure overseas. Novels began to treat the familiar theme of the American in Europe, and a new kind of travel magazine appeared which combined traditional narrative with an analysis of foreign institutions. *Around the World* and *The 400,* founded in 1893, offered accounts of travel, exploration, and science. They were soon followed by *National Geographic* and *Four Track News* (renamed *Travel Magazine* in 1906). Americans were marrying foreigners at a rate never again equaled—so rapidly, in fact, that by 1906 no less than six heads of foreign missions in Washington had taken American partners. German universities like Göttingen and Heidelberg, which had trained a good number of Americans in the 1850s, were now educating six or seven times as many.[52] In addition, some who traveled, married, or studied overseas were so attracted by the charm of an older culture that they adopted it in preference to their own. Others went abroad for the opportunity of living more comfortably on a reduced income. But for whatever reason, the list of émigrés swelled to include such names as Henry James, H. Marion Crawford, Emily Carow (Roosevelt's sister-in-law), Lafcadio Hearn, and Edith Wharton.

Along with the increased urge to travel went a rising fascination with Czarist Russia and the Orient. Soon after the Civil War, Assistant Secretary of the Navy Gustavus Fox had made a good-will trip to St. Petersburg to express American relief at the czar's narrow escape from assassination. In 1891, a Russian famine prompted Americans to

mount the most effective relief effort of any nation in the
world. At the same time, with friction growing between re-
actionary and radical, thousands of Jewish refugees fled the
pogrom in search of a new life in America. Carrying with
them the deeply etched memory of Czarist oppression and a
corresponding interest in the darker side of Russian politics,
they provided a natural market for George Kennan's celebrated exposé of the Czarist police in *Century Magazine*. It
was to this sentiment that the exiled Kropotkin appealed
when he published his *Autobiography of a Revolutionist* in
the *Atlantic Monthly* (1889). Such spirit helped account for
the enthusiasm which greeted the flowering of Russian literature. Novels by Turgenev and Dostoievski gained a wide
audience, while Tolstoi's *Confession* was serialized in American magazines. A Tolstoi club convened the first of many
meetings in Boston, and annual pilgrimages began making
their way to the door of Tolstoi's native home, Yasnaya
Polyana.[53] By this time, too, Boston's Museum of Fine Arts
had acquired the bulk of its valuable Far Eastern collection.
A group of new magazines made their appearance under
such titles as *Artistic Japan,* the *Journal of the Asiatic Association,* and the *Asiatic Journal of Commerce.*[54]

Interest in foreign affairs was reflected dramatically in
such journals as *Forum, North American Review, Harper's,*
and the *Nation,* which now devoted over half their space to
foreign news. Publications dealing exclusively with the outside world included *Modern Mexico,* the *Chicago International, International Monthly, Pan-American Magazine,* and
Armenia, all of them founded between 1895 and 1904.
Magazines from abroad sold a rising number of subscrip-
tions and even began, in some cases, to publish in the
United States.[55]

One of these periodicals, the London *Review of Reviews,* was introduced in 1891 by a leading proponent of
Anglo-American unity, William T. Stead. Within a year, it
was in the hands of American owners, but with its original
layout and editorial policy intact. American current events
were listed under the caption "The Progress of the World,"

and a special section, "The Spirit of the Foreign Reviews," offered a brief digest of periodical literature in France, Britain, Japan, Italy, and Germany. There were accounts of foreign taste in literature, German opinion of Russia, French thought on the British Empire, and what foreigners in general were saying about America and its president. Perhaps the owner, Albert Shaw, summed it up neatly enough some twenty years after releasing his first copy. Regarding himself as a pioneer in devoting "what in the United States was an unwonted and novel attention to foreign questions," he recalled that in 1895 only a limited public had been familiar with such matters, or "eager to know about them. A marvelous change has come about in the range of American information and opinion. We have now a great American public caring about the concerns of mankind from Norway and Sweden to Morocco, and from Tibet to Venezuela."[56]

As will be seen in the essays which follow, each of the intellectual currents thus far discussed left its imprint on the diplomacy of Theodore Roosevelt. Dogmatic pronouncement, the code of the gentleman, a personal approach to negotiation, the emphasis upon material strength—even the enthusiasm for empire and that curious admixture of the patriotic with the cosmopolitan—all became in some way or other a mark of the man as well as the age. If, therefore, T.R. can be said to have been unique among presidents in the way he formulated ideas or planned his strategy, it is helpful to bear in mind that this novelty had its counterpart, if not its origin, in the spirit of the time. Similarly, the success or failure which attended his policy should also be assessed within the larger context.

Notes

1. Bradford Perkins, *The Great Rapprochement*, pp. 42, 44–45, 157–58.

2. John St. Loe Strachey to Roosevelt, 23 September 1901, Strachey Papers, House of Lords Library, London.

3. He once wrote of his experience with London society that "having begun by treating all the Englishmen I met with austere

reserve," he had "perhaps in consequence become quite a lion."
Roosevelt to Corinne Roosevelt Robinson, 22 November 1886,
Theodore Roosevelt, *The Letters of Theodore Roosevelt*, 8 vols.,
ed. Elting E. Morison and John M. Blum, 1:116 (hereafter cited
as *Letters*). Likewise, to his friend Lodge, some months later: "I
really think our utter indifference and our standing sharply on our
dignity have been among the main causes that have procured us
so hospitable a reception." Ibid., p. 126.

4. Foster Rhea Dulles, *America's Rise to World Power*,
p. 60.

5. The Russian gesture came just as England was seriously
weighing the merits of intervention on behalf of the Confederacy.
Historians have since noted that the czar had more than one
motive for sending his ships. But whatever the cause of their presence, it signified a mutual desire to thwart British designs and had
an electrifying effect on Union morale.

6. By 1898, almost a quarter of the Hawaiian population
was Japanese, and an envoy sent there by Tokyo to look after the
interests of Japanese nationals became so depressed by his government's inability to stand up to American expansion that he at-
tempted suicide. Akira Iriye, *Pacific Estrangement: Japanese and
American Expansion, 1879-1911*, pp. 50, 53. Iriye gives an excellent account of the clash between Japanese and American imperialism. Ibid., pp. vii, 26, 48, 54.

7. *Yale Review* 11 (May 1902): 7. From 1884 to 1891, not
only were all operas sung in German, but most of the works performed were by Wagner, and most of the singers were from Germany. William H. Seltsam, comp., *Metropolitan Opera Annals*,
pp. 8, 14, 19, 25, 30, 36, 41.

8. Dexter Perkins, *A History of the Monroe Doctrine*, pp.
208-11.

9. The treaty with Denmark was signed by Hay on 24
January 1902 and approved by the Senate soon after. It might
also be noted that the chief interpreter for Santo Domingo was a
German. See the *New York Tribune*, 25 January 1902; Stephen
Bonsal, "Greater Germany in South America," *North American
Review* 176 (January 1903): 58; J. Fred Rippy, "The Initiation of
the Customs Receivership in the Dominican Republic," *Hispanic
American Historical Review* 17 (November 1937): 422, 425, 430-
35; Dexter Perkins, *History of the Monroe Doctrine*, pp. 209, 213;
Dana Munro, *Intervention and Dollar Diplomacy in the Carib-
bean, 1900-1921*, pp. 5-7; *Outlook* 72 (1902): 474-75.

10. Warren Schiff, "German Military Penetration into Mexico During the Late Diaz Period," *Hispanic American Historical Review* 39 (November 1959): 568–69; Willis Fletcher Johnson, *Four Centuries of the Panama Canal,* pp. 134, 136, 139.

11. William R. Braisted, "The United States Navy's Dilemma in the Pacific, 1906-1909," *Pacific Historical Review* 26 (August 1957): 235–36; Alfred Vagts, "Hopes and Fears of an American-German War, 1870-1915," *Political Science Quarterly* 54 (December 1939): 530, 532, 534; Richard W. Leopold, *Elihu Root and the Conservative Tradition,* p. 60; Theodore Roosevelt to Henry Cabot Lodge, 27 March 1901, Henry Cabot Lodge, ed., *Selections from Correspondence of Theodore Roosevelt and Henry Cabot Lodge, 1884-1918,* 2 vols., 1:485 (hereafter cited as *Roosevelt-Lodge Correspondence*). Typical of the poisoned atmosphere was Lodge's suspicion that the Germans, under cover of the Danish Asiatic and Hamburg-American companies, were trying to establish a large coaling station on the island of St. Thomas. To all outward appearances, the kaiser still appeared to be "hankering over those islands." Lodge to Roosevelt, 10 June 1905, ibid., 2:135–36.

12. Joseph Conrad, "Autocracy and War," *North American Review* 181 (July 1905): 49, 54–55; Albert Keller, "The Colonial Policy of the Germans," *Yale Review* 11 (May 1902): 59, 122–23; *Atlantic Monthly* 89 (1902): 764–70; Yves Guyot, "German Designs on Holland and Belgium," *North American Review* 184 (January 1907): 22–28; *Review of Reviews* 28 (July 1903): 17. The swindler, one William Voigt, was a shoemaker who bought his uniform at a second-hand clothing store. Marching into Koepenik, he took command of a dozen soldiers, entered City Hall, and ordered the mayor and his counselors to hand him the keys to the municipal safe. He then carried off $12,000, which he claimed in the name of the emperor, sent the mayor off to Berlin under escort, and disappeared. The story was eventually made into a popular movie, *The Captain of Koepenik. Review of Reviews* 34 (December 1906): 664–65.

13. See, for example, Philip C. Jessup, *Elihu Root,* 2 vols., 1:542: "Fears of German expansion were . . . unnecessarily entertained in Washington." Also, Vagts, "Hopes and Fears," pp. 530–32.

14. Prince Bernhard von Bülow, *Memoirs of Prince Von Bülow,* trans. F. A. Voigt, 4 vols., 1:660–61. The italicized portion reads, in the original German version (published in 1930), as

follows: Die Verhältnisse in Süd und Zentralamerika möge der
Prinz aus eigener Initiative nicht besprechen und selbstverständ-
lich keinerlei Absichten Deutschlands auf jene Gegenden zugeben
oder gar durchblicken lassen. Bülow, *Memoirs,* 4 vols. (Berlin,
1930), 1:575.

15. British War Office, Division of Military Intelligence,
"Memorandum on Our Military Responsibilities with Regard to
Belgium, Holland, Norway, Sweden and Portugal," bound item
#49739, Arthur James Balfour Papers, British Museum, London;
Vigilans Sed Aequus [pseud. for William T. Arnold of the *Man-
chester Guardian*], *German Ambitions as They Affect Britain and
the United States.*

16. Sydney Brooks, "The Voyage of the American Fleet,"
Fortnightly Review [London], O.S. 89 (February 1908): 204.

17. Walter Houghton, *The Victorian Frame of Mind, 1830-
1870,* pp. 137, 139-45.

18. Alan Clark, ed., *'A Good Innings': The Private Papers of
Viscount Lee of Fareham,* p. 49; Bradford Perkins, *Great Rapprochement,* p. 102.

19. Merle Curti, *The Growth of American Thought,* pp. 519
ff., 586; Frank Luther Mott, *A History of American Magazines,
1885-1905,* 5 vols., 4:276; *Outlook* 72 (1902): 363-64; *Review of
Reviews* 32 (September 1905): 374-75. The *North American Review* returned again and again to such topics as the papacy,
science and religion, and the reunion of Christendom. In one year,
it carried such articles as "Religious Education of Children," "The
War against Christianity in France," "Religion Strong," "The Im-
mortality of the Soul," and "The Trial of Christianity." The list of
books published in 1902 includes *Light for Daily Living, Homely
Virtues, Representative Men of the Bible, Christian Point of View,
The Reasonableness of Faith, Through Science to Faith,* and
Spiritual Heroes.

20. Houghton, *Victorian Frame of Mind,* p. 247.

21. Ibid., p. 359 n.; Kenelm Digby, *The Broadstone of
Honour,* 5 vols.

22. Others whom T.R. classed as "gentlemen" in his private
correspondence included Arthur Lee and Mackenzie King. Roosevelt to Elihu Root, 2 September 1899; Roosevelt to Arthur Lee,
2 February 1908, Arthur H. Lee Papers, Courtauld Institute,
Portman Square, London.

23. H. L. Elmendorf, "Some Things a Boy of Seventeen
Should Have Had an Opportunity to Read," *Review of Reviews*

28 (December 1903): 713–17. Other titles recommended by Elmendorf included Charles Kingsley, *The Heroes of Greek Fairy Tales;* Hamilton W. Mabie, *Norse Stories Retold;* the *Iliad* and the *Odyssey;* Sir Thomas Malory's *Morte d'Arthur;* Tennyson's *Idylls of the King;* Sidney Lanier, *The Boy's King Arthur;* Andrew Lang, *The Book of Romance;* and Mrs. Joseph B. Gilder, *The Bible for Children.*

24. Henry James, *The American* (New York: Dell Publishing Co., 1962), p. 259; *North American Review* 175 (August 1902): 194–200; *Review of Reviews* 28 (September 1903): 350; 32 (August 1905): 251; *Outlook* 72 (1902): 472; Richard Harding Davis to Arthur Lee, 1 October 1899, Arthur H. Lee, viscount of Fareham, ed., *Letters That Remain (Friendly and Otherwise) From the Postbag of Arthur and Ruth Lee, 1891-1941,* p. 209.

25. Kenton J. Clymer, *John Hay: The Gentleman as Diplomat,* pp. 110–11, 173, 181.

26. Authur H. Lee, viscount of Fareham, *A Good Innings and a Great Partnership, Being the Life Story of Arthur and Ruth Lee,* 3 vols., 1:327; Theodore Roosevelt, *The Strenuous Life,* in *The Works of Theodore Roosevelt,* ed. Hermann Hagedorn, 20 vols., 13:527. Roosevelt, in early 1907, observed that the British government had behaved especially well under very trying circumstances, and he felt that he had endeavored in return to be "just as gentlemanly and considerate as possible." But he complained that the San Franciscans were "howling and whooping and embarrassing me in every way, and their international manners are inexcusable." In a similar vein, he insisted during World War I that his sons be permitted to take their place on the fighting front "as honorable gentlemen should." Roosevelt to Kermit Roosevelt, 4 February 1907, to Anna Roosevelt Cowles, 22 January 1907, to Arthur Lee, 20 June 1917, Theodore Roosevelt Collection, Houghton Library, Harvard University, Cambridge, Mass.

27. Princess Victoria, sister of Edward VII, became the mother of Kaiser Wilhelm. Queen Alexandra, wife of Edward, had a sister who became the mother of Czar Nicholas, as well as a brother who became King George of Greece. In addition, Princess Ena, who was Edward's niece, married King Alfonso of Spain.

28. For a good discussion of the ascendancy of individualism, as well as the signs of its demise, see Curti, *Growth of American Thought,* chap. 25; Houghton, *Victorian Frame of Mind,* p. 338.

29. Although Alger wrote 119 hero books, he was not alone in the field. Freeman Hunt, Orison S. Marden, Charles C. B.

Seymour, and William Makepeace Thayer also turned out books on the rags-to-riches theme.

30. According to *World's Work*, Roosevelt was "the best public hero that has come in this generation," Mott, *History of American Magazines*, 4:170.

31. Mott, *History of American Magazines*, 4:369–70; John Higham, *Writing American History* (Bloomington: Indiana University Press paperback ed., 1972), pp. 77–85. In the 1906 Olympics, the United States won eleven out of twenty-nine gold medals, five silver medals, and three bronzes. Altogether, the American team totaled nearly twice as many points as its closest rival, which was Britain. *Review of Reviews* 33 (June 1906): 664.

32. Houghton, *Victorian Frame of Mind*, pp. 205–11.

33. Ibid., p. 203.

34. Ibid., pp. 204–205.

35. Jean Jules Jusserand, *What Me Befell*, pp. 142, 144.

36. *North American Review* 176 (February 1903): 247; Roosevelt to Theodore Roosevelt, Jr., 1 March 1903; Roosevelt to David Gray, 5 October 1911, *Letters*, 3:437, 7:405; Nelson M. Blake, "Ambassadors at the Court of Theodore Roosevelt," *Mississippi Valley Historical Review* 42 (September 1955): 201; David H. Burton, "Theodore Roosevelt: Confident Imperialist," *Review of Politics* 23 (July 1961): 360; Jusserand, *What Me Befell*, p. 142; Roosevelt to Kermit Roosevelt, 23 November 1906, Roosevelt Collection, Harvard University.

37. *Atlantic Monthly* 89 (1902): 610–11; Roosevelt, *The Strenuous Life*, in Hagedorn, ed., *Works*, 13:323–24.

38. *North American Review* 176 (April 1903): 528–29.

39. Roosevelt to Arthur Lee, 6 October 1909, Lee Papers, Courtauld Institute; *Review of Reviews* 30 (July 1904): 117. Ernest May has traced the trans-Atlantic influence on American imperial thought, and he is particularly effective at showing how an alternating pattern in the British imperial impulse was paralleled by the waxing and waning of American thought. May, *American Imperialism: A Speculative Essay*, chaps. 6 and 7.

40. Roosevelt, *The Strenuous Life*, in Hagedorn, ed., *Works*, 13:332–33, 336–37.

41. Clymer, *Hay*, p. 129.

42. Rippy, "Customs Receivership," pp. 438, 443; Howard C. Hill, *Roosevelt and the Caribbean*, p. 102; *Review of Reviews* 34 (July 1906): 31.

43. *Review of Reviews* 33 (December 1903): 659; 31 (February 1905): 267; William H. Harbaugh, *The Life and Times of Theodore Roosevelt,* p. 189. The claims of the American Santo Domingo Improvement Co. against the Dominican Republic had been submitted to arbitrators, who ruled in July 1904 that the United States should take charge of the customs receipts at Porto Plata and Monte Christi for the benefit of the American citizens to whom money was due.

44. *Review of Reviews* 31 (March 1905): 294, quoting Prof. John Bassett Moore.

45. Ibid., p. 296. The Santo Domingo Improvement Co. collected from 1893–1901.

46. See, for example, Joseph Chamberlain (British colonial secretary) to Lord Minto, 13 May 1902, MG 26 G, Vol. 753, No. 215496, Wilfrid Laurier Papers, Public Archives of Canada, Ottawa (hereafter cited as PAC). Stead aired many of his views in *The Americanization of the World* (New York: H. Markley, 1901), and he later perished in the sinking of the *Titanic,* midway between the two English-speaking worlds he had done so much to unite.

47. *Atlantic Monthly* 89 (1902): 401; *Outlook* 72 (1902): 2, 569; Lord Strathcona to Sir Wilfrid Laurier, 5 May 1902; Laurier to Strathcona, 9 May 1902, MG 26 G, Vol. 753, Nos. 215488, 215492, Laurier Papers, PAC.

48. For American optimism regarding the future of democracy, see May, *American Imperialism,* p. 173.

49. *Review of Reviews* 33 (May 1906): 608–609; 34 (July 1906): 44, 48.

50. Ernest May, *Imperial Democracy: The Emergence of America as a Great Power,* p. 32; Daniel Smith, ed., *Major Problems in American Diplomatic History,* 2 vols. (Lexington, Mass.: D. C. Heath, paperback, 1968), 2:288–90.

51. Clymer, *Hay,* p. 115.

52. Mott, *History of American Magazines,* 4:223–24; Curti, *Growth of American Thought,* p. 566; May, *American Imperialism,* pp. 88–94. Heads of mission married to Americans included the following: Baron Moncheur of Belgium, who had wedded a handsome girl from Louisville, Kentucky; Jonkheer R. de Marees van Swinderen of the Netherlands, married to the daughter of the president of the Riggs National Bank of Washington, D.C.; M. C. Hauge of Norway, who married a wealthy widow and died just after building a fine home; Baron Speck von Sternburg of

Germany; and Jules Jusserand of France. Mme. Jusserand, it might be noted, was American by birth only, having been reared in France. Lord Bryce to Edward Grey, 6 March 1908, FO 414/202, Public Record Office, London (hereafter cited as PRO).

53. Mott, *History of American Magazines,* 4:232.
54. Ibid., pp. 233–34.
55. Ibid., pp. 223–24, 237.
56. *Review of Reviews* 32 (July 1905): 3.

CHAPTER 2

The Question of Credibility

TURNING now to Roosevelt's actual record, the first question to be examined is that of his credibility. Of all the presidents whose veracity has been challenged before the bar of history, Roosevelt is among the most prominent. This may seem improbable when one recalls that the Rough Rider spent much of his life crusading for honesty in various branches of government, first as New York State assemblyman, then as civil service commissioner, police commissioner, governor, and president. He was as much admired for his straightforward ways as he was outspoken in denouncing others for duplicity. But since his death in 1919, and particularly in recent years, historians have come to doubt his credibility and have described him as something of a "self-glorifier" with "an acknowledged tendency toward exaggeration."[1]

The issue of credibility is not unimportant in the case of T.R. since his writings, if trustworthy, constitute an indispensable source for reconstructing his career. Nor does the problem appear to be insoluble.

Most charges of exaggeration rest upon a limited number of incidents which deserve more scrutiny than they have thus far received. To take one example, Roosevelt claims to have warned Germany and France, in the early stages of the Russo-Japanese War, to refrain from intervening on the side of the czar. He was prepared, as he put it, to "proceed to whatever length was necessary" should either power try to deprive Japan of the fruit of her military victory.[2] Scholars have found it hard to imagine so explicit a warning in view of the staunch isolationist tradition of the United States and the fact that there is no mention of it in the French, German, or American archives.[3] However, in addition to the fact that such a warning would have squared with Roosevelt's conception of the national interest, Prof. Edward Parsons showed in 1969 that German officials, anxious to back Russia, were genuinely concerned about the possibility of American intervention and the form it might take. This is confirmed by a warning given to the German foreign office by Friedrich von Holstein, its chief adviser: "The greatest drawback of our going with Russia is the fact that we would draw further away from America which could revenge itself on us in some way or other, even without war."[4] There is also the fact that Roosevelt concentrated an unusually large number of warships at Gibraltar during the early months of the war for the first large-scale demonstration of American naval power outside home waters. Later, he wrote his friend, George von Lengerke Meyer, American ambassador to Italy, that he wanted "to avoid any blustering or threatening," but "be able to act decidedly when any turn of events menaces our interests, and to be able to make our words good once they have been spoken."[5]

Another reason for accepting Roosevelt's claim is the existence of some remarkable evidence which would seem to support a similar claim in reference to the Anglo-German blockade of Venezuela. The time was late in the year 1902, and again the president claimed to have issued an ultimatum. Again, there was a display of naval power. And again, there is no concrete documentation. Since attacks on Roosevelt's Venezuela claim constitute the principal challenge to his credibility, they are worthy of careful consideration.

According to T.R., he threatened Germany with war in December 1902 unless she agreed within ten days to arbitrate a monetary dispute with Venezuela. He also saw Theodor von Holleben, the German ambassador, on three occasions: first to issue the ultimatum; then, when it became clear that Germany was holding out, to advance the deadline by twenty-four hours; finally, at the eleventh hour, to be notified that the American demand for arbitration would be met.[6] In the meantime, German ships, acting with the Royal Navy, had sunk Venezuelan gunboats, bombarded Venezuelan forts, landed troops, and clamped a blockade on the principal ports.[7] Although Roosevelt was in complete sympathy with European claims and regarded President Cipriano Castro of Venezuela as little better than a highwayman, he feared that military operations might lead to prolonged occupation of Venezuelan soil by Germany, which would do violence to the Monroe Doctrine and jeopardize the American plan for exclusive control of an isthmian canal.

The earliest accounts of the episode do not question Roosevelt's story.[8] But as soon as it became apparent that there was no evidence for it in the British, German, or American archives, one skeptical voice after another began to make itself heard. In 1927, Howard Hill, followed by J. Fred Rippy, speculated that Roosevelt might have confused December 1902 with January 1903 and mistaken Holleben for his successor, Hermann Speck von Sternburg. In 1935, Alfred Vagts, followed by Dexter Perkins, rejected the story out of hand and wrote off the naval maneuvers as a political device for winning military appropriations from Congress.[9] Seward Livermore in 1946, Howard Beale in 1956, and Edward Parsons in 1971 published fresh evidence and marshaled strong arguments on the side of Roosevelt's claim. Nicholas Roosevelt, son of T.R.'s first cousin, J. West Roosevelt, recalled several occasions on which the ex-president told him personally of an ultimatum to Holleben: "As I recall it, T.R. . . . said ten days." Yet the general trend has been to deny the existence of a pointed diplomatic crisis and to ascribe British and German acceptance of arbitration to the subtle influence of public opinion as it became known in the United States and England.[10]

There is no need to summarize the many arguments for and against T.R.'s dramatic story. This has been done quite succinctly by Professor Beale. It may be useful, however, to extend the limits of the debate, to present additional facts, and to adduce some new lines of reasoning.

Evidence already published, but not yet fully utilized, indicates that American naval operations for the year beginning in December 1901 virtually guaranteed a crisis of the magnitude Roosevelt describes, apart from any alleged swell in public opinion. This can be seen by observing that the president accompanied every step in the diplomatic confrontation with a corresponding buildup of American power.[11] When Germany, on 13 December 1901, first warned Roosevelt of her plan to use force against Venezuela, the president admitted Germany's right to coercion. But he also spoke out against long-term occupation or acquisition of Venezuelan territory. On 17 December, he ordered the navy to prepare a base of operations off the coast of Puerto Rico (Culebra) "in case of sudden war."[12] This precipitated a war scare which was reflected in the diary of Andrew White, American ambassador to Germany. White wrote as follows on 30 December: "Gave to [the] press an interview in answer to sensational cablegrams from N. Y. to [the] effect that the leading US military and naval authorities look on war with Germany anent Venezuela as certain." Roosevelt proceeded to ask Congress for appropriations to stage Caribbean fleet exercises of unprecedented size, and he ordered the navy to begin investigating German activities in Venezuela.[13] In February, the State Department was told to gather information on Venezuela's chief roads and landing areas so that a plan of defense could be prepared by the General Board of the navy. Soon after, in response to a German note asking whether, in case of annexation of Holland by Germany, the United States would object to German acquisition of the Dutch colonies in America, T.R. sent the kaiser what he claimed to be the strongest message ever composed on the subject of the Monroe Doctrine.[14]

By the time Germany was ready to act, she had decided to do so in conjunction with England, and the month was November. This was the month in which a Naval Staff memorandum to the administration labeled war as "most probable."[15] It was also the month the American Caribbean squadron arrived at Culebra (5 November), followed by the arrival of the North Atlantic battle squadron (21 November). On 25 November, the allied powers gave formal notification of their intention, and four days later, the remaining units of the American battleship fleet, the South Atlantic and European squadrons, dropped anchor at Trinidad, just off the threatened coast. On 1 December, Admiral Dewey, the navy's highest ranking officer and a man well known for his anti-German sentiment, sailed to take personal charge. With him was Rear Adm. Henry C. Taylor, the nation's second ranking officer, in command of all battleships. On 8 December, the day Germany and Britain severed diplomatic relations with Venezuela in preparation for attack, Dewey hoisted his flag aboard the presidential yacht *Mayflower.*[16]

The most critical day of all was 16 December, for it was on this day that Roosevelt decided in Cabinet to order important units of the fleet, now at Culebra, back into the blockade zone. Four battleships were to be dispatched to Trinidad and two cruisers to Curaçao, both destinations only a few miles from the Venezuelan coast. Although this Christmas rendezvous had been planned for some time, it does not lessen the significance of Roosevelt's decision to go ahead with it, for, as Admiral Taylor cautioned, Trinidad was "only across the road from Venezuela" and one did "not know how the [*sic*] delicate the situation might be down there."[17] The sixteenth was also the day on which Roosevelt supplied the press with military maps of the danger zone; it was the day the British cabinet met and decided privately to accept arbitration; and it was the day Secretary Hay *formally* demanded that the allies accept arbitration.[18] On 18 December, Admiral "Fighting Bob" Evans arrived at Manila with orders to gather the entire Asiatic squadron for extensive maneuvers; Taylor was publicly ordered to move into the Trinidad-Curaçao theatre; Albert von Quadt, the German chargé in Washington, rushed to Hay in great alarm, demanding an explanation; and Whitehall announced its decision to yield to Roosevelt's wishes, with Germany following suit the next day.[19]

Dewey hauled down his flag on 5 January, and six small

cruisers returned to Europe. But not until April, when the diplomatic storm clouds had passed, did Roosevelt's battleships leave the Caribbean-Gulf area; for, as the president wrote in late December, he was not yet "out of the woods." The precise form of the arbitral arrangements had yet to be determined, and this demanded time and patience.

One of the problems with Roosevelt's story is that the official White House calendar of appointments shows only one visit by Holleben. Appointments are shown for 6 and 8 December, with the first of the two dates crossed out. In addition, Roosevelt's personal Memorandum of Engagements, much of it written in his own hand, shows an uncanceled meeting for the sixth with nothing for the eighth.[20] If we are to believe testimony given by Roosevelt's personal secretary many years later, the gap between the first and second meeting was only two or three days, making the eighth a likely second date. It was on the eighth that the press first began carrying reports of Holleben's expected retirement.[21] On the other hand, Holleben may have received the ultimatum at the White House on 8 December and returned for two other meetings, both of them unrecorded. White House calendars are not necessarily accurate.[22] Nor should Roosevelt's Memorandum of Engagements be considered a reliable guide, since it includes a meeting with Sternburg on 18 February 1903, while omitting another one known to have been held on 31 January.[23] Finally, there is no difficulty, as has been suggested, with the fact that Holleben left Washington for a trip to New York City toward the end of the critical period. Roosevelt, in his famous letter of 1916, does not say that the ambassador notified him *in person* of Germany's decision to yield, only that he notified him. And there is also a possibility, judging from Holleben's continuous communication with the State Department during this period, that he may have been in New York for only one day (16 December) before returning to the capital.[24]

Before confronting the question of why the ultimatum fails to appear in any official record of the three major powers concerned, it should be noted that Roosevelt unquestionably levied sharp and urgent demands upon the British, who had far more naval power in the area than Germany. On 15 December, Henry White, American chargé in London, made three important representations. He told Foreign Minister Lansdowne of his "grave apprehension." He expressed "grave fears" to other government officials with whom he was on friendly terms, and he conveyed the same sentiment to Prime Minister Balfour, visiting him at his private rooms in the House of Commons and unburdening himself "very frankly." White was exceedingly well connected in British society, even to the point of being regarded as "deep in the counsels of the cabinet." Furthermore, he believed he had made a vivid impression on each of his listeners, having heard "in special confidence" on the same day that the government was not planning to land additional troops. Later, during a parliamentary debate in the evening, he was treated to the rare experience of hearing Lord Cranborne, undersecretary for foreign affairs, proclaim that "no nation in the world is more anxious than England to assist them [the United States] in maintaining that doctrine [the Monroe Doctrine]." Cranborne's remarks were greeted by enthusiastic cries of "Hear! Hear!" On the morrow, 16 December, the British cabinet made the crucial decision to accept arbitration, pending German acquiescence, with Lord Lansdowne replying to Lord Spencer during question time in the House of Lords: "It is not intended to land a British force, still less to occupy Venezuelan territory." On 17 December, White wrote Hay that he had carried out his instructions to represent to Lansdowne the desirability of arbitration and that he had done so "urgently." On 18 December, the ministry announced its acceptance of arbitration (it had received word of Germany's decision the day before). White also wrote Hay that Lansdowne "would, I know, appreciate highly the suppression, if possible, when correspondence is published, of instructions I carried out yesterday to represent desirability of acceptance. In any case, please erase word 'urgently' in my cablegram." Hay complied with White's request by having the word "urgently" placed in brackets with the notation alongside, "not for publication."[25]

This evidence of a heated Anglo-American confrontation is confirmed by the disappearance of nine telegrams sent by the British ambassador in Washington to the Foreign Office during the period 5 November to 31 December.[26] There is also Roosevelt's later recollection that the British had "behaved badly," as well as White's judgment that John Bull had retreated in response to "urgent representations."[27] Surely, if Roosevelt had expressed himself so strongly to the English, whom he trusted, his approach to the Germans, whom he did not trust, would have been equally adamant.

Second, if the British wished to suppress all evidence of Roosevelt's demands, the Germans, who never denied receiving an ultimatum, would have had even more reason to purge the record. Most of the German letters, diaries, correspondence, and official documents for this period were published shortly after World War I when the Fatherland was in urgent need of foreign aid.[28] Former Chancellor Bernhard von Bülow expressed a common sentiment in 1930 when he reminisced about Prince Henry's highly acclaimed good-will tour of the United States some twenty-eight years earlier: "Would to God that we had had a Prince Henry to send to America to work on behalf of our welfare in those black days that followed our collapse in November, 1918, days when we needed a friendly attitude on the part of America so badly."[29] To publish Roosevelt's ultimatum in the 1920s would not only have caused a loss of face; it would have jeopardized good relations with the United States when they were at a premium.

The hypothesis that a body of material was destroyed for diplomatic reasons is further supported by an astonishing gap that appears in all the published German material for the critical weeks leading up to and following 6–16 December 1902. The diary and letters of Holstein, edited by Norman Rich and H. M. Fisher, are completely void from 13 November 1902 to 1 April 1903, with only a few entries for

the months immediately before and after. Not until 1904
does the collection resume its normal proportions. Nor does
Rich's full-length biography of Holstein shed any light on
the subject.[30] The same gap appears in papers handed down
by Chancellor von Bülow and the kaiser.[31] The first of the
published Bülow letters is dated 25 October 1903, and
Bülow's memoirs are remarkable for the fact that, in two
pages devoted to the Venezuelan incident, there is no mention of either Roosevelt or the United States. More curious
still is the complete absence of any mention of how the crisis
was resolved—only the misleading statement that "Mr.
Castro . . . accepted my suggestion that the case be submitted to arbitration at the Hague Court." The kaiser's
memoirs follow a similar pattern, containing a chapter on
Bülow's chancellorship without one reference to the United
States or its president. The published records of the German
foreign office contain only three pieces of correspondence
from the German embassy in Washington during the entire
year beginning 20 January 1902. There is nothing at all during the climax period, 25 November to 16 December. And
the one published cable from Ambassador Holleben (16 December) was received after Germany had unofficially made
its decision to yield.[32]

Unpublished records of the German foreign office include a great deal of correspondence from the German embassy in Washington to the Wilhelmstrasse from 1 December to 12 December. But the traffic is trivial and without
reference to the urgent confrontation at hand.[33] Furthermore, while the German archives have not produced a single
piece of significant German-American correspondence for
this period, they reveal two very significant gaps. First the
*Catalogue of Files and Microfilms of the German Foreign
Ministry Archives, 1867–1920*, published in 1959 by the
American Historical Association, lists no agents' reports
from North America dated later than June 1902, nor are
they anywhere to be found.[34] Second, the German foreign office series known as "Beziehungen der Vereinigten Staaten
zu Venezuela" (U.S.-Venezuela Relations) from 1888 to 1904

contains fifty-one manuscript pages of reports for 1901, forty-two pages for 1904, but only nine pages (on very trivial matters) for the critical years 1902–1903.[35]

Even if Roosevelt had never issued an ultimatum, the impending naval confrontation would have warranted lively discussion. Instead, we have Holleben's queer remark on 12 December that Roosevelt had expressed admiration for the German navy. We have his report, four days later, that the press was beginning to stir, with business showing signs of concern. And we have Quadt's observation, after hearing the alarming news of the dispatch of the fleet to the Trinidad-Curaçao area, that Roosevelt and Hay "reposed entire trust in us." Not a single word on naval operations.[36]

One can go further. The mysterious disappearance of records is not confined to Germany. It occurs on the American side as well. There is an amazing gap in the correspondence between Secretary Hay and Roosevelt's secretary, William Loeb, with no word whatever from 17 September 1902 to 25 February 1903. Hay's surviving general correspondence for the month of December contains only two items, one a message to Senator Cullom, chairman of the Senate Foreign Relations Committee, that makes no reference to Venezuela, the other a sonnet, dated 24 December and composed in honor of T.R.[37] The American embassy in Berlin, in its record of "Notes Sent to the German Foreign Office," shows a complete void for the period 17 October to 12 December. Volume 57, labeled "April 26, 1901, to December 11, 1902," ends in mid-sentence of a note dated 17 October! Pages 275–658 are entirely blank. Volume 60 begins on 12 December with the arrival of the new American ambassador, Charlemagne Tower (his predecessor, Andrew White, had presented his recall on 28 November). Volumes 58 and 59 contain dispatches from the embassy to Secretary Hay and reveal an identical gap. Volume 58 ends unexpectedly on page 35 with a dispatch dated 18 October. The remaining 615 pages are void. Volume 59 begins with a dispatch for 11 December. At the same time we know from the embassy register of outgoing correspondence, as well as from actual surviving papers of the State Department, that dispatches did go out in early December and that at least two of them (dated 3 and 10 December) were related to Venezuela. In addition, there are items missing in the collection of "Diplomatic Instructions from the State Department to the United States Embassy in Berlin." Three instructions that appear on the embassy register are nowhere to be found, while key instructions for December 1902 appear months later, by which time the department had decided to make them public and actually marked them "for publication."[38]

The lack of documentary evidence on the American side has a great deal to do, naturally, with Roosevelt's diplomatic style. Henry Adams once remarked that the absence of any reference to the Venezuela incident in Hay's papers was attributable to his penchant for secrecy, and that it was his habit to "settle all questions, if possible, by word of mouth, and to write few papers." But what Adams said of his good friend Hay is doubly applicable to Hay's chief, who prided himself on the "kind of diplomacy that consists of not uttering one word that can be avoided."[39]

Roosevelt's domestic record is studded with instances of presidential silence. We are still mystified by the way in which he managed to persuade Congress to approve legislation for the regulation of railroads. It is thought that he may have conferred privately with such figures as Speaker Cannon and Senator Aldrich and agreed to drop his campaign for tariff reduction in return for their support on the railway bill. The evidence, however, is missing. His famous settlement of the anthracite coal strike involved a secret understanding with General Schofield as well as covert negotiations between Secretary of War Root and J. P. Morgan in New York City. Roosevelt made careful preparations for deploying the National Guard; but, as he later remarked, "I did not wish to talk about it until and unless I actually acted."[40]

In the realm of diplomacy, Roosevelt was more apt to communicate vital information on the tennis court or on a

strenuous hike through Rock Creek Park than he was to
commit it to writing. During a crisis, he might hold a night-
time conference with Ambassador Jusserand, whose advice
he valued. He would converse on horseback with Secretary Root and Ambassador Sternburg (better known as
"Specky"). He made a practice of "stopping by" at Secretary Hay's home after Sunday services to discuss matters of
state and hear firsthand stories about Lincoln. Every so
often he met Hay for an after-supper walk, and on at least
one occasion he crossed Lafayette Square incognito to dine
in the company of Hay and the British ambassador. At the
same time, he was just as apt to bypass the State Department altogether on important occasions and have recourse
to private envoys such as Oliver Wendell Holmes or Henry
Cabot Lodge, who delivered his confidential messages while
abroad.[41]

He even went so far as to rely on trusted representatives of other countries. We find the British chargé in Washington writing the Foreign Office in the spring of 1902 that
T.R. insists "on sending his recent messages either through
Spring Rice or Kitson on the ground that everything which
passes through the State Department is liable to be asked
for by senators" (Col. G. C. Kitson was the military attaché).[42] Later, when Whitehall sent a new ambassador in
the person of Sir Mortimer Durand, Roosevelt judged him
"incompetent for any work of delicacy or importance":

If I ask him informally to lunch he treats it as a diplomatic function. If I ask him to walk, he can't or doesn't walk. With Jusserand and Speck I walk, ride, or play tennis and can talk with
them intimately—as man to man. In this way our most valuable
work has been done. But if I attempt to be confidential with
Durand, or to give him privately information (say about Germany)
with the request that he should not make it the subject of an official despatch, he perceptively freezes and apparently suspects
me of some dark Machiavellian motive. . . . I hope there are no
troubles ahead . . . [but] if any difficult question *does* arise your
government will have to send over, specially, somebody with
whom we *can* work.

The only subject that really seemed to interest Durand was "an attempt to persuade the State Department to pardon a British subject who had been sent to States Prison—for rape!"[43] Consequently, T.R. chose to conduct his diplomacy by summoning foreign friends upon whom he felt he could rely from places as distant as St. Petersburg. They crossed the Atlantic for secret tête à tête conferences and reported to their governments in person. On 27 December 1904, Roosevelt wrote Cecil Spring Rice, secretary of the British Embassy in Russia: "I wish to Heaven you could come over if only for a week or two, and I think it would be very important for your government." The Englishman answered the call in late January and stayed with Henry Adams without ever revealing the purpose of his visit. Senator Lodge and Secretary Hay did not know why he had come. Roosevelt feigned surprise. And there was no mention of any foreign visitor by the press.[44]

In much the same manner, T.R. came to regard the American ambassador to Germany as completely under the spell of the kaiser and thus decided to use Sternburg to contact the imperial authorities directly. Typical is the following message from Bülow to the kaiser dated 24 December 1904 (Berlin): "Sternburg has arrived here charged with special messages from President Roosevelt and commissioned to act as his mouthpiece. The state of his health is given as the ostensible object of his journey." Equally typical is a reference by someone in New York to the fact that "while the Morocco Conference was going on a casual emissary from Berlin went to Washington (the job was not the sort to be confided to a man like Speck v. Sternburg). This person lunched with the President and gradually broached the Morocco matter."[45]

On the eve of the Venezuela crisis, Roosevelt had three special guests at the White House: Sternburg, who had not yet been assigned to the United States; Strachey of the *Spectator;* and Arthur Lee, member of Parliament and former officer in the British army. Although the real purpose of two of these visits has never been disclosed, there can be little doubt. Sternburg returned immediately to Berlin and reported in person to the kaiser at the most critical moment of the crisis. According to the published papers of Lee, he visited the United States in August of 1902 to see his wife's parents, and no reason is given for his invitation to the White House except that T.R. might deliver himself of some "solid home-spun" sentiment. Yet we know from his private papers that he and Roosevelt covered the entire range of differences between Britain and the United States. The president referred specifically to his plans for a powerful navy and to the fact that "dear Dewey" was "doing his proper work" and "training what navy we have got for war." T.R. also made it clear that he would seize the Dutch Caribbean islands if they were ever threatened by a German takeover.[46]

Three months later, in November, the frail Strachey made a flying visit to the United States so that he could spend a few days in New York, a few more in Washington, and two at the executive mansion (24–25 November). He spent most of his time crossing and recrossing the Atlantic. Yet he offers absolutely no explanation for the trip in his autobiography. His wife, who also published a book, mentions that her husband spent one afternoon with T.R. galloping through the driving rain and talking hard all the while; also, that he rode with Secretary of War Root. She speaks of discussions between Strachey and the president on the Alaskan boundary, but she is absolutely mute on the far more sensitive subject of Venezuela, which could scarcely have been ignored.[47]

Though the foregoing facts are not in themselves a conclusive demonstration of the truth of Roosevelt's ultimatum story, they certainly suggest the kind of crisis atmosphere one would expect. Furthermore, they are significant for what they say about the Roosevelt style. Benjamin Franklin and John Jay employed British diplomats during the peace negotiations of 1781–82 to represent the American position in London, and they did quite well.[48] T.R. was unique, however, in requesting that foreign governments send his personal choice of ambassador. The kaiser responded favorably by giving him Sternburg, while the Court of St. James's ignored his preference for Lee or Spring Rice and instead sent him the scholarly Bryce. Nonetheless, Roosevelt and "Springy" kept up such a vigorous and irregular correspondence on world affairs that, out of deference to the Foreign Office, Spring Rice addressed all letters to Mrs. Roosevelt, and his superiors studiously refrained from any reference to them in their official dispatches.[49]

Foreigners were especially appreciative of Roosevelt's insistence on strict confidentiality, since they found that it compensated for a number of weaknesses in the American political process. One British cabinet report to the Crown referred to Washington, D.C., "with its omnipresent unscrupulous press, its senators who have to be separately conciliated, and its diplomatic methods unchecked by any long diplomatic tradition," as "probably the most difficult theatre in [the] world for carrying on delicate negotiations."[50] Similarly, in talks leading to the Portsmouth Peace Conference, the Japanese hesitated to confide in Roosevelt because they deemed the democratic system unreliable in the handling of sensitive matters. As evidence, they cited the recent case of Ambassador Takahira, who had expressed confidential views on Manchuria only to see them printed in the pages of the *New York Sun* three days later.[51] Roosevelt gave them little real cause for concern, though, for he not only met their envoys at ten o'clock in the evening to avoid detection by reporters, but also waited three weeks to inform his own secretary of state that Russia and Japan had asked for his good offices to end the war. During the actual conference at Portsmouth, Baron Rosen of the Russian delegation was awakened at 2:00 A.M. to be advised that the president wanted to see him and that he might avoid publicity by catching a 7:00 A.M. train for Oyster Bay. Roosevelt received him the following afternoon on the tennis court, racquet in hand, and they conversed during "intervals of the game." Other members of the Portsmouth delegations conferred with T.R. at his summer home without public notice, and he maintained a discreet silence to the end of his life about the role he had played in effecting a compromise agreement between the two sides.[52]

It is not hard to find other instances of Roosevelt's capacity for silence. During negotiations prior to the Algeciras Conference, he confided in neither Hay nor the leading ambassadors. It took historians twenty years to uncover his Taft-Katsura memorandum with Japan.[53] One can mention the secret investigations ordered in connection with crises that arose in Panama, Venezuela, and the Dominican Republic, as well as his decision to burn evidence of the kaiser's indiscretion which was to have been shown to Lord Lansdowne.[54] The list is long.

Roosevelt was thus true to form when he managed his negotiations over the Venezuela blockade in such a way as to keep them from the press and off the official record. In his annual address to Congress of 2 December 1902, he stated blandly that there was "not a cloud on the horizon." Lodge helped him forestall debate in the Senate just before the Christmas holidays, and he allowed himself to be reported as late as 16 December not thinking the situation in the Caribbean especially grave.

As for the thesis that it was public opinion in Britain and the United States rather than Roosevelt's hard line and ready arm that caused the allies to accept arbitration, a slight ripple of public indignation did follow allied bombardment of Puerto Cabello on 13 December. But the *New York Herald* ran an article the next day under the caption "Senators Trust Venezuela Question to the President." Secretary Root told a House committee that there was "no possibility" of war. And even when the press began to reflect more serious concern, on the fifteenth of the month, its general tone remained mild. The *Outlook* gave Venezuela no special prominence in its issues of 13 and 20 December. It simply announced on the thirteenth, almost as if under orders from the White House, that "as far as the United States is concerned, there seems to be no likelihood of friction." The *Chicago Tribune* reported that Roosevelt wanted no inflammation of public opinion since he hoped the situation would be adjusted by arbitration. At the same time, officials emphasized that the well-publicized American fleet maneuvers were not to be interpreted as hostile to Germany or Great Britain. By this time, British leaders were in retreat and Germany had decided unofficially to yield.[55] Despite some rumblings in Congress and several days of stock market jitters, editorial opinion never became heated. A canvass of the *New York Times, Chicago Tribune,* and *Evening Star* indicates that the December editions showed "firmness and intelligent concern . . . rather than bellicosity."[56] In addition, British opinion seems to have been as dilatory as American, judging from a list of hostile petitions received by Lord Lansdowne, none of which is dated prior to 16 December.[57]

Another reason for accepting Roosevelt's version of the Venezuela affair is that he did not manufacture it on the spot in 1916. Professor Beale has cited letters penned long before 1916 which bear this out, and there are others written at the time of the crisis which tend to confirm the point. A few days after the initial concessions by Germany and Britain, T.R. told publisher Albert Shaw that he had experienced "no little difficulty" and felt he had won "a great triumph" even though he was not yet "out of the woods." To Taft, on the same day, he wrote that his victory had been "second only to that of the coal strike in real importance."[58] These are strong words for Roosevelt, and he continued to mention Venezuela in subsequent letters as one of the chief successes of his first term.[59] Two letters addressed to Whitelaw Reid, American ambassador to Britain, are particularly revealing. In the first, dated 27 June 1906, he described his ultimatum as one which brought the kaiser "to terms at once." In the second, dated 4 December 1908, he promised someday to give Reid the "inside history" of Venezuela and to tell him of "the message" he sent the kaiser and of its "instantaneous effect." To Henry White, on 14 August 1906, he came close to outlining the details of his confrontation: I "had to make a display of force and to convince him definitely that I would use the force if necessary. . . . I saw the German ambassador privately myself. . . . I do not know whether it was a case of *post hoc* or *propter hoc;* but immediately afterwards, the Kaiser made to me the proposition that I should arbitrate myself." Significantly, he added that "where I have forced him to give way, I have been sedulously anxious to build a bridge of gold for him."[60]

In the second of the above-mentioned letters to Reid, Roosevelt compares the Venezuela incident to the world cruise of the great white fleet. He sees both as examples of how to speak softly and carry a big stick—or, in other words, the use of force in polite and friendly style. Similar comparisons appear elsewhere, as, for instance, in a letter to Arthur Lee in which he claims to have "brought both Germany and Japan to a sharp account and made them instantly back water when we came into contact with them, and *especially with Germany* on points where I thought they were wrong."[61] (Italics added.) The parallel is interesting not only for what it reveals about the way the Venezuela affair was settled, but also because it introduces still another challenge to the credibility of the president.

Roosevelt states in his *Autobiography* that the major purpose of sending his battleships on a world cruise in 1907 was to impress the American people (presumably to obtain more funds for the navy) and to afford practice for the fleet maneuvers. "Practice" was also the explanation that he gave to naval officers and to Congress in his annual address. Yet, in a fifty-page letter to the British historian Sir George Otto Trevelyan, he explained his motivation in terms very similar to what he told Reid: that while doing his best to be polite and courteous to Japan, he had begun to detect a "very very slight undertone of veiled truculence in their communications in connection with things that happened on the Pacific Slope. . . . It was time for a show down. I had great confidence in the fleet."[62]

These divergent accounts have baffled scholars for years. Some accept the public explanation given in the *Autobiography* and annual address. Others rely on the private version. Still others give equal weight to both or add theories of their own.[63] To confuse things still further, Raymond Esthus found no evidence in the Japanese or American archives that would seem to justify Roosevelt's reference to "veiled truculence" in Japanese communications relating to the west coast.[64]

A brief review of the historical context will demonstrate that Roosevelt was not and could not be altogether candid in his autobiographical account. Ever since the Japanese victories over Russia in 1904 and 1905, he had been concerned about the possibility of a raid on the Philippines, Hawaii, or even California. The Japanese had launched their surprise attack on Russia just as the trans-Siberian railway was nearing completion. Might they not strike the United States at an equally opportune time, prior to the building of the Panama Canal, with the United States on the verge of adding powerful new warships to its fleet? Were they not strengthening their diplomatic ties with Colombia to establish a base for the seizure of the Canal Zone? It would be easy enough for them to seize Hawaii and Panama and then announce to a sympathetic world that they were going to build an "international" canal. They were buying large quantities of ammunition and, in Roosevelt's view, were in "great danger of having their heads turned."[65] They had rioted for two days in response to his blocking of their extreme demands at Portsmouth; and his portrait, once prominently displayed in Tokyo shop windows, had been turned to the wall. Even before Portsmouth, he had expressed concern that the Japanese in Hawaii outnumbered the whites and were "showing signs of an insolent temper." After Portsmouth, when some Japanese seal fishermen were shot for poaching on American preserves, Secretary Root did not like "the spirit" shown by Japanese officials.[66]

It was the outbreak of serious anti-Japanese discrimination on the west coast, however, that led to a war scare in the summer of 1907. Californians vented their anger at the increasing influx of oriental labor by requiring Japanese students to attend segregated schools. There were mob as-

saults on Japanese persons and property. Roosevelt replied
with a scorching condemnation, pointing out that he was
duty-bound to mobilize the National Guard to protect the
rights of all persons living in California. At the same time,
he inserted complimentary references to Japan in his annual
message of 1906. And he prevailed upon Tokyo, by means of
the famous Gentlemen's Agreement of February 1907, to
promise voluntary restriction of emigration, thus allowing
her to save face while affording California a measure of
relief.[67]

The problem was that Japan did not honor the Gentlemen's Agreement; the west coast disturbances did not end;
and Roosevelt feared that Tokyo would construe his sympathetic response as a form of weakness. There were signs of
approaching danger. Early in 1907, the heads of the Japanese chambers of commerce wrote to their American coun-
terparts in language that threatened a crippling boycott of
American goods. Rumors circulated that the mild-mannered
and conciliatory Aoki, Japanese ambassador to the United
States, might be replaced by a spokesman for the hard line.
Roosevelt told his son Kermit that the Japanese were acting
"cocky and unreasonable" and that there might be trouble
with them at any time. On 26 July, he wrote Root that
"their heads seem to be swollen to a marvellous degree." In-
stinctively, he wished to conciliate a potential foe by in-
serting face-saving phrases in his annual message of 1907
while at the same time standing firm on the matter of American rights. He was dissuaded from doing so, however, by
Luke Wright, American ambassador to Japan, as well as by
Francis Huntington Wilson, third assistant secretary of
state. Their impression of Nippon coincided with his own:
she was altogether too "cocky." As for Secretary of War
Taft, he had thought the Japanese *"tête monté"* ever since
the war.[68]

It is abundantly clear from confidential correspondence,
written both at the time of the decision and after, that Roosevelt's primary aim was to let Japan know that the United
States was not to be intimidated when it came to such mat-

ters as immigration policy and the occupation of the Philippines—that she was ready and willing to fight, if necessary, to defend her vital interests and safeguard the national honor. He did not, however, expect the cruise to lead to war. On the contrary, he believed it to be the best guarantee of peace; and when he called it a "good will cruise" by "sixteen messengers of peace," his words were sincere, whatever they may have concealed.[69] It must be remembered that the navy did not wish to send the fleet beyond California; indeed, many naval experts from abroad considered a round-the-world trip to be virtually impossible. In no sense, therefore, was Roosevelt's decision a response to official pressure.[70] At the same time, he could not afford to be entirely candid, for if he had revealed all aspects of the delicate situation, he would not only have triggered a full-blown war scare but made it virtually impossible for Japanese leaders to find a graceful exit from their difficult corner. As he told his son, he dared not advertise his concern lest he bring on the "grave trouble" he hoped to avoid. It was for this reason that he concealed the final destination of the fleet for as long as possible and introduced it to naval officers and the general public as a "practice cruise."[71] Admiral Mahan proceeded to write an article on the "practice cruise" for *Scientific American* which echoed Roosevelt's line and helped to mislead historians.[72] Meanwhile, the American commander in the Philippines was alerted to expect hostilities "momentarily" and to prepare the defense of the islands "as quietly as possible and without ostentation."[73]

The fleet had not been long at sea when, in Roosevelt's words, "every particle of trouble with the Japanese government and the Japanese press stopped like magic."[74] Tokyo put the best face on the cruise by inviting it to stop for a visit along the way and offered a cornucopia of diplomatic concessions. These included an arbitration agreement (5 May 1908), two treaties for the protection of trade marks in Korea and China (19 May), a favorable settlement of the long-pending Kapsan mining case (17 June), full compliance with the Gentlemen's Agreement, and, in November, the

Root-Takahira Agreement, which confirmed the American
position in the Philippines and the Open Door for China.[75] In
addition, Japan agreed in early 1909 to consider restrictions
on her right to hunt seals off the American-owned Pribilof
Islands. This last concession was particularly significant in
light of Tokyo's past record of intransigence and the fact
that up to 1908 the Nipponese fishing fleet had been challenging American sealers in ever-increasing numbers. Suddenly, in 1909, the number of Japanese fishing schooners off
the Pribilofs dropped nearly 50 percent.[76]

Up to this point, Roosevelt's effort to camouflage his
motives and cover his tracks was aimed as much at arresting the war scare on both sides of the Pacific as it was at
saving face for Japan.[77] But he continued to play the
diplomatic game long after the threat of war subsided. In a
unique gesture of good will, he asked Congress for funds to
participate in the upcoming Tokyo world's fair. Then, when
the fair had to be postponed to the chagrin of its sponsors,
he presented Congress with a graceful explanation. This was
the Roosevelt who reflected, as the fleet steamed home, that
the use of power "should be accompanied with every mani-
festation of politeness and friendship—manifestations
which are sincere, by the way, for the foreign policy in which
I believe is in very fact the policy of speaking softly and
carrying a big stick. I want to make it evident to every foreign nation that I intend to do justice; and neither to wrong
them nor to hurt their self-respect."[78] Hence it was that he
composed an autobiographical account of the cruise, years
later, giving only the most peripheral account of his
motives.

Roosevelt's penchant for face saving is the key to much
of the mystery surrounding his foreign policy, and in order
to appreciate it, one must cast aside the common impression
of him as a person of unalloyed bluntness. Critics, referring
to his fondness for the slogan "Speak softly and carry a big
stick," have charged that he was "incapable of speaking
softly." According to Thomas Bailey, his soft-spoken language resembled "the bellowing of a bull moose during
mating season." His public boast in 1911 of having "taken"

the Canal Zone is often cited as evidence of an unbridled tongue.[79] This is only a small part of the story, however. A sharp tongue he had. He was not one to suffer fools gladly, and he called a spade a spade. Examples of his spleen abound: William Jennings Bryan was "a professional yodeler," a "human trombone"; Castro of Venezuela an "unspeakably villainous little monkey"; Sir Mortimer Durand a man of "mutton-suet consistency" with a "brain of about five guinea pig power"; King Leopold of Belgium, a "dissolute old rake" (a remark blurted out at a dinner for friends and officials).[80] But this same Roosevelt could be a master of discretion when the occasion required it. It would not be an exaggeration to say that in the field of diplomacy he was nearly *always* tactful and courteous. The finesse with which he arranged and hosted the Portsmouth peace talks was recognized the world over, nor was Baron Rosen of the Russian delegation alone in praising him for "admirable" tact which seemed so natural.[81]

Portsmouth is only one example of many. The instructions he drafted for American participation in the International Conference of American States (1901) are indisputably the work of a deft and sophisticated statesman.[82] One can cite his repeated use of the word "tact," which he often linked with two other words: "firmness" and "courtesy."[83] In his history of New York, he speaks of Governor Stuyvesant as a man who "knew how to show both tact and firmness in dealing with his foes." In like manner he characterizes Governor Nicolls's administration as "an iron hand beneath the velvet glove."[84] Even before reaching the presidency, he urged McKinley to appoint insular governors who combined these three qualities, and he insisted on the importance of tact as a standard ingredient in the conduct of foreign policy.[85]

Although he mellowed under the weight of increased responsibility, he was not without tact even in his earliest years.[86] The first foray he ever made into public life brought him to within a few votes of the speakership of the New York State Assembly, and he was notably careful, in the Governor's Mansion as well as in the White House, to avoid

frontal assaults on boss politicians. He did not wish "to
humiliate them or to seem victorious over them," despite
his contempt for what they represented. So he flattered,
cajoled, consulted, and threatened them in strictest secrecy.
He built an impressive case against Lou Payn, the corrupt
state commissioner of insurance, and quietly removed him
in the face of formidable opposition from Boss Platt's
machine. He chose not to publicize evidence of Payn's dis-
honesty, preferring instead to enunciate, for the first time,
his now famous maxim: "Speak softly and carry a big
stick." He raised the eyebrow of many a reformer by sitting
down to regular breakfasts with Platt. But the appearances
were deceptive, for while he catered to Platt's vanity, he was
extracting the hard coin of concession. In the case of the anthracite coal strike, he delighted in hitting upon a face-
saving expedient which satisfied the mine operators as well
as the union.[87] Thus he was consistent, pursuing the same
tactics in domestic politics as in the field of foreign affairs.

One historian has written that Roosevelt was the first
president to make prestige an important factor in American
foreign policy.[88] One might add that he was just as con-
scious of the *amour-propre* of other nations as he was of his
own. It was not out of character for him to praise the kaiser
for preserving Chinese territorial integrity in 1904 or to
credit the czar with holding a second Hague Peace Conference even though, in both these instances, the initiative had
come from him. Rarely did he win a contest that he did not
go out of his way to bind up his opponent's wounds. He
backed the Algeciras Conference in order to "save the
Emperor's esteem" and assured France that she would receive "the kernel of the nut" in return for her cooperation.
When the conference voted decisively against German proposals, he congratulated the kaiser on an "epoch-making
success" and warned France to "abstain from a noisy
celebration of victory."[89]

Both Admiral Dewey and General MacArthur boasted
that the Venezuelan incident had been "an object lesson to
the Kaiser," and both were immediately silenced. Dewey's

gaffe was reported in the *New York Herald* on 27 March 1903. The next day, he was summoned to the White House for a sharp reprimand; and on 30 March, Roosevelt wrote him that "we are too big a people to be able to be careless as to what we say." Admiral Taylor also received a warning against "boasting, or saying anything that will hurt the feelings of powers with which we are at peace." At the same time, Roosevelt came out publicly against strident claims and applied the expression "speak softly" to the context of foreign affairs.[90] To sweeten Germany's pill in the Venezuela crisis he ordered an American battleship to make a special appearance at the Kiel naval show. He even approved of German influence in South America and said he would favor a German state if it could be carved from the territory of Brazil.[91] This is as close as one can come to a clear-cut deception on Roosevelt's part and can only be understood in terms of his policy always to allow a vanquished foe to save face.[92]

One final case deserves special mention. This is the way in which Roosevelt chose to settle the Alaskan boundary dispute with Canada. Although he did not believe the Canadians had a legal leg to stand on, he agreed to allow their leaders to save face by submitting the question to a quasi-judicial joint commission with the private understanding that he would never be forced to recede from his fundamental position. There is an impression that he rubbed Canada's face in the dirt by appointing American commissioners who were outspokenly opposed to the Canadian claim while the agreement called for "impartial jurists of repute"; also, that he bludgeoned the commission into accepting his basic position.[93] There may be truth in this, although the merit of Roosevelt's position deserves further analysis and will be considered more carefully in the next chapter. What is important here is the manner in which he applied pressure on England.

Without making a single public threat, he confided to Arthur S. Raikes, the British chargé, that he was prepared to be "ugly" if the decision were not favorable (Pauncefote,

the regular ambassador, was fatally ill at the time). To
George Smalley, New York correspondent for the London
Times, he said in private that he meant "to be drastic" if
need be. He conveyed this attitude to trusted members of
the diplomatic corps, including Sternburg, and transmitted
it to important British officials through such intermediaries
as Oliver Wendell Holmes, Joseph Choate, Henry White,
and his three commission appointees.[94] On 8 August 1903,
Joseph Chamberlain reported to Prime Minister Balfour
from his post at the Colonial Office that Justice Holmes had
called upon him that day to read a private letter sent by the
President. The gist of it was that the Canadians had no case
whatever and that,

only his intense desire to remain on good terms with England had
induced him to allow such a matter to be the subject of discussion
at all. He went on to say that, if the arbitration did not result in a
satisfactory agreement, he would appeal to Congress in such
terms that he felt sure they would give him the appropriation for
which he asked, and he would then take possession of the line to
which the United States was clearly entitled.

For a final diplomatic thrust, Roosevelt recruited steel-
master Andrew Carnegie. On 23 July 1903, Carnegie wrote
Balfour that Canadian claims in Alaska were "trumped up."
"Is your career to be dimmed by disaster? Because of my
deep interest in you and in my native land, I wish to record
my conviction that nothing but disaster can follow an attempt to prefer Canada over the Republic."[95]
   In the meantime, T.R. had emitted another quiet, yet
rather more tangible, signal of his determination—namely,
the sending of eight hundred cavalrymen to the disputed
boundary area. The reason generally alleged at the time and
still accepted by some historians is that more troops were
needed for police duty lest angry miners clash over new dis-
coveries of gold.[96] Like Roosevelt's public account of the
world cruise, however, this constituted only a partial explanation at best. England had resisted an effort by Hay to
send troops in 1899, and all investigations of the border,

both Canadian and American, beginning with Senator Fairbanks's report of July 1899 and extending through the reports of 1901 and early 1902, minimized the danger of a clash. This is reflected in Lord Lansdowne's cable to Lord Pauncefote on 24 January 1902, in which Lansdowne reported that the United States Government considered the rumors of disturbances in the Yukon district "to be much exaggerated. . . . In the opinion of the Canadian government there is no cause for alarm . . . the necessary police precautions have been taken." Later, on 28 March, only one day after the troop order had been issued from the White House, the British ambassador reported a sudden and serious hardening of the American position which would rule out any kind of arbitration in the formal sense. It is also known that by May Colonel Kitson was sending information to London "as affecting the defense of Canada" in "reply to some enquiries."[97] Whitehall, at least, seems to have had little difficulty interpreting the meaning of the president's action.

Roosevelt came to the point in a letter to Lodge some years later: "I actually moved troops up into Alaska so as to be able immediately to take possession of the important disputed points and hold them against small bodies of Canadians in the event that the effort to come to an agreement resulted in nothing." Lodge had wanted troops sent to the area for precisely this reason, and his wish was granted over the protest of Secretary Hay just after he had conferred with Roosevelt at the White House. Hay, a confirmed Anglophile, suggested that if troops were to be sent, they should be sent "very quietly."[98] They were. Roosevelt remained true to his original intention, which, in Hay's words, was "to enable the British government to get out of an absolutely untenable position with dignity and honor." He never boasted of victory, as he is said to have done.[99] On the contrary, he said in retrospect that the settlement "offered signal proof of the fairness and good will with which two friendly nations can approach and determine issues." And he congratulated the British for doing as well as they had,

adding that if he had ever appointed men of true judicial
stature, Canada would not have come out nearly as well as
she did.[100]

Because Roosevelt was such a positive person, his every
word fairly bristling with controversy, he has drawn the fire
of a great many critics, and it is hard to distinguish between
those who merely challenge his judgment and those who
question his credibility. When his opponents accuse him of
fomenting the Panamanian Revolution, it is clearly his credibility which is at stake, for this is a matter of objective fact
which he vigorously denied. But when they take issue with
him for claiming that he acted legally and morally to sustain
the independence of Panama, the issue is just as clearly one
of judgment. Thus far, he has been vindicated by history in
the first matter, while in the second there is considerable
room for disagreement. Other matters of judgment on which
he is commonly questioned include the magnitude of Germany's threat to the Western Hemisphere, the efficacy of
his actions in connection with the Alaskan boundary tribunal and world cruise, and the extent of his role in the
Portsmouth and Algeciras conferences.[101]

One of the things that Arthur Lee remembered about
T.R.'s visit to London in 1910 was something the Roosevelt
children said while they and their parents were staying at
his home. Ethel and Kermit complained to Mrs. Roosevelt
that their father talked too much about himself, and they
asked Lee whether he couldn't do something to "persuade
Father not to write his name so large" in the visitor book![102]
This is a side of Roosevelt that has been forgotten more by
his friends than by his enemies, and it tends to suggest that
his judgment is least reliable when he is assessing his own
importance in world affairs. As will be seen in chapter five,
he did win an unprecedented measure of esteem for the
United States and became the most internationally popular
figure ever to occupy the White House. As long as he remained in the White House, his voice carried real weight
wherever international counsel was taken. The issue, however, is one of degree. It would have been a humbling experi-

ence for the Rough Rider to peruse the memoirs of world leaders whom he had known. He would have found that Holstein, in 400 pages of published correspondence and diary for the years 1901 to 1909, mentioned his name only three times, once in connection with Portsmouth and twice casually in conjunction with Algeciras. He would have encountered a similar void in the memoirs of Kaiser Wilhelm, who mentions him once in 342 pages only to minimize his importance in ending the Russo-Japanese War. Bülow refers to Roosevelt and the United States in the most perfunctory manner, and British statesmen seem to have assessed his world role as distinctly minor.[103]

He was particularly proud of his part in expediting a negotiated settlement of the Russo-Japanese War, believing that if the belligerents had not met at Portsmouth, "they would not have made peace."[104] There may be substance in this, for he intervened at frequent intervals to offer advice. Privately, he urged each belligerent to moderate its demands on the other; he also worked hard to shape world opinion for a compromise settlement.[105] Both parties, however, were thoroughly tired of war, Russia because of continual military reverses and domestic unrest, Japan because of an empty purse. The Wilhelmstrasse gave strong support to Roosevelt's good offices because it feared Anglo-French intervention and expected, in return, to receive American support on the Moroccan issue.[106] Furthermore, both Russia and Japan were prepared from the outset to yield the lion's share of their preconference demands. The key stipulations formulated by Japan were for an indemnity and Sakhalin Island. Yet the Japanese delegation was authorized, even before setting foot in the United States, to give way on both points rather than prolong the war. The czar was also far more flexible than appearances might suggest. Publicly, he ruled out any concessions on Sakhalin and refused to pay a single kopek in reparations. At the same time, his chief delegate, Count Serge Witte, offered at one point in the talks to give up all of Sakhalin.[107] Later, after yielding South Sakhalin and agreeing to pay for an exchange of prisoners,

Witte claimed to have "achieved more than was expected of me."[108]

The best evidence of the czar's underlying flexibility is an interview he granted American ambassador George von Lengerke Meyer on 23 August in which he stated flatly that he would cede South Sakhalin. When Meyer then suggested a payment for retention of the north, Nicholas did not rule it out. Rather, he asked, "How can that be ascertained?" and insisted that he "would not pay a substantial sum." The presence of a finance minister on the Russian peace delegation suggested all along that St. Petersburg was prepared to pay something by way of compensation.[109] The Russians would not have come to Portsmouth had they been unwilling to retreat on one or both of the major issues, nor would they have been so quick to make minor concessions in peripheral areas.

Roosevelt felt that his last-minute intercession as the Russians were packing their bags and threatening to bolt had been decisive. Perhaps. But the servants of the czar were not the first diplomats in history to pack their bags under pressure. A Roosevelt message to St. Petersburg did abort an apparent order from Nicholas to break up the conference. But a little while later, the czar again ordered his delegation to pack, and this time it chose to make peace. Witte was wily enough to use the orders of his imperial master to full advantage. The Russians had a strong hand with one powerful trump card, and they knew it. In addition to breaking the American diplomatic code, they were well aware of the crucial weakness in the Japanese bargaining position—finances. It is interesting to observe that although England was Japan's only ally, the British foreign minister was still puzzled as to why Tokyo finally backed down, attributing it to the influence of Marquis Itō as well as to Roosevelt's "powerful argument." Roosevelt himself, however, spoke to the crux of the issue a bit earlier, when he predicted that his role as mediator would succeed if the matter was one of "punctilio" but fail if there was any substantial difference between the opposing sides.[110]

T.R.'s famous boast that he stood the kaiser "on his head" during the Algeciras Conference is another claim that is hard to substantiate. As Roosevelt saw it, he secured a pledge from Ambassador Sternburg that if he supported a conference to consider the disposition of French interest in Morocco, Germany would then follow his lead in the event of stalemate. A stalemate did occur, he threatened to reveal Sternburg's pledge, and the kaiser yielded. The assumption is, therefore, that because Germany yielded on the aftermath of American pressure, she must have yielded because of it, *post hoc ergo propter hoc.* [111] In actual fact, there are many possible reasons. Between the time that the kaiser originally demanded the conference and the time it convened, France's ally extricated herself from a debilitating war with Japan and rebuffed Germany's anxious offer of an alliance. The Bjorko agreement, so inauspicious for French security, had come to nothing. Germany's position had thus been substantially reduced by the time she reached Algeciras, whatever T.R. may have said or done.

Nor did the conference represent as much of a loss on the part of Germany as might be supposed. The mere fact that it was held, coupled with the fact that France bowed before a German ultimatum and suffered the resignation of her foreign secretary was a stunning victory for Berlin. Bülow wrote on 7 June 1905: "Delcassé's fall . . . ought to close the acute phase of the Morocco question, whether the conference takes place or not." [112] The kaiser seems to have agreed with his chancellor, since he seized upon the occasion to make him a prince. Certainly, France regarded any interference in her colonial affairs by an international body as gravely humiliating. And although Germany did not emerge from the talks as strongly as she had hoped—particularly in her failure to split the Anglo-French entente—nonetheless, her interests were more secure than they had been before. Two years prior to the conference, the Quai d'Orsay had persuaded Morocco to place her entire debt into the hands of a French consortium which would collect revenue at eight ports. A French syndicate was to have an option on all future loans, and France was to oversee the coinage and purchase of silver and gold—in other words, almost complete financial control. In October, Paris and Madrid proceeded to divide North Africa into neat spheres of influence. In July, France was authorized to begin training the military police of Tangier. She could therefore look forward to nothing less than control of the two key aspects of life in Morocco: constabulary and banking.[113]

From this position of virtually no influence in Morocco, Germany advanced by means of the conference to an assurance that her financial interests would be protected, at least temporarily, from a French monopoly. Before setting foot in Algeciras, Bülow had secured general agreement to three principles: the territorial integrity of Morocco, the absolute independence of the sultan, and the open door for commerce. Both the chancellor and the kaiser later claimed, with some justification, that although Germany had not done as well as she would have liked in the actual settlement, she had done as well as could be expected. She had gained a form of compromise on the two key issues. Four of the important police posts were to be under French control, two under Spanish, and the two most important (Tangier and Casablanca) under a force trained by Spanish as well as French officers and supervised by the inspector of a neutral power. The bank was to be international (with each signatory to have one share against three for France) and it would operate under four supervisors to be appointed by France, Spain, Britain, and Germany.[114]

None of this is to suggest that Roosevelt's role in the conference was not large, perhaps even decisive, in a tactical sense. Nor is it to deny that Germany made significant concessions. British records indicate that T.R. was active from the beginning of the talks to the end, albeit secretly. It would seem, too, that his ultimatum to the kaiser did produce an "instantaneous" effect, and that with one or two false starts, he helped to shape the final settlement on police organization. France, nevertheless, had to accept a much more modest role in Morocco than that which she was prepared to play when the kaiser landed at Tangier, and, as one diplomat observed, "if she wishes hereafter to get rid of the German incubus, she must make a bargain with Prince Bülow or his successors as she did with Lord Lansdowne." As for standing Wilhelm on his head, T.R. was most likely exaggerating his anti-German bias in order to mend his reputation in London. It was to his ambassador at the Court of St. James's that he addressed his celebrated account of head standing, and, as Professor Perkins has observed, he generally "tailored his foreign correspondence to the nationality of the recipient, using it either to instruct or to flatter."[115]

What, then, are we to conclude with regard to Roosevelt's credibility? Like any mortal, he was fallible in matters of personal judgment, and his memory, as he readily admitted, could fail him on occasion. One might argue that world peace did not depend on his contribution to the Portsmouth and Algeciras conferences to the extent he liked to believe. But the real issue is whether his word can be trusted on matters of fact, and of this there is scant room for doubt. In the oft-cited case of Venezuela, the absence of documentary evidence in official archives supports his story far more than it weakens it, especially when viewed as part of an obvious gap in the surviving record. In addition, what we know of his bargaining style in domestic and foreign affairs confirms the idea that he was just as capable of speaking softly as he was of carrying a big stick. Soft speaking, in Roosevelt's sense, did not mean the mincing of words or any hedging on issues. T.R. addressed himself forcefully, even pointedly, to foreign envoys. But he did so privately and in such a way as to afford a graceful exit from awkward confrontation.

He never misrepresented the broad outline of his policy, as other presidents have done. Even in the case of the world cruise, he did not label his battleships "messengers of peace" in order to disguise a policy he knew would lead to war, but rather because he anticipated peace and regarded his action as the surest step in that direction. Admittedly, the secrecy in which he wrapped sensitive negotiations is a stumbling block for those who insist on conclusive evidence for each of his claims. His policy of allowing vanquished opponents to save face did not always permit candid public accounting. In such cases, one must read between the lines and search out the truth in private letters. Even here, he may have exaggerated, on occasion, to achieve an effect. On balance, though, the circumstantial evidence is heavily on his side wherever he made a statement of fact. It would require more than a single essay to examine every last challenge to his credibility. But it is fair to say that, as far as one can judge from the diplomatic record, his original reputation for honesty stands upon solid ground.

Notes

1. See, for example, Thomas A. Bailey, *Presidential Greatness,* pp. 307–308; John Morton Blum, *The Republican Roosevelt,* pp. 126–27; Robert A. Friedlander, "A Reassessment of Roosevelt's Role in the Panamanian Revolution of 1903," *Western Political Quarterly* 14 (June 1961): 535, 541, 543; Edward B. Parsons, "Roosevelt's Containment of the Russo-Japanese War," *Pacific Historical Review* 38 (February 1969): 34 n. (a reference to Alfred Vagts). According to Max Beloff, "retrospective exaggeration was a well-known Rooseveltian failing." Beloff, *The Great Powers,* p. 222.

2. Roosevelt to Cecil Spring Rice, 27 December 1904, 24 July 1905, *Letters,* 4:1087, 1284.

3. Historians who question Roosevelt on this point include A. Whitney Griswold, Alfred Vagts, John Morton Blum, Samuel Flagg Bemis, and Edward Zabriskie. For the most recent defense of Roosevelt's claims and a brief historiographical summary, see Parsons, "Roosevelt's Containment."

4. Ibid., pp. 36–37; Friedrich von Holstein, *The Holstein Papers: The Memoirs, Diaries, and Correspondence of Friedrich von Holstein, 1837–1909,* ed. Norman Rich and H. M. Fisher, 4 vols., 4:278, (hereafter cited as *Holstein Papers*). See also Oron James Hale, *Germany and the Diplomatic Revolution, 1904–1906;* Raymond A. Esthus, *Theodore Roosevelt and Japan,* p. 45.

5. Roosevelt to George von Lengerke Meyer, 26 December 1904, quoted by Mark A. DeWolfe Howe, *George von Lengerke Meyer, His Life and Public Services,* p. 110; Seward W. Livermore, "The American Navy as a Factor in World Politics, 1903–1913," *American Historical Review* 63 (July 1958): 869.

6. Roosevelt made his claim in three letters to William Roscoe Thayer, 21, 23, 27 August 1916, *Letters,* 8:1101–1108. It should be noted that there are two versions of what T.R. wrote on 21 August. Compare *Letters,* 8:1103: "A week later . . . the Ambassador notified me" with Joseph B. Bishop, *Theodore Roosevelt and His Time Shown in His Letters,* 2 vols., 1:224: "A few days later . . . the Embassy notified me." Bishop, whose version was reprinted by others, including Howard Hill and Dexter Perkins, may have been trying to make Roosevelt appear more credible. In any case, it is the Morison version that squares with the original manuscript. One should also note that Roosevelt's accounts of the ultimatum are not entirely consistent, leaving unclear the precise interval between Holleben's visits. Compare, for example, his letters to Thayer with Thayer's account in *The Life and Letters of John Hay,* 2 vols., 2:287–88; also, two of T.R.'s speeches of 1917, cited in Howard C. Hill, *Roosevelt and The Caribbean,* pp. 132–33 n. The differences are so minor, however, as to be nearly imperceptible. Roosevelt admitted, in his letter of 23 August, that his recall may have been a trifle faulty. Nor does such inconsistency vitiate the main thrust of his claim, which is that he gave the Germans an extremely sharp ultimatum that included a specific time limit.

7. Historians disagree on the details of the allied operations. James Ford Rhodes, J. G. Latané, and others name Germany as initiator of the joint naval action. But more recent accounts lean to England: Hill, *Roosevelt,* p. 110; Chester L. Jones, *The Caribbean Since 1900,* p. 221; and Charles S. Campbell, Jr., *Anglo-American Understanding, 1898–1903,* p. 271. Warren G. Kneer, *Great Britain and the Caribbean 1901–1913: A Study in Anglo-American Relations,* holds that Germany and Britain share responsibility, pp. 13 ff. Some say Germany sank three gunboats as, for example, Hill, p. 117 n. Others put the number at two: Campbell, p. 276; Dexter Perkins, *The Monroe Doctrine, 1867–1907,* p. 337; Kneer, *Great Britain,* p. 32. According to the German Embassy in Washington, the kaiser's navy was forced to sink two gunboats because they were unseaworthy; but an American observer, Lt. Comdr. F. B. Diehl, reported that the original intention had been to hold the gunboats in custody at Curaçao and that they were sunk only when the German ship *Panther* had to leave them in order to go to the aid of the German consul in La Guayra; Memorandum, 18 December 1902, Notes from the German Embassy in the United States to the Department of State, Record Group 59, Microfilm M58, Reel T32 National Archives, Washing-

ton, D.C.; Diehl to the Secretary of the Navy, undated, Naval Records Collection of the Office of Naval Records and Library, Record Group 45, Area File 8, December 1902–January, 1903, Microfilm M625, Reel 261, National Archives. As for what day the Germans bombarded Fort San Carlos, it was 17 January, according to Perkins, pp. 354, 370; 18 January, according to Howard K. Beale, *Theodore Roosevelt and the Rise of America to World Power,* p. 423; 17 *and* 18 January, according to Edward B. Parsons, "The German-American Crisis of 1902–1903," *The Historian* 33 (May 1971): 437, 447; 21 January, according to Campbell, p. 292, and Kneer, p. 44. As to how many ships fired on it, Beale, *Roosevelt,* p. 423, gives the number as three, while Bradford Perkins, *The Great Rapprochement,* p. 190, gives it as one. See Hill, p. 137 n. for a list of common misconceptions about the nature of the blockade and claims settlement.

8. Works by such scholars as Thayer, Bishop, James Ford Rhodes, and A. L. P. Dennis; also, the celebrated newspaperman and White House fixture throughout the T.R. years, O. K. Davis, *Released for Publication.*

9. Hill, *Roosevelt,* pp. 106–47; J. Fred Rippy, *Latin America in World Politics* (New York: Alfred A. Knopf, 1928), pp. 194–95; Alfred Vagts, *Deutschland und die Vereinigten Staaten in der Weltpolitik,* 2 vols., 2:1555–1630; Perkins, *Monroe Doctrine, 1867–1907,* pp. 335–95, especially pp. 377 ff. The latest confirmation of a lack of evidence in English archives is Kneer, *Great Britain,* p. 37.

10. Nicholas Roosevelt, *Theodore Roosevelt: The Man as I Knew Him,* pp. 143–45; See also notes 7 and 11 for reference to Beale, Parsons, and Livermore. More recently, Ronald Spector has claimed that neither T.R. nor his naval staff had much confidence in the ability of the U.S. to defeat Germany on the seas; Spector, "Roosevelt, the Navy, and the Venezuela Controversy: 1902–1903," *American Neptune* 32 (October 1972): 257–63. For additional criticism of Roosevelt, see Lionel M. Gelber, *The Rise of Anglo-American Friendship,* pp. 113–17; J. Fred Rippy, *The Caribbean Danger Zone,* pp. 34–35; Samuel Flagg Bemis, *A Diplomatic History of the United States,* p. 525; Bemis, *The Latin-American Policy of the United States,* pp. 146–48. Others who question the Roosevelt story include Foster Rhea Dulles, *America's Rise to World Power,* p. 74 n.; and Julian S. Amery, *The Life of Joseph Chamberlain,* 4 vols., 4:200–201. Great emphasis is laid upon public opinion by Bemis, *Latin-American Policy,* p. 147;

Thomas A. Bailey, *A Diplomatic History of the American People,*
p. 503; Bradford Perkins, *Great Rapprochement,* pp. 191–92; and
Campbell, *Anglo-American Understanding,* chap. 13. Campbell
flatly denies the truth of Roosevelt's account (p. 283 n.), while
Paul S. Holbo suggests that Roosevelt resorted to an ill-advised
"public diplomacy"; in other words, he served his ultimatum
through the press and by means of ambiguous naval operations
rather than through the channels outlined in his 1916 letter to
Thayer. Holbo, "Perilous Obscurity: Public Diplomacy and the
Press in the Venezuelan Crisis, 1902–1903," *The Historian* 32
(May 1970): 428–48. Spector, in his recent biography of Dewey,
seems to side with those who doubt "the dramatic manner" of
T.R.'s ultimatum story, and he wonders if the Caribbean maneuvers were even "designed to impress the Germans." Spector,
Admiral of the New Empire, pp. 141–42.

11. Still indispensable for understanding American naval
maneuvers in the Caribbean is Seward W. Livermore, "Theodore
Roosevelt, the American Navy, and the Venezuela Crisis of
1902–1903," *American Historical Review* 51 (April 1946): 452–71.
See also Spector, *Admiral,* pp. 140–44.

12. Beale, *Roosevelt,* p. 416. The mildness of Roosevelt's
public reply on 16 December has been erroneously interpreted to
signify that he received the German warning "without a tremor."
Dexter Perkins, *A History of the Monroe Doctrine,* p. 218. See also
Dexter Perkins, *Monroe Doctrine, 1867–1907,* p. 326.

13. Andrew D. White, *The Diaries of Andrew D. White,* ed.
Robert Morris Ogden, p. 376. Roosevelt made it clear that the
fleet exercises were his idea and not the navy's; Roosevelt to T. C.
Platt, 28 June 1902, *Letters,* 3:283.

14. Roosevelt to George W. Hinman, 29 December 1902,
Letters, 3:400; Lord Pauncefote to Lord Lansdowne, 28 April
1902, FO 800/144, Lord Lansdowne Papers, PRO.

15. Parsons, "German-American Crisis," p. 442.

16. It might also be noted that on 3 December Admiral
Sperry, commander of the Far East Squadron stationed at Amoy,
China, weighed anchor for the American naval base at Manila via
Hong Kong. Rear Admiral Charles S. Sperry Papers, Box 1, Let-
terbooks, Library of Congress.

17. George Dewey Papers, Letter Book on Winter Maneu-
vers, Container 54, Library of Congress; Henry Clay Taylor to
William Moody, 14 December 1902, William Henry Moody
Papers, Library of Congress; Dewey to the Secretary of the Navy,

14 December 1902, Naval Records Collection of the Office of Naval Records and Library, Record Group 45, Area File 8, Microfilm M625, Reel 261, National Archives.

18. Castro was preparing to defend Caracas, and it was estimated that the allies might need upwards of twenty thousand troops to capture it; *New York Herald*, 14 December 1902, p. 3.

19. In Lansdowne's words, Germany was concerned that Roosevelt might exchange "the role of post office for one of a more active character," Lansdowne to Sir F. Lascelles, 18 December 1902, George P. Gooch and Harold Temperley, eds., *British Documents on the Origin of the War, 1898-1914*, 11 vols., 2:162.

20. Theodore Roosevelt Papers and Diaries, Library of Congress Microfilm, Reel 430, Series 9-Venezuela.

21. *New York Herald*, 8 December 1902, p. 11; Henry Pringle, *Theodore Roosevelt*, pp. 202-203. The reports on Holleben were, of course, denied by the German Foreign Office.

22. Holleben's ostensible reason for calling at the White House on 8 December (to accompany a German cultural group; Holbo, "Perilous Obscurity," p. 430 n.) in no way precludes a private meeting with the president. One is reminded of the time when Benjamin Franklin, representing the United States in Paris, received a call from a Russian prince and returned the honor by signing the guest register at the Russian embassy. The official record of both visits was erased, however, at the request of an embarrassed Catherine, who had not yet recognized the infant republic and did not wish to jeopardize her lucrative position as a neutral.

23. Hill, *Roosevelt*, p. 144 n.

24. Although Dexter Perkins, in his *History of the Monroe Doctrine*, p. 220, argues that Holleben was in New York from 14 December to 26 December, and although Holleben did indeed cable the foreign office from New York on 16 December, we also have notes from Holleben to the Department of State dated 15, 17, and 18 December, all of them bearing his unmistakable signature and stamped "Rec'd" on 16, 19, and 24 December respectively. Notes from the German Embassy to the Department of State, Record Group 59, Microfilm M58, Reel 58, National Archives; J. Lepsius, A. Mendelssohn Bartholdy, and F. Thimme, eds., *Die Grosse Politik der Europäischen Kabinette, 1871-1914*, 40 vols., 17:264 (hereafter cited as *Grosse Politik*).

25. White to Hay, 15, 16, 17, 18 December 1902, Despatches from United States Ministers to Great Britain, Record Group 59,

Microfilm M30, Reel 193, National Archives; White to Hay, 31 December 1902, Henry White Papers, Box 4, Library of Congress; Campbell, *Anglo-American Understanding,* pp. 276–82. According to Mrs. St. Loe Strachey, wife of the influential editor, "a recently joined member of Mr. Balfour's cabinet" had inquired, " 'Can you tell me who it is who comes to Cabinet meetings whom Mr. Balfour always calls Harry?' It was, of course, Mr. Harry White, Chief Secretary of the American Embassy, who himself was deep in the counsels of the Cabinet," Amy Simpson Strachey, *St. Loe Strachey: His Life and His Paper,* p. 144. Parenthetically, Lord Balfour told the House of Lords on the seventeenth what Lansdowne had told Commons the day before.

26. FO 5/2489, PRO. A glance at FO 566/566, which is the guide to FO 5 for the years 1901–1905, reveals that all nine of the missing cables are related either to Venezuela or Alaska, as one might expect: the two questions were most likely interlocked for bargaining purposes. Even though Sir Michael Herbert was far from the center of the diplomatic crisis (Roosevelt bypassed him completely), he was still close enough to the heat to have his communications removed from the sight of posterity.

27. Arthur H. Lee, *A Good Innings and a Great Partnership, Being The Life Story of Arthur and Ruth Lee,* 1:335; Roosevelt to Henry Cabot Lodge, 29 June 1903, *Roosevelt-Lodge Correspondence,* 2:37; Bradford Perkins, *Great Rapprochement,* p. 189; Allan Nevins, *Henry White: Thirty Years of American Diplomacy,* p. 212. Herbert cabled Lansdowne on 29 December that "the administration has been most friendly throughout," but this was hardly the case; Roosevelt simply made his contact with British leaders through White, whom he believed to be "the most useful man in the entire diplomatic service." Theodore Roosevelt, *An Autobiography,* p. 388.

28. Characteristic of the gaps in the surviving British records is the collection of British documents edited by Gooch and Temperley. Its material on the subject of the Venezuela crisis is so incomplete that it does not contain the slightest hint as to how or why Britain and Germany came to accept Roosevelt's demand for arbitration.

29. Prince Bernhard von Bülow, *Memoirs of Prince von Bülow,* trans. F. A. Voigt, 4 vols., 1:662.

30. The average number of pages, annually, for the three years before and after 1903 is forty-six. For 1903, however, the pages number only three. Holstein, *Holstein Papers,* vol. 4. Rich's

biography, based almost entirely on *Grosse Politik* and the published *Papers*, says only that Holstein spent some time in the Hartz mountains in September 1902. Norman R. Rich, *Friedrich von Holstein*, 2 vols., 2:672.

31. Kaiser Wilhelm II, *My Memoirs, 1878-1918*, pp. 92-119; Bülow, *Memoirs*, 1:641-42. In his history of imperial Germany, Bülow makes the misleading statement that "at the beginning of the new century, America never once opposed our policy," quoted in Hill, *Roosevelt*, p. 136.

32. Bülow, *Memoirs*, 1:641; *Grosse Politik*, 17:239-93, esp. 256, 264; Bülow, *Letters of Prince von Bülow*, trans. Frederic Whyte. These sources should be compared to *Grosse Politik*, vol. 17, which contains an unusually large section on the Venezuela crisis (albeit stripped of critical detail). To be exact, it contains fifty-four pages on the Venezuela crisis, as compared with only thirty for the Franco-Russian entente and twenty for the Anglo-Japanese alliance.

33. German Foreign Ministry Archives on record at The National Archives of the United States, Microfilm T149, Reel 246 (Ver. St. v. Nord Amerika 7: Die americanische Diplomatie); Microfilm T139, Reels 109 (Ver. St. v. Amerika 1: Allgemeine Angelegenheiten von Nord Amerika), 114 (No. 16: Beziehungen der Ver. St. zu Deutschland), 119 (No. 20: Die Allgemeine Politik der Vereinigte Staaten; No. 20a: Die Monroe Doctrin), 120 (No. 5: Militär-Angelegenheiten der Ver. St. von Nord Amerika; No. 17: Beziehungen der Ver. St. v. Nord Amerika zu England), 122 (No. 2: Die Presse der Ver. St. von N. Amerika), 123 (No. 1: Amerikanische Staatsmannen), 125 (No. 11: Präsidenten der Ver. Staaten).

34. Research in the archives of both East and West Germany (Potsdam and Bonn) confirms that they are indeed missing.

35. Aktenzeichen Ver. Staaten ver Amerika No. 22, Bd. 1, Abteilung A, Auswärtiges Amt, Bonn.

36. *Grosse Politik*, 17:264; E. T. S. Dugdale, ed., *German Diplomatic Documents, 1871-1914*, 4 vols., 3:164; Parsons, "German-American Crisis," p. 443. Needless to say, such statements are "queer" only because their context is missing.

37. John Hay Papers, Special Correspondence and General Correspondence, Library of Congress.

38. Records of the United States Embassy in Berlin, Record Group 84, volumes 57-60 and separate register, National Archives; Diplomatic Instructions from the Depatment of State to

the United States Embassy in Berlin, Record Group 59, Microfilm M77, Reel 72, National Archives. An instruction for 8 December appears in the embassy register but not in the State Department register, M17, Reel 17; nor is it anywhere to be found. Also missing is the second of two instructions for 12 December as well as for 16 December. See National Archives Microfilm M44, Reel 96, for dispatches from the American embassy in Berlin preserved by Hay. I am indebted to Sylvia Kasey Marks for this note.

39. Roosevelt, *Autobiography,* p. 110; Livermore, "Venezuela Crisis," p. 470 n.

40. Roosevelt, *Autobiography,* p. 513. See also Blum, *Republican Roosevelt,* pp. 80–81.

41. Hay to John St. Loe Strachey, 16 October 1902, Strachey Papers, House of Lords Library; Lodge to Roosevelt, 2 July 1905, *Roosevelt-Lodge Correspondence,* 2:161–62; Raymond A. Esthus, *Theodore Roosevelt and The International Rivalries,* p. 5; Jean Jules Jusserand, *What Me Befell,* p. 271.

42. Arthur S. Raikes to the British Foreign Office, 9 May 1902, FO 800/144, Lansdowne Papers, PRO.

43. Lee, *Good Innings,* 1:325–26.

44. Arthur Lee came in the fall of 1906 to relay the president's views on Portsmouth and Algeciras; Beale, *Roosevelt,* pp. 134–35; Esthus, *Rivalries,* p. 11; Baron Roman Rosen, *Forty Years of Diplomacy,* 2 vols., 1:256; A. Whitney Griswold, *The Far Eastern Policy of the United States,* p. 113; Hay to White, 23 January 1905, Henry White Papers, Special Correspondence, Box 28, Library of Congress.

45. Sir Mortimer Durand to Lord Lansdowne, 5 February 1905, FO 800/116, Lansdowne Papers, PRO; Esthus, *Rivalries,* p. 18; Beale, *Roosevelt,* p. 418; Bülow, *Letters,* p. 84; Extract from a New York letter, unaddressed and dated June [1906] RA W49/49, Royal Archives, Windsor Castle. This citation and those that follow from the Royal Archives have been included by permission of Her Majesty the Queen.

46. Alan Clark, ed., *'A Good Innings'; The Private Papers of Viscount Lee of Fareham,* p. 83; Lee Memorandum, dated 13 September 1902, in box marked "Personal," Arthur H. Lee Papers, Courtauld Institute, Portman Square, London; Lee, *Good Innings,* 1:260.

47. Amy Simpson Strachey, *Strachey,* pp. 138–39, 142, 144–45, 147; John St. Loe Strachey, *The Adventure of Living: A Subjective Autobiography,* pp. 409–16. It should also be noted that

another intermediary whom T.R. used and who was then the British military attaché in Washington returned to England in late August 1902, after having forwarded copious information to Lansdowne. Arthur S. Raikes to Lord Lansdowne, 25 August 1902, FO 5/2487, PRO.

48. Richard Oswald and Benjamin Vaughan.

49. John St. Loe Strachey to Louis [?], 23 November 1906, FO 800/111, PRO; Blanche Elizabeth Campbell Dugdale, *Arthur James Balfour, First Earl of Balfour,* 2 vols., 1:386, 389; Esthus, *Rivalries,* p. 11.

50. Cabinet Report to the King, 8 February 1903, RA R23/38, Windsor Castle. See also, Kneer, *Great Britain,* p. 58.

51. Lloyd Griscom to Hay, 15 March 1905, Hay Papers, Special Correspondence, Library of Congress Microfilm, Reel 8.

52. Eugene Trani, *The Treaty of Portsmouth: An Adventure in American Diplomacy,* pp. 11, 51, 139–42; Beale, *Roosevelt,* pp. 282, 288, 297, 311; Tyler Dennett, *Roosevelt and the Russo-Japanese War,* p. 339.

53. Disclosure of the Taft-Katsura Memorandum would have undercut his influence with the czar. The Russians were upset that Taft was even stopping in Japan. Roosevelt did divulge his Algeciras role in a letter to Whitelaw Reid on 28 April 1906, but not publicly until he had retired (on a visit to Sir Edward Grey). Beale, *Roosevelt,* pp. 369, 388–89; Lodge to Roosevelt, 25 July 1905, *Roosevelt-Lodge Correspondence,* 2:170.

54. *Le Temps* [Paris] made public the details of the American plan for Algeciras after Roosevelt had insisted that his role be kept secret. Thomas T. Lewis, "Franco-American Relations During the First Moroccan Crisis," *Mid-America* 55 (January 1973): 33. J. Fred Rippy suspected Roosevelt of having Hay hold secret talks with Jusserand on the Dominican Republic crisis. Rippy, "Customs Receivership," p. 436. See also Esthus, *Rivalries,* pp. 127–29; Thomas Bailey, *Theodore Roosevelt and the Japanese-American Crises,* pp. 150, 166; Nevins, *White,* p. 290; Roosevelt to Arthur Lee, 23 November 1908, Lee Papers, Courtauld Institute.

55. Cabinet Report to the King, 15 December 1902, RA R23/25, Windsor Castle Library; *Outlook* 72 (13 December 1902): 867; (20 December 1902): 909–10; Holbo, "Perilous Obscurity," pp. 428–48. On the evening of 15 December, Balfour announced to the House of Commons that Britain would not go to war for Venezuela bondholders. *New York Herald,* 16 December 1902, p. 3.

56. Holbo, "Perilous Obscurity," p. 431. This is confirmed

by a survey of the *New York Herald* for 4-21 December (see especially 20 December, p. 4).

57. Campbell, *Anglo-American Understanding*, p. 284 n.

58. Roosevelt to Albert Shaw, to William Howard Taft, 26 December 1902, *Letters,* 3:396, 399. To Cleveland, he wrote on the same day that his victory in "getting England and Germany explicitly to recognize the Monroe Doctrine" was comparable to what the ex-president had achieved in the crisis of 1895. Ibid., p. 398.

59. To Root, for example, he wrote on 2 June 1904 that he considered the "striking enforcement of the Monroe Doctrine" in the Venezuela crisis one of his chief accomplishments. To Spring Rice, he wrote on 1 November 1905: "I succeeded in impressing on the Kaiser quietly and unofficially . . . that the violation of the Monroe Doctrine by territorial aggrandizement . . . meant war, not ultimately, but immediately and without any delay." *Letters,* 4:811; 5:63. See also Roosevelt to Edwin A. Van Valkenburg, 5 September 1916, ibid., 8:1113; Roosevelt to John Hay, 9 August 1903, Theodore Roosevelt Collection, Houghton Library, Harvard University.

60. Roosevelt to White, 14 August 1906, to Reid, 27 June 1906, 4 December 1908, *Letters,* 5:319, 358-59; 6:1410. White was not surprised. He had a recollection of "similar warnings given privately." Beale, *Roosevelt,* p. 418. Later, at about the time Roosevelt related the incident orally to Thayer, he wrote the details to Frederick Scott Oliver, 22 July 1915, *Letters,* 8:956-57. This was followed by the three well-known letters to Thayer of 1916.

61. Roosevelt to Lee, 17 June 1915; to Kipling, 30 November 1918, *Letters,* 8:936, 1408.

62. Roosevelt, *Autobiography,* p. 593; Roosevelt to Trevelyan, 1 October 1911, *Letters,* 7: 393.

63. For an account that emphasizes the practice value of the cruise, see Livermore, "The American Navy," p. 872. Accounts that emphasize Roosevelt's desire to wring appropriations from Congress include Vagts, *Deutschland,* 2:1525-1636; Charles Neu, "Theodore Roosevelt and American Involvement in the Far East, 1901-1909," *Pacific Historical Review* 35 (November 1966): 441; and Harold and Margaret Sprout, *The Rise of American Naval Power,* pp. 265-66. The following accounts accept Roosevelt's private version: Thomas Bailey, "The World Cruise of the American Battleship Fleet, 1907-1909," *Pacific Historical Review* 1 (September 1932): 398-99; Bailey, *Japanese-American Crises,*

p. 222; Gordon C. O'Gara, *Theodore Roosevelt and the Rise of the Modern Navy*, pp. 74–77; Donald C. Gordon, "Roosevelt's 'Smart Yankee Trick,'" *Pacific Historical Review* 30 (November 1961): 351; Dulles, *America's Rise*, p. 71; and Louis Morton, "Military and Naval Preparations for Defense of the Philippines During the War Scare of 1907," *Military Affairs* 13 (September 1949): 95–104. Authors who adopt both of Roosevelt's accounts, or add an explanation of their own, include Beale, *Roosevelt*, pp. 328–29; William H. Harbaugh, *The Life and Times of Theodore Roosevelt*, pp. 287–88; Robert A. Hart, *The Great White Fleet*, pp. viii, x, 25; Lawrence F. Abbott, *Impressions of Theodore Roosevelt*, pp. 110–11; Richard D. Challener, *Admirals, Generals, and American Foreign Policy, 1898-1914*, p. 181; Esthus, *Roosevelt and Japan*, pp. 182–83; Akira Iriye, *Pacific Estrangement: Japanese and American Expansion, 1879-1911*, p. 163. Esthus lists, first of all, Roosevelt's desire for congressional funds; then the practice value; and last, the desire to impress Japan. In his subsequent book *Rivalries*, he emphasizes Roosevelt's desire to silence the foreign press (p. 119). Hart belives the cruise was "a search for prestige" and quotes Mark Twain: "All for show, all for advertisement." According to Iriye, it was "part of preparedness." According to Charles Neu, it was "principally" to educate public opinion; Neu, *An Uncertain Friendship: Theodore Roosevelt and Japan, 1906-1909*, pp. 117, 312.

64. Esthus, *Roosevelt and Japan*, p. 184. It should be noted that when Roosevelt referred to "veiled truculence" in his letter to Trevelyan of 1 October 1911, he distinguished between the Japanese "war party" and the "Elder Statesmen [Genro]."

65. Meyer Diary, 22 September 1907 in Howe, *Meyer*, pp. 371, 377; Roosevelt to Lodge, 8 September 1905, *Roosevelt-Lodge Correspondence*, 2:192; Roosevelt to Lodge, 5 June 1905, *Letters*, 4: 1205. The United States expected to complete three battleships and three cruisers within a few months as compared to Japan's plans for only four cruisers and no battleships in two years. William R. Braisted, *The United States Navy in the Pacific, 1897-1909*, p. 194. See also Roosevelt to Kermit Roosevelt, 11 November 1908, Roosevelt Collection, Harvard University.

66. Roosevelt to Taft, 9 February 1905, *Letters*, 4:1118; Esthus, *Roosevelt and Japan*, pp. 133–34; Meyer Diary, 13 August 1907, in Howe, *Meyer*, p. 365; Sir Mortimer Durand to Sir Edward Grey, 26 January 1906, FO 800/81, Edward Grey Papers, PRO.

67. Bailey, *Japanese-American Crises,* pp. 150–66.

68. F. D. Lugard [governor of Hong Kong] to the Earl of Elgin, 13 October 1907, FO 115/1433, PRO; Esthus, *Roosevelt and Japan,* pp. 156, 175, 177; Oscar Straus, *Under Four Administrations: From Cleveland to Taft,* pp. 225–26, 228; Neu, *Uncertain Friendship,* pp. 146–47; Roosevelt to Root, 26 July 1907, *Letters,* 5:730; Roosevelt to Kermit Roosevelt, 9 February 1907, Roosevelt Collection, Harvard University.

69. It is important to distinguish between fear and expectation. Roosevelt's *fear* of war was genuine, but he did not consider it likely; and the cruise was intended to reduce the possibility still further.

70. Challener, *Admirals,* p. 253.

71. Sir Edward Grey to Sir F. Bertie, 12 December 1906, FO 115/1394, PRO; Grey to Bryce, [April?] 1908, James Bryce Papers, Bodleian Library, Oxford University; *New York Evening Post,* 5 July 1907; Lord Bryce to Foreign Office, 12 July, 31 August 1907, FO 115/1436, PRO; Roosevelt to Kermit Roosevelt, 19 April 1908, *Letters,* 6:1012; Iriye, *Pacific Estrangement,* pp. 147, 157, 168 (Iriye is particularly good on the war scare atmosphere). Roosevelt wrote Root on 13 July 1907: "In the first place, I think it will have a pacific effect to show that it can be done. . . . [it is also] "absolutely necessary for us to try in time of peace to see just what we could do in the way of putting a big battle fleet in the Pacific." *Letters,* 5:717. For other evidence that T.R. did indeed fear war by the summer of 1907, see Charles W. Toth, "Elihu Root," in Norman Graebner, ed., *An Uncertain Tradition: American Secretaries of State in the Twentieth Century,* pp. 49–50; Challener, *Admirals,* p. 246; Howe, *Meyer,* p. 383; Esthus, *Roosevelt and Japan,* p. 177; Bailey, "World Cruise," pp. 398, 403.

72. Sydney Brooks, "The Voyage of the American Fleet," *Fortnightly Review* [London], O.S. 89 (February 1908): 209; Alfred Thayer Mahan, "The True Significance of the Pacific Cruise," *Scientific American* 97 (December 1907): 407.

73. Edward Zabriskie, *American-Russian Rivalry in the Far East, 1895–1914: A Study in Diplomacy and Power Politics,* p. 135; Morton, "Defense of the Philippines," p. 97.

74. Roosevelt to Trevelyan, 1 October 1911, *Letters,* 7:394.

75. Bailey, *Japanese-American Crises,* p. 292; Esthus, *Roosevelt and Japan,* pp. 250–51; Straus, *Under Four Administrations,* p. 228. Scholars have contended that this last agreement was a concession rather than a gain for the United States because

of the omission of the word "territorial" (territorial integrity). Toth calls the Root-Takahira Agreement "a significant diplomatic victory" for the Japanese; Toth, "Root," in Graebner, ed., *Uncertain Tradition*, p. 50. The same opinion is found in Michael H. Hunt, *Frontier Defense and the Open Door*, p. 139; Griswold, *Far Eastern Policy*, pp. 129–30; and Hart, *Fleet*, pp. 233, 236 (quoting Willard Straight). However, Japanese Foreign Minister Hayashi used the words "territorial integrity" on subsequent occasions without the slightest compunction. It was the Lansing-Ishii Agreement, signed under the pressure of World War I, not Root-Takahira, that was deemed a concession to Japan. Count Tadasu Hayashi, *The Secret Memoirs of Count Tadasu Hayashi*, ed. A. M. Pooley, pp. 252–53; Roy Hidemichi Akagi, *Japan's Foreign Relations*, pp. 293–94; Seiji Hishida, *Japan Among the Great Powers*, pp. 218, 220; Thomas A. Bailey, "The Root-Takahira Agreement of 1908," *Pacific Historical Review* 9 (March 1940): 35. According to Esthus, the Root-Takahira Agreement was a definite gain for the United States. Root wanted the word "integrity" inserted, and he succeeded in this despite Japanese opposition. He did not push for the word "territorial," and Japan made no distinction. Esthus, *Roosevelt and Japan*, chap. 16.

76. Rivalry of a similar kind in the 1880s between American and Canadian sealers had led to friction of a serious nature. Now, the challenger was Japan, with a total of thirty-one boats in 1906, thirty-five in 1907, thirty-eight in 1908, but only twenty-three in 1909; Alexander DeConde and Armin Rappaport, eds., *Essays Diplomatic and Undiplomatic of Thomas A. Bailey*, pp. 173–79, esp. 173 n., 179 n.

77. The Japanese fleet was on war maneuvers in the Bonin Islands, and foreign observers were not optimistic about the chances for peace. Lloyd's of London was offering even odds; the kaiser had volunteered the use of German ships and equipment; and Russian citizens were signing up to fight in the American armed services. See Hart, *Fleet*, pp. 17–19; Fletcher Pratt, *A Compact History of the United States Navy*, p. 195.

78. Roosevelt to Reid, 4 December 1908, *Letters*, 6:1410. See also Roosevelt to Arthur Lee, 20 December 1908; Roosevelt to Sydney Brooks, 28 December 1908, ibid., pp. 1432, 1444–45; Bailey, *Japanese-American Crises*, p. 302; Esthus, *Roosevelt and Japan*, pp. 213, 253–55; United States Department of State, *Papers Relating to the Foreign Relations of the United States* (1907), pt. 1, p. lxv; ibid., (1908) p. xlviii (hereafter cited as *Foreign Relations*).

79. Alexander E. Campbell, *Great Britain and the United States, 1895–1903*, p. 116; Bailey, *Presidential Greatness*, p. 306. See also Kenneth Davis, *FDR: The Beckoning of Destiny*, p. 154; "In neither foreign nor domestic affairs was his voice notably soft."

80. Other gems include his description of George Bernard Shaw as a "blue-rumped ape" and Maurice Low (*London Post* correspondent) as a "circumcised skunk"; Roosevelt to Lee, 2 February 1908, 1 August 1914, 4 September 1914, Lee papers, Courtauld Institute; Lee, *Good Innings*, 1:325; Lloyd Griscom, *Diplomatically Speaking*, p. 222.

81. Rosen, *Forty Years*, 1:265, 276.

82. The instructions are contained in a letter to Hay dated 8 October 1901, *Letters*, 3:164–70.

83. See, for example, Roosevelt to Sir Edward Grey, 18 December 1906, on the need to handle a dispute over the fisheries with "tact and patience and forebearance"; also his letter to Hay, 1 July 1899, warning that "in Cuba we may lay up for ourselves infinite trouble if we do not handle the people with a proper mixture of firmness, courtesy, and tact." On 31 July 1902, he wrote to Taft, with reference to moving against the Philippine friars: "Whatever is done should be done as tactfully and inconspicuously as possible." To the Republican chairman of the House Military Affairs Committee, he spoke of the need to pay "proper courtesy to all foreign nations". *Letters*, 2:1024–25; 3:305; 5:529; Roosevelt, *History of New York*, in Hagedorn, ed., *Works*, 10:376, 386, 398; Beale, *Roosevelt*, pp. 64, 327; Roosevelt, *The Strenuous Life*, in Hagedorn, ed., *Works*, 13:429. See also Roosevelt to Lodge, 21 July 1889, *Letters*, 2:1038.

84. The references are to Peter Stuyvesant and Richard Nicolls, both of whom were colonial governors of New York and men whom Roosevelt admired. Roosevelt, *History of New York*, in Hagedorn, ed., *Works*, 10:386, 398. One of Nicolls's successors is described, significantly, as a man whose "tact was not equal to his courage and probity." Ibid., p. 431.

85. Beale, *Roosevelt*, p. 64; Roosevelt to Lodge, 21 July 1899, *Letters*, 2:1038.

86. Roosevelt's tact even as a New York State assemblyman was recognized by the press. Bishop, *Roosevelt*, 1:29. For the view that Roosevelt changed in personality and approach over the years, see Dulles, *America's Rise*, p. 70; Harbaugh, *Roosevelt*, p. 260; Pringle, *Roosevelt*, p. 196.

87. Roosevelt, *Autobiography*, pp. 305, 508.

88. Alexander Campbell, *Great Britain,* p. 108.

89. Frank C. Lascelles to Lord Lansdowne, 11 February 1904; Lansdowne to Durand, 23 March 1904, FO 115/1307, PRO; Lansdowne to Durand, 14 January 1905, FO 115/1350. Roosevelt, *Autobiography,* p. 416; Roosevelt to Reid, 28 April 1906, *Letters,* 5:242; Beale, *Roosevelt,* pp. 384–85; Lewis, "Franco-American Relations," pp. 32–33.

90. Roosevelt to Henry C. Taylor, 28 March 1903, quoted in Bishop, *Roosevelt,* 1:239; John G. Clifford, "Admiral Dewey and the Germans, 1903: A New Perspective," *Mid-America* 49 (July 1967): 217–19; Roosevelt to Taft, 7 March 1904, *Letters,* 4:744. As a face-saving gesture, he also said, in his Chicago speech (2 April 1903), that "both powers Germany [and Great Britain] assured us in explicit terms that there was not the slightest intention on their part to violate the Monroe Doctrine, and this assurance was kept with an honorable good faith which merits full acknowledgement on our part." Quoted in Hill, *Roosevelt,* p. 131. Roosevelt's first *public* use of the phrase "Speak softly and carry a big stick" seems to have occurred during his vice-presidency in an address at the Minnesota State Fair, 2 September 1901. Roosevelt, *The Strenuous Life,* in Hagedorn, ed., *Works,* 13:474.

91. Sternburg to Foreign Office, 19 February 1903, *Grosse Politik,* 17:291–92; Roosevelt to Hay, 22 May 1903, *Letters,* 3:478; Clifford, "Admiral Dewey and the Germans," p. 220.

92. Dexter Perkins and Howard Hill, taking Roosevelt at his word, have interpreted these and other statements as being inconsistent with the kind of "flaming belligerence" that "would have dictated an ultimatum." Perkins, *Monroe Doctrine, 1867–1907,* pp. 382, 384–86; Hill, *Roosevelt,* p. 131. It is interesting to note that even Castro saved face because, under the misleading rubric of "arbitration," Roosevelt prevailed upon him to accept all the major allied claims. Only minor issues were actually submitted to arbitration. Ibid., pp. 138, 142–43.

93. Thomas A. Bailey, "Theodore Roosevelt and the Alaska Boundary Settlement," in DeConde and Rappaport, eds., *Essays,* pp. 163, 167. According to Bailey, Roosevelt employed "clumsy tactics" and "browbeat the British."

94. Sternburg to Foreign Office, 19 February 1903, *Grosse Politik,* 17:292; Bailey, "Alaska," in DeConde and Rappaport, eds., *Essays,* pp. 162–64; Beale, *Roosevelt,* pp. 114, 125–30; Campbell, *Anglo-American Understanding,* pp. 327–28; Memorandum of a Conversation between Spring Rice and Joseph Pope, "A Half

Century of Service, Being the Memoirs of Sir Joseph Pope," film
M 585, pp. 184–85, PAC. Smalley spent long hours with Hay and
Roosevelt before reporting to Canadian Prime Minister Sir Wilfrid
Laurier. Smalley to Laurier, [?] January 1902, MG 26 G, vol. 218,
nos. 61212–61214, Wilfrid Laurier Papers, PAC.

95. Carnegie to Balfour, 23 July 1903; Chamberlain to Balfour, 8 August 1903, Arthur James Balfour Papers, British
Museum.

96. Beale, *Roosevelt,* p. 129; Campbell, *Anglo-American
Understanding,* pp. 243–44; Jessup, *Elihu Root,* 1:391–92; John
A. Garraty, *Henry Cabot Lodge,* p. 244. According to Bradford
Perkins, the troops were sent "at least in part" for police duty.
Perkins, *Great Rapprochement,* p. 167. There is, indeed, evidence
of intended police duty in a letter from Roosevelt to Hay, dated 16
July 1902, but the problem here, as elsewhere, is that the evidence
is inconclusive.

97. Hay to Pauncefote, 7 January 1902, Confidential Print,
FO 414/173, PRO; Lansdowne to Pauncefote, 24 January 1902,
FO 5/2484, PRO; Arthur S. Raikes to the Foreign Office, 30 May
1902, FO 5/2486, PRO. See also Lord Minto to Joseph Chamberlain, 20 December 1901 (according to the Canadian mounted
police, "no apprenhension of danger now exists"), MG 26 G, vol.
753, no. 215422, Laurier Papers, PAC.

98. Roosevelt to Lodge, 28 January 1909, *Letters,* 6:1492;
Beale, *Roosevelt,* p. 114.

99. Hay to White, 20 September 1903, quoted in Nevins,
White, p. 198. According to Alexander Campbell, Roosevelt was
"incapable of speaking softly" and "determined . . . to make clear
the extent of his diplomatic victory." Campbell, *Great Britain,* p.
116.

100. Roosevelt to Lee, 7 December 1903, *Letters,* 3:665–66;
Pringle, *Roosevelt,* p. 206.

101. Roosevelt claimed that his threats with regard to the
Alaskan boundary were "very important and probably decisive"
in vindicating the basic American position. Roosevelt to Theodore
Roosevelt, Jr., 21 October 1903, *Letters,* 3:635. Accounts which
differ include Nevins, *White,* pp. 201–202; also Bailey, "Alaska
Boundary," in DeConde and Rappaport, eds., *Essays,* p. 166.
Accounts that agree with Roosevelt include G. Wallace Chess-
man, *Theodore Roosevelt and the Politics of Power,* p. 95. Oliver
Wendell Holmes considered Roosevelt's assumption "extremely
probable." Holmes to Roosevelt, 21 October 1903, quoted in

Bailey, "Alaska Boundary," in DeConde and Rappaport, eds., *Essays*, p. 165. As for the battleship cruise, Roosevelt believed that it helped avert war and bring about an improvement in Japanese-American relations. Accounts which share this view include Griswold, *Far Eastern Policy*, p. 357, which maintains that the cruise "helped to clear the air," and Bailey, "World Cruise," pp. 400, 421, which holds that it may have been "his most notable contribution to peace." Others are not so sure, as, for example, Zabriskie, *American-Russian Rivalry*, p. 135 n.; Beale, *Roosevelt*, pp. 331–32; and Harbaugh, *Roosevelt*, p. 288. Still others view the cruise as "a failure" that "lost more than it gained." Hart, *Fleet*, pp. ix, 298.

102. Lee, *Good Innings*, 1:421.

103. Holstein, *Holstein Papers*, 4:236–620; Kaiser Wilhelm II, *Memoirs*, p. 200; Bülow, *Memoirs*, 1:658–62. Sir Edward Grey devotes over 150 pages of his memoirs to the period 1901–1909, but within this space he makes only two passing references to Roosevelt, one of them in a footnote. These two comments, plus one other, are the only acknowledgment for that period that there was a country by the name of the United States. Grey, *Twenty-Five Years, 1892–1916*, 2 vols., 1:53, 118 n., 189. One finds a similar disregard in biographies of British statesmen; for example, Dugdale, *Balfour*.

104. Roosevelt to Alice Roosevelt, 2 September 1905, *Letters*, 5:2. He also credited Meyer with convincing the czar to cede South Sakhalin and was convinced that peace was made "only by disregarding the old conventional diplomatic methods. . . . I communicated personally with the Czar, the Mikado, the Kaiser, Balfour, Rouvier, and so forth." Roosevelt to Francis V. Greene, 5 September 1905, ibid., p. 12. See also Roosevelt to Lodge, 2 September 1905, ibid, p. 8.

105. Roosevelt, *Autobiography*, pp. 585–87; Roosevelt to Lodge, 16 June 1905, *Letters*, 4:1229–30. For accounts that support Roosevelt's view, see Esthus, *Rivalries*, pp. 33–34; Esthus, *Roosevelt and Japan*, pp. 81–84, 94; Trani, *Portsmouth*, pp. 156–57; Roosevelt to Kermit Roosevelt, 11 June 1905, Roosevelt Collection, Harvard University.

106. Kaiser Wilhelm II, *Letters from the Kaiser to the Czar*, ed. Isaac D. Levine and N. F. Grant, pp. 183–90, 203–205; Erich Brandenburg, *From Bismarck to the World War: A History of German Foreign Policy, 1870–1914*, trans. Annie Elizabeth

Adams, p. 232; Hale, *Germany and the Diplomatic Revolution,* pp. 153, 155 n.

107. Esthus, *Rivalries,* p. 33; Esthus, *Roosevelt and Japan,* pp. 87–88. Witte also expressed an interest in paying for the privilege of keeping North Sakhalin. Trani, *Portsmouth,* p. 141. See also Lloyd Griscom to Hay, 15 March 1905, Hay Papers, Library of Congress Microfilm, Reel No. 8. Griscom reported the Japanese, even this early, as being "extremely anxious for peace."

108. Count Serge Witte, *The Memoirs of Count Witte,* trans. and ed. A. Yarmolinsky, p. 152. Since Japan held more prisoners than Russia, and each side agreed to pay the other for the cost of prisoner care, Russia was in fact agreeing to pay the difference. The figure, as announced in 1907, came to approximately $20 million (a small amount compared to the $600 million originally asked by Japan as indemnity). *New York Times,* 24 November 1907, Part 3, p. 2. I am indebted for this note to Mr. Christopher Dukas.

109. Esthus, *Roosevelt and Japan,* pp. 86, 88–89; Rosen, *Forty Years,* 1:263.

110. Lansdowne to Balfour, 3 September 1905, Balfour Papers, British Museum; Roosevelt to Whitelaw Reid, 3 August 1905, to Alice Roosevelt, to Lodge, 2 September 1905, *Letters,* 4:1298; 5:2, 8; Esthus, *Roosevelt and Japan,* pp. 84–85. Roosevelt remained under the illusion that his last-minute plea to Kaneko had been decisive and that Ambassador Meyer had convinced the czar to yield South Sakhalin.

111. Roosevelt to Lodge, 11 July 1905, to Reid, 28 April, 27 June 1906 ("when it became necessary at the end I stood him [the kaiser] on his head with great decision"), *Letters,* 4:1272; 5:236, 239–42, 249, 251, 319. Holstein, at one point, claimed that Germany had thrown down the gauntlet to France only to suffer a dangerous retreat that would determine her future credibility. Holstein to Pascal David, 13 May 1906, Holstein, *Holstein Papers,* 4:424. This has become the theme of many historians who doubt Roosevelt's wisdom in siding with France. See, for example, Raymond Sontag, "German Foreign Policy, 1904–1906," *American Historical Review* 33 (January 1928): 297–301. Esthus feels that Roosevelt, by blocking an increase in German prestige commensurate with her rising power, helped plant the seeds of World War I. Esthus, *Rivalries,* pp. 23–24, 110. For accounts which view Roosevelt's role as wise and evenhanded, as well as decisive, see

Beale, *Roosevelt,* pp. 383–89; Nevins, *White,* pp. 271–82; Chessman, *Theodore Roosevelt;* Lewis, "Franco-American Relations." For accounts which question Roosevelt's claim to a major role, see Dulles, *America's Rise,* p. 78; Hale, *Germany and the Diplomatic Revolution,* p. 164. Sir Edward Grey thought Roosevelt's claim perfectly possible. *Twenty-Five Years,* 1:118 n.

112. Bülow to Count von Tattenbach at Fez, 7 June 1905, Dugdale, ed., *German Diplomatic Documents,* 3:230.

113. Prince Bernhard von Bülow, *Imperial Germany,* pp. 79–80; Hale, *Germany and the Diplomatic Revolution,* pp. 80–81, 86, 88, 99; Baron von Mentzingen [German minister at Tangier] to Count von Bülow, 5 April 1904, Dugdale, ed., *German Diplomatic Documents,* 3:219.

114. Bülow told the Reichstag on 14 November 1906, that America "maintained its neutral position throughout. . . . This was the second great service which America rendered to the peace of the world." Quoted in James B. Scott, "Elihu Root," in Samuel Flagg Bemis, ed., *The American Secretaries of State and Their Diplomacy,* 10 vols., 9:208. See also the *Review of Reviews* 33 (March 1906): 272; 33 (May 1906): 532; Bülow to Wilhelm, 24 June 1905, 27 and 30 June 1907; Wilhelm to Bülow, 26 June 1907, Bülow, *Letters,* pp. 129–30, 135–36, 214–15, 218, 220; Freiherr von Schoen, *The Memoirs of an Ambassador by Freiherr von Schoen,* trans. Constance Vesey, p. 94; Bülow, *Imperial Germany,* p. 50; Hale, *Germany,* pp. 152, 160; Christian Gauss, ed., *The German Emperor as Shown in his Public Utterances,* p. 241; Holstein to Radolin, 28 March 1906, Holstein, *Holstein Papers,* 4:404; Nevins, *White,* p. 279 ("the Kaiser telegraphed Radowitz 'Bravo! Well done!' ").

115. Grey to Durand, 22 March 1906, FO 115/1391, PRO; Charles Hardinge [British ambassador to Russia] to King Edward, 9 March, 23 March 1906, RA W48/84, 94, Donald M. Wallace to Honorable Sidney Greville, fourth son of the fourth earl of Warwick and private secretary to Queen Alexandra, 21, 23, 25 March 1906, RA Add X21/8,9,10, Windsor Castle; Lee, *Good Innings,* 1:331–33; Bradford Perkins, *Great Rapprochement,* p. 103. Sir Mortimer Durand complained of T.R.'s "intimacy with the Germans." Durand Diary, 4 December 1906, in Sir Percey M. Sykes, *The Right Honourable Sir Mortimer Durand.*

CHAPTER 3

The Moral Quotient

HAVING examined the question of Roosevelt's credibility and observed how he handled challenges involving the use of power, it would seem logical at this stage to broaden the analysis. Such tactics as secrecy and face saving offer only partial insight into T.R.'s underlying approach to foreign relations. One may assume that domestic politics, combined with the national interest, motivated much of his everyday conduct. But this does not account for all the unique features of his style. Elihu Root allegedly addressed the president on one occasion as follows: "What I admire most about you, Theodore, is your discovery of the Ten Commandments."[1] Root was being facetious, of course. Yet his playful wit raises an important question. To what degree were Roosevelt's public actions motivated by a personal conception of morality?

Although he consistently invoked a higher law and expressed himself in the language of ethics, there is a tendency for historians to discount Roosevelt the moralist and to concentrate instead on Roosevelt the warrior. Scholars have emphasized his spectacular use of power and the oft-repeated words, "Speak softly and carry a big stick." Richard Hofstadter spoke of his "worship of strength," and Thomas Bailey referred to him as "an apostle of Mars."[2] Whenever notice is taken of his preaching, the assumption is apt to be that it was either hypocritical or blindly "self-righteous." To some students, he appears authoritarian, to others highhanded. He has been accused of refusing to meet an opponent halfway and of reacting paranoically to opposition. According to Bailey, he browbeat other nations into submission, "especially the smaller ones." According to Eugene Trani, he deemed "any war in which Americans fought" to be "just." Howard Beale goes so far as to say that Roosevelt was convinced that "his country could never act unjustly or wrongly" and that "when his pride was aroused or his will crossed," he reacted "like a child determined to have his own way." If America "could not get what she wanted and do as she pleased without war, then she must fight."[3]

Such charges, usually made *en passant*, are unfortunate. They overlook the complexity of Roosevelt's thought and ignore a large body of contradictory evidence. But more important, they conceal the fact that T.R.'s moralistic approach to international relations requires a rethinking of the traditional interpretation of "Big Stick" diplomacy, especially with regard to such controversial episodes as the acquisition of the Canal Zone and the settlement of the Alaskan boundary dispute. Although it is impossible to "prove" motivation, it can be shown that Roosevelt was prone by instinct to approach issues in terms of right and wrong and that he was just as much of a preacher as Woodrow Wilson. His preaching may have conformed to the spirit of the age and added much to his popular appeal, but it is hard to avoid the conclusion that he preached with genuine conviction. In addition, his view of the major events of his administration is worth taking into serious account if for no other reason than the fact that there was usually a substantial basis for it.

Before turning to specific cases, it is important to recall the man himself. Two of the leading figures of the age, Woodrow Wilson and Charles Evans Hughes, were sons of ministers. Roosevelt might just as well have been, for his father took part in charitable causes and reform movements, taught Sunday school in the local church, and gave occasional talks on "patriotism, good citizenship, and manly morality." The senior Theodore exerted an unusual amount of force on his sickly son, urging him to build his body and, as a college freshman, to put his morals ahead of his health or studies. The son idolized the father for his purity, cleanliness, courage, and integrity; and his death drove him to months of mournful diary entries. Like his father, he taught Sunday school for seven years and even considered missionary work. He neither smoked nor drank to the customary degree; indeed, he might well have been judged a prig by his schoolmates had it not been for an unfailing good nature and the amazing feats of physical prowess which he would demonstrate to the end of his life.[4]

One of the paradoxes of Roosevelt's personality was its combination of a sharply moralistic outlook with a rollicking sense of humor and a repugnance toward all forms of sanctimony. Girls who had known him as a youth could recall how they had laughed at his amusing and original twists of conversation. His cabinet meetings were famous for anecdote and repartee. To his postmaster general, George von Lengerke Meyer, he once confided that he found Catholics and strict Episcopalians impossible to get on with at the end of Lent because they had fasted so much and that if he were picking a husband or wife, he would rather have them a little less moral. On another occasion, when reminded of Franklin's aphorism, "Eat not to dullness, drink not to elevation," he replied: "I always did dislike Franklin's sayings."[5]

The fact remains, however, that by all outward appearances T.R. aimed at virtue to a degree rare among mortals. While a student at Harvard, he chose his friends for such qualities as manliness, refinement, and gentlemanliness. Later, in a touching passage written shortly after his marriage to Alice Lee, he revealed that he had never appreciated before their wedding "how wonderfully good and unselfish she was."[6] As New York State assemblyman and civil service commissioner, he fought well-known battles against graft, nepotism, and machine politics. Appointed police commissioner in 1895, he set records in crime reduction and galvanized the Men in Blue by arresting idle officers on marathon prowls through the streets of New York. His midnight inspections earned him the sobriquet "Haroun al Roosevelt" after the ancient caliph of Baghdad who gained equal notoriety by personal raids on places of iniquity. Atop his Mulberry Street desk was a tablet inscribed with the words: "Aggressive fighting for the right is the noblest sport the world affords."[7] He dubbed his presidency the "Square Deal" and set his face like flint against those whom he called "malefactors of great wealth." He distinguished between "good" and "bad" business combinations, finding no reason to prosecute a monopoly which operated in the public interest so long as it had been justly built. His letters are full of the language of good and evil, and the amusing *Autobiography* contains a chapter entitled "The Peace of Righteousness," with the words "honest" and "honesty" appearing no less than three times in a single sentence.[8] Some may object to his views on marriage, abortion, childbearing, or the value of strenuous exercise. But none can deny that he poured forth a continuous stream of moral imperatives from his "bully pulpit," the White House.

Nowhere is his moralistic bent more visible than in his artistic and literary taste. It was easy for him to reject the sensuous Rubens in favor of the more ascetic Rembrandt. Among his favorite works of literature he counted Wordsworth's "The Happy Warrior," Julia Ward Howe's "Battle Hymn of the Republic," Germany's *Nibelungenlied,* Longfellow's *Saga of King Olaf,* and Browning's "Childe Roland"—all of them featuring some theme of valor and courage. Why, he wondered, should Tolstoi condemn war while taking a detached view of adultery? Was the infidelity of Anna Karenina not as great an evil as war? War, he admitted, was an evil, but a lesser evil compared to some of its alternatives.[9] He tended to favor didactic novelists such as Scott, Thackeray, and Dickens; and he preferred the moralistic historians, Gibbon, Macaulay, and Thucydides. As president of the American Historical Association, he insisted that "the greatest historian should also be a great moralist." Nor did he hesitate, in his own works of history, to condemn the United States when he believed it to be in the wrong. The early American concept of "manifest destiny" he depicted as a piratical longing for neighboring land; the Mexican War he denounced as unjust. He deplored the indiscriminate massacre of Indians at Wounded Knee and beside the stockade on Wall Street as much as he did Jefferson's refusal to take a military stand against the British in 1807.[10]

He lectured his countrymen as they were never lectured before or since for infringing the rights of oriental immigrants. In his Annual Message to Congress of 1906, he castigated Californians for discriminatory practices, which he labeled "wicked nonsense," and he insisted that "no nation is fit to teach unless it is willing to learn." His attitude toward the Chinese was equally sympathetic. They had long been the victims of American racial prejudice, and when China finally struck back with a boycott of American goods and terminated an American railway concession, T.R. warned his fellow citizens that "we cannot receive equity unless we are willing to do equity." He took pains to see that the navy was ready to defend American interests, but he also proposed a partial remission of the Boxer indemnity and accepted the appointment to the United States of an abrasive Chinese ambassador: "He is a bad old Chink and if he had his way he would put us all to heavy death . . . [but] I do not object to any Chinaman showing a feeling that he would like to retaliate now and then for our insolence." He also instructed customs officials that any discourtesy to the Chinese would be punished by immediate dismissal from government service. Despite the murder of American missionaries in China, Roosevelt did not forget that "grave injustice and wrong have been done by this nation to the people of China."[11]

This was a man who again and again inveighed against crass materialism, particularly along the east coast, and who attributed the fall of ancient civilizations to sybaritic indolence. In his biography of Oliver Cromwell, he described the first forty years of the seventeenth century as a time of ignoble and evil peace, characterized by a rotting of the na-

tional fiber and leading inevitably to a bloodbath. Newsmen
were startled when the president advised them to resign
their jobs rather than tolerate a shift in the editorial opinion
of the paper for which they worked. To do otherwise, he
argued, would make it appear that their minds were for
sale.[12] Needless to say, the White House was closed to persons of dubious moral reputation, and its occupant was not
bashful about chiding the celebrated Russian writer, Maxim
Gorki, for trying to crash American society in the company
of an actress passing herself off as his wife.

In the realm of foreign relations, Roosevelt believed
that nations were bound by the same moral code as individuals, and that the United States should adhere to the
Golden Rule as scrupulously as any of its citizens. He was
realistic enough to see that the application of morality was
not always the same for international as for interpersonal
relations, but he believed the standard should be the same in
both cases. A powerful nation should act with restraint
toward a weaker one, even though weakness was no license
for wickedness; imperialism could be justified only when it
benefited the subject as much as it did the subjugator; and
the United States owed a great deal more to its overseas ter-
ritories than roads, schools, and hospitals.[13] One of the most
bitter and protracted struggles of his political career was
his fight for congressional enactment of a tariff that
would place the Cuban and Philippine economies on a more
prosperous footing.

In keeping with his credo that responsibility goes hand
in hand with power, he felt that the nation had a moral duty,
noblesse oblige, to work actively in all parts of the world for
justice as well as peace. On at least one occasion, he declined
to aid a foreign ruler who sought power by corrupt means.
President Amador Guerrero of Panama was pro-American,
and, in the interest of stability, it might have been expedient to support him in spite of his dubious methods. But
Roosevelt refused to compromise on the principle of honest
elections, and the result was an executive turnover. In 1908,
when he sent American troops to monitor a Panamanian

election, he explained to Taft that "fraudulent methods which deny to a large part of the people opportunity to vote constitutes a disturbance of the public order which under Panama's constitution requires intervention, and this government will not permit Panama to pass into the hands of anyone so elected." The Roosevelt Corollary to the Monroe Doctrine was based on the same general line of thought—that no state should be permitted to plunder under cover of the American flag. Thus, if Europe was to keep "hands off" the Western Hemisphere, the United States would have to act as a self-appointed guardian of foreign life and property.[14] Lawlessness was as deplorable in the Caribbean as it was in the Sudan, as frightful in America's back yard as it was on the plains of Armenia. One of Roosevelt's chief motives for favoring imperialism over self-determination was his belief that the colonial power often exerted a force for law and order. No person or nation deserved to be independent until it could maintain stability at home and carry out its international obligations. Self-reliance was a cardinal virtue for the group as well as for the individual.

Above all, Roosevelt believed that a man's word was his bond. His devotion to the idea of honor attracted him to a study of *Bushido,* the Japanese feudal code of knight errantry, and he felt constrained, whenever he had committed himself and his country to a particular course of action, to do the utmost to deliver what he had promised. This was as true of his arbitration treaties settling Anglo-American differences on Newfoundland and the Great Lakes as it was of his reciprocity agreements with Cuba and the Philippines. When the arbitral award on the Newfoundland fisheries went against the United States and Congress refused to vote the required funds, he worked "four gibbering years" beyond his term as president to obtain it.

He was especially proud that the United States had withdrawn from Cuba on the basis of the Platt Amendment, believing this to be the first case in history when such a promise had been kept in letter as well as in spirit. The British had promised to leave Egypt (an unwise promise, in

his opinion, but a promise nonetheless), and the promise was
not kept. Japan had made a similar pledge to Korea with a
similar failure to deliver. Some years later, after he had left
the White House, Britain challenged the assumption that
American vessels passing through the Panama Canal were
entitled to a special tolls exemption as compared with the
shipping of other countries. Many in Congress were unwilling at the time to place justice ahead of partisanship and in-
stinctively rejected a British offer of arbitration. But Roosevelt's reaction was consistent. In one of the rare cases in
which he sided with President Wilson, he declared: "I feel
that we are pledged to arbitration and I believe in keeping
promises scrupulously, just as I disbelieve in making promises recklessly." It was this spirit, as well as his country's
power and neutral status, that won for him the role of peacemaker and the title of "honest broker" in the Russo-
Japanese peace talks of 1905.[15]

His insistence on the binding nature of even informal
agreements sometimes led him to do things that might appear inexplicable under normal circumstances. Take, for
example, the way in which he acquired the Panama Canal
Zone—one of the most heavily criticized moves in the
annals of American diplomacy. Failing, in sustained effort,
to obtain the Zone by treaty with Colombia, he used force to
prevent Colombian suppression of an isthmian revolt and
proceeded to negotiate directly with the newborn republic,
leaving Colombia in a state of impotent rage. Descriptions
range all the way from "rape of Colombia" to "cowboy
diplomacy." Even Samuel Flagg Bemis, never one to dwell
upon the negative side of American history, calls this "the
one really black mark in the Latin American policy of
the United States, and a big black mark."[16] Almost every
account of the incident stresses Roosevelt's "Big Stick"
philosophy and maintains that the Colombians had every
right to disapprove their treaty with the United States; that
they were at a distinct disadvantage in a contest of strength
with their northern neighbor; and that Roosevelt's personal

prestige as well as the national interest was tied to the speedy acquisition of a canal zone at Panama. Only a few critics have taken the president at his word when he described the basis for his action as one of high moral principle.[17]

Roosevelt's case is an interesting one, however. To begin with, it was well known at the time that the province of Panama had never been fully integrated into the workings of the Colombian government. It had always conducted its own postal relations with the outside world and never adopted the national paper money, preferring to rely on silver specie. Nor had Panama always been a province of Colombia. When it first obtained independence from Spain in 1821, it established its own government. Thereafter, it voluntarily entered the Granadian Confederation which in 1832 broke apart to form Equador, Venezuela, and New Granada (Colombia). Panama remained with New Granada until 1840, when she resumed independent status. From 1842 to 1855, she was again with the larger state. In 1855, the national constitution was amended to divide power more evenly between central government and provinces, and three subsequent constitutions adopted with the approval of Panama allowed still more local control. Panama thus existed as a virtually sovereign state in confederation with others for twenty-three years until in 1886 her legislature, along with the legislatures of other provinces, was abolished by decree of Bogotà, and she was summarily stripped of nearly all her autonomy. The two Panamanian delegates who attended the constitutional convention of 1886 were both appointed by Bogotà, and neither had ever lived in Panama. Nor was the new instrument of government ever submitted for approval to the Panamanian people.[18]

With three-quarters of the people reportedly in favor of separation, the year 1885 saw the outbreak of the first in a series of three full-scale insurrections which led eventually to complete independence. Twice, the people fought to exhaustion only to be put down by United States marines. In the rising of 1901–1902, they outnumbered their opponents on the isthmus by seven thousand to four thousand and had routed them in battle before American forces intervened to frustrate their bid for final victory. The revolution of 1903 was therefore the third major effort on the part of the Panamanian patriots.[19] It was also a revolution which, by democratic standards, had every right to succeed, since the relationship between central government and province had always been one of exploitation rather than of reciprocal benefit. For decades, Colombian politicians had derived a good portion of the national revenue from isthmian railway tolls without returning a pittance for the building of schools, hospitals, and other public facilities. President Marroquín's apparent willingness to gamble with the economic future of the isthmus by trying to squeeze the United States and the New Panama Canal Company was thus only one more grievance on a list of many.

It should also be recalled that even in physical terms Bogotá was separated from the isthmus by impassable jungle and awesome mountain terrain. At an altitude of 8,700 feet, the capital could not be reached from the sea in less than twelve days, three by mule and nine by rail. Provincials could make the trip to Washington, D.C., more quickly than they could arrive at the seat of their own government.

Elihu Root summed up the ethical issue when he pointed out that a strong Colombia had long held a weak Panama "in unlawful subjection," and Roosevelt was able to note in his Annual Address of 1903 that Panama had experienced fifty-three outbreaks, rebellions, and revolutionary disturbances in the fifty-three years since the United States had agreed to guarantee free and open transit across the isthmus. In addition, it is clear that the Colombian government had requested the aid of American troops to enforce order on the isthmus at least six different times (Roosevelt mentioned only four).[20]

At the very time the treaty talks were taking place, American marines were again in Panama on behalf of a Colombian dictator engulfed in the worst civil war of his nation's history and threatened with invasion by Venezuela. It would have been easy to take advantage of the situation, especially since the Panamanian rebels promised a liberal canal treaty. Nevertheless, Secretary of State Hay sustained negotiations with Colombia for over two years until the dictator, José Marroquín, triumphed over all his rivals. Several times during this period, Hay reluctantly agreed to pay higher sums of money for a treaty which included such minimum security provisions as control of local police and establishment of American courts. The Colombian minister to the United States had been instructed to accept all of Hay's terms except those relating to price. Money was therefore the main stumbling block at the beginning, as it was to be at the end.[21]

The crux of the issue for both Roosevelt and Hay was the expectation that once Marroquín had committed himself to the treaty as the best obtainable in competition with Nicaragua, he would be honor-bound to recommend it to his countrymen. Technically, Colombia had the right to reject the treaty, since it was a sovereign state with a constitution requiring congressional approval under normal conditions. But the canal negotiations had been initiated by Colombia. Three Colombian ministers had urged the treaty upon the United States for two years. The United States had agreed to purchase the rights and property of the French New Panama Canal Company with the express consent of Colombia, which held one million francs' worth of stock in the company, and whose representative at a stockholders' meeting had voted accordingly. It was on such assurances that the United States had concluded its agreement with the French company and that Congress had reversed itself, under strong administration pressure, from its original decision to designate Nicaragua as the preferred site. Thus, as Hay indicated to the Colombian minister of foreign affairs, "the United States, in view of the foregoing facts and of the responsibilities which it has thus been induced to incur, considers that the pending treaty is in the nature of a con-

clusive agreement on the part of Colombia." Marroquín's
support was, in other words, not only something that had
been promised, but also a "warrantable expectation."[22]

In actual fact, Marroquín acted from the moment the
treaty was signed to mobilize opinion against it. He not only
failed to endorse it in his New Year's Message of 1903 but
encouraged open debate, saying he would let the masses
decide. General Fernandez, minister of finance, issued a cir-
cular to the Bogotá press inviting public discussion and
reaffirming that the government "had no preconceived
wishes for or against." One of Marroquín's more obvious
moves was to solicit the opinion of three well-known
lawyers, who responded with a uniformly critical view. Certainly, for the victor of a Latin-American civil war that had
claimed over one hundred and fifty thousand lives, this was
tantamount to inviting the treaty's defeat. The British
minister to Bogotá observed that "the measures employed
by the Colombian government to prevent public discussion
of affairs of state [over a period of many years] have had the
effect of destroying anything like public opinion." And he
was correct. What passed for "public opinion," said to be
enthusiastic at first, now shifted quickly to the negative.
The Marroquín government continued to claim that it had
no feelings for or against the treaty, while the American
minister in Bogotá reported nothing but criticism coming
from a press which he described as having "suddenly
sprung into existence." He could not find a single journal
or newspaper willing to publish an article in favor of the
treaty, even though the articles that did appear gave no hint
of Nicaraguan competition in the bidding and ridiculously
exaggerated the profits expected to accrue to the United
States.[23]

Equally significant is the fact that when the time arrived to elect delegates for a congress specially called to consider the treaty (and the first to meet since 1898), the governor of Panama, who was a Marroquín appointee, named an
antitreaty man as government candidate for the congress.
This individual was then declared elected, despite the fact

that the overwhelming sentiment in the province of Panama favored the treaty.[24]

Historians have claimed that Marroquín was not to blame because he was politically weak.[25] But the truth of the matter was well put by the Colombian consul in New York, who insisted that there was no party in Colombia "strong enough to defeat the wishes of the President." As soon as the congress convened, Marroquín showed himself firmly in control by mustering a vote of thirty-eight to five against an opposition party motion demanding to see all executive correspondence on the treaty. Marroquín supporters were elected president and vice-president of the senate, and the government went on to carry every important question in the course of the debate. Secretary Hay suspected that Marroquín might submit the treaty without recommendation. But the Colombian president went considerably beyond this to stall the proceedings and pave the way for the treaty's defeat should the United States refuse to pay large additional sums of money. In his opening address, he announced that he would only suggest that Colombia was in a good position to demand better terms. He withheld the treaty for several weeks and then cavalierly submitted it without his signature, an act unprecedented in Colombian history. Two weeks of debate thus revolved around the question of whether congress had the right to consider an unsigned document. In the meantime, he sought additional sums from representatives of both the United States and the French Panama Canal Company, intimating that this was the only way to ensure senate approval.[26]

Mysterious things happened. There was a secret meeting on 30 June between the senate and Marroquín's foreign minister at which he revealed a strongly worded plea from the United States. There was also an unusual failure of telegraph service for three critical weeks during which a senate committee decided to attach nine amendments to the treaty, including a stipulation for more money. On 4 August, the committee issued its report; on 5 August, telegraph service resumed, and the American minister was presented with an urgent and long-delayed wire from Hay. Other cables were unaccountably lost.[27]

In the end, Marroquín's special congress voted unanimously to reject the treaty, and the Panamanians carried out their long-threatened revolt. Bogotá failed to send early reinforcements, despite Roosevelt's frank warning that in such a situation he would avail himself of his legal right to maintain peace along the Panama railroad and prevent all troops from landing within a radius of fifty miles. Four hundred of Marroquín's troops did manage to land at Colón before Roosevelt acted, but they could do little on their own and were actually saved from an encounter with eager Panamanian forces nearly four times as large when the American naval commander refused them access to Panama City.[28]

The Colombian government now asked for American aid in putting down the revolt and offered, in return, to approve the ill-fated Hay-Herrán Treaty either by presidential decree or by summoning an extra session of congress with new and friendly members. This only confirmed T.R.'s suspicions of double-dealing and steeled him all the more in his support of Panamanian independence. It is unnecessary to recall the long history of Panamanian separatism, the periods when the province had enjoyed various degrees of autonomy, or the many times Colombian authorities had been unable to put down insurrection on the isthmus without American aid. Suffice to say that in the opinion of both Hay and Roosevelt, a failure to intervene would have resulted in "endless guerrilla warfare." Hay had advised Roosevelt that we "shall be forced" to do something "in the case of a serious insurrectionary movement in Panama to keep the transit clear. Our intervention should not be haphazard, nor this time should it be to the profit, as heretofore, of Bogotá." And the president, for his part, harbored a fear of intervention by some European power and appreciated his responsibility to protect the lives of American citizens.[29]

Even more to the point, the issue was conceived in

terms of moral principle. Roosevelt might have shifted the
negotiations to Nicaragua; he might have discouraged revolutionary sentiment on the isthmus; he might even have
helped Colombia put the revolution down. But, apart from
political and practical considerations, such actions would
have been entirely out of character. It would have earned
him, in his own words, a place in Dante's inferno "beside
the faint-hearted cleric who was guilty of *il gran rifiuto.*"
Marroquín's last-minute demands for more money struck
him as outrageous, and he filled his personal correspondence
with words such as "homicidal corruptionists," "extor-
tion," and "blackmail." Marroquín, an absolute dictator
with power to "keep his promise or break it," had "determined to break it." The Colombian congress was an assembly "of mere puppets," a "sham," and the country "had
forfeited every claim to consideration." Nor was that
"stating the case strongly enough; she had so acted that
yielding to her would have meant on our part that culpable
form of weakness which stands on a level with wickedness."[30]

Roosevelt was so convinced, in fact, that Marroquín had
broken faith and brazenly flouted his part of the agreement
that he was ready to seek congressional support for a direct
takeover of the Canal Zone. Had he decided to do so, he
could have counted on the enthusiastic support of at least
two powerful members of the Senate Foreign Relations
Committee, Senator Shelby Cullom of Illinois, the chairman, and Senator Henry Cabot Lodge of Massachusetts. He
would also have been backed by Prof. John Bassett Moore
of Columbia University, the nation's leading scholar in the
field of international law. Mild-mannered, gentlemanly John
Hay thought even less than Roosevelt of Colombia's conduct, labeling Marroquín and his advisers "greedy little an-
thropoids" and railing against "the jack rabbit mind." On
one occasion, he wrote the president that "the jack rabbits
are in a great funk." On another, he declared that the Colombians "have had their fun—let them wait the requisite

number of days for the consequent symptoms." As for a
unilateral takeover, it might lead to war, but the war "would
be brief and inexpensive."[31]

Some of the most telling indictments of Marroquín
came, not from Americans, but from Colombians. Miguel
Antonio Caro, former president and leader of the senate
opposition, not only charged the government with lack of
good faith in not defending a treaty of its own making and
"endeavoring to throw the whole responsibility for its
failure on Congress"; he also accused Marroquín of stage-
managing the proceedings in such a way as to make it seem
that the senate had rejected the treaty as a result of
American threats. In accordance with a motion made by
Marroquín's son, who participated in the debate as a
senator, some of the more pointed communications from
Hay to Marroquín were read aloud to the full senate. This
tactic, which had been employed once before at a critical
moment during a secret session of congress, now evoked
loud murmurs of disapproval from the gallery. British
observers who had seats in the chamber agreed with Caro
that Marroquín's men were trying to "exculpate themselves
for their action by throwing the responsibility, as much as
possible, on the United States Minister as being the result
of his so-called undiplomatic action." This is how the scene
looked as they saw it:

Senator Caro rose and vehemently attacked the government for
its attitude in the conducting of the whole negotiations. He also
taunted the Minister for Foreign Affairs for his action in having
the correspondence between the American minister and himself
read aloud as an attempt to elude the responsibility resting on the
government and cover it by courting the applause of the gallery as
the champion of the rights of the Colombian Senate, which
Senator Caro pointed out, had never been called in question by the
American minister. The same attitude was taken by Senator
Arango in a short speech.[32]

José Concha, Marroquín's ambassador to the United
States in 1902 and a former secretary of war, charged his
chief with acting in bad faith when he led the United States

to believe that he would support the treaty. "I have not believed," he wrote, "that just because the Colombian Congress has the right to approve or disapprove the treaty under consideration, an agent of the Executive Power can sign it in any form, exempting himself and his superiors from all moral and legal responsibility." It was Concha, incidentally, who had earlier assured Hay that the treaty would "not be hampered by pecuniary considerations." Tomás Herrán, Colombian chargé d'affaires and signer of the treaty, went even further. He asserted that the dispute had been sought by Marroquín's "imbecilic government." Finally, the people of Bogotá registered their dissatisfaction by parading the streets in large crowds, chanting "Down with Marroquín!" and stoning the home of Marroquín's son.[33]

The Panama incident is not the only one in which Roosevelt thought he had arrived at an understanding with foreign leaders only to find his trust misplaced. If such were the case and one did not know Roosevelt, one might deem the moral issue minor in the face of so large a national interest as an isthmian canal. The conclusion would then be that the president spoke in moral terms while acting unscrupulously and on impulse. There are other incidents, however, which follow a curiously similar pattern, one of which is the Alaskan boundary settlement.

Again, the story can be simply told. When gold was discovered in 1896 in the Klondike region of Canada, Canadians began to challenge the validity of the eastern boundary of the Alaskan panhandle, which barred their miners from access to the Pacific. A Canadian commission claimed to have evidence which placed the boundary line farther west. Roosevelt thought the claim preposterous, as there had never been a serious question about the border in the seventy years since its original definition. Almost every map, including the one hanging in Parliament House at Ottawa, argued against it.[34] He rejected all Canadian demands for arbitration, for he was unwilling to concede any of the major points at issue, and arbitration implied splitting the difference. The most he would do was to continue a *modus vivendi*, dating back to 1899, whereby the British deferred their claim in return for de facto control of a narrow strip of land about the size of the state of Rhode Island. But he insisted that even this was strictly gratuitous on any basis of law or morals. Canada had no more right to it "than the United States did to Cornwall or Kent."[35]

The British were in a stronger position by January 1903 than they had been for many years. The Boer War was over, and Roosevelt wanted their cooperation in defusing an explosive challenge to the Monroe Doctrine along the coast of Venezuela. It is possible that he was anxious to eliminate the boundary dispute before gold was discovered any closer to the American line. He may even have been influenced by the wishes of the Anglophile Hay. In any case, he now agreed to settlement by a joint commission in which each side was to appoint three "impartial jurists of repute." Ottawa would appoint two of the commissioners, London the third.

The heart of the matter for Roosevelt was his assumption that the British and Canadian authorities were asking for only one thing: to be permitted to save face. Prime Minister Laurier of Canada and his governor general, Lord Minto, had staked their political future on the promise of a settlement, and they told Roosevelt that they sought only to salvage their reputation at home by obtaining some kind of a judicial verdict. According to Henry White, secretary of the American embassy in London, the Canadian prime minister had said that "what he would like is an arbitration in order to 'save his face,' so to speak, *vis à vis* his people. . . . He added that he is well aware of your difficulties in respect to the Senate with any negotiation of that kind." Laurier offered to yield all essential points and accept British compensation elsewhere if for any reason the settlement should go against the United States. In particular, he said that he would not expect to take Dyea or Skagway, even if awarded, since these were "American towns which the Dominion government would not desire to take over." Ambassador

Choate gathered from Laurier that Canada would gladly accept "a 'compromise line' drawn either provisionally or as a permanent arrangement."[36] And the British, for their part, made it known that they desired no more than a *pro forma* solution on behalf of an ally who had rendered yeoman service in the Boer War; indeed, they signed the convention without even consulting Canada on final terms.[37]

Finally, Roosevelt made it crystal clear, both before he signed the convention and after, that he would not yield an inch on any essential point. He would appoint his three men. They would vote as expected. One or more members on the opposite side would concur, perhaps the British appointee, Chief Justice Lord Alverstone, and a potentially serious cause of Anglo-American discord would evaporate. Canada would save face, and justice would be done. This is what he expected, and this is the understanding he felt he had with the British and Canadians. Just before the final verdict, Secretary Hay wrote White that Roosevelt had "agreed to try the experiment, to enable the British government to get out of an absolutely untenable position with dignity and honour." Hay added that he had "heard from Laurier and Pauncefote directly, *that they have no case.*"[38] (Hay's italics.)

Secure in this belief, Roosevelt was confounded when Canada persisted to the very end in an effort to obtain some form of regular arbitration or refer the case to the Hague Tribunal. He was equally exercised when the British began maneuvering to delay the decision and all three of their judges came out adamantly against important aspects of the American brief. "Dangerously near blackmail," he stormed. The British must be kept "right up to the mark."[39] It was at this point that he repeated, in unmistakably strong language, something he had hinted many times before: that he would use force, if necessary, to back his position. His warnings were discreetly passed by word of mouth, but the English must have marked them well for, as we have seen, he had already dispatched eight hundred cavalrymen to the panhandle, and American public opinion was solidly against compromise. On 5 June 1903, the moderate-liberal *New York Times* reminded its readers that "no American commissioner could possibly continue to reside in this country if he gave up a single tittle of the American claim."[40]

All along, Roosevelt tried to ease the way for British concessions. After a visit to the White House in 1902, Arthur Lee reported to Lord Lansdowne that Roosevelt was prepared to refer the Alaskan question to an advisory commission but that it was "absolutely impossible for the United States government to yield upon what they conceived to be indubitable. At the same time, he [Roosevelt] recognized our difficulty with Canadian public opinion and seems to have suggested that if the other Canadian issues were referred to the same commission, he would be willing to see a verdict given in favor of Canada upon some of these in order to mitigate disappointment over Alaska. . . . with this view the President would even go so far as not to press the United States case upon these other points to its full value."[41] Such a development never occurred, of course. But T.R. did let it be known, as the London talks drew to a close, that he was willing to yield a narrow strip of land along the border as well as a number of other American claims by way of compensation.

In spite of this, however, the result hung perilously in the balance. A dramatic series of conferences took place between Lord Alverstone and British leaders, between Alverstone and the American envoys, and between the Americans and the highest officials of the British government. Until the very last moment, Roosevelt remained in suspense, wondering whether he might yet be forced to go to Congress, as he had threatened, and ask for authority to "run the line" himself. Only at the eleventh hour did Lord Alverstone break the deadlock by siding with substantive elements of the American brief.[42]

Canada raised an outcry at the final verdict, branding it a betrayal on the part of Alverstone and charging that Roosevelt's appointees had been anything but "impartial

jurists of repute." For a short while, the American flag was
hissed in theaters from Ottawa to Montreal. On the other
hand, Canadian officials had never considered their argument very compelling, however much they may have hoped
to benefit from the normal course of adjudication. The impression they gave to British and American officials as to
their ambivalence and willingness to compromise reflected
their actual state of mind. As Lord Minto confided to Sir
Michael Herbert, "I do not say that the Canadian case is a
very strong one on all points . . . but it is a good arguable one
in some points." Significantly, Undersecretary of State
Joseph Pope felt so dubious about the Canadian claim that
he hoped not to be chosen as agent, remarking that "in
respect of its really important feature, the ownership of the
heads of inlets, [it] was not overstrong." Ottawa's choice
of agent fell instead to Secretary of the Interior Clifford
Sifton, a polished lawyer who struck Pope as "much better
fitted than myself to make the best . . . of a case not con-
spicuous for its strength." As for Laurier, he had immediately given up on "any idea of obtaining the Lynn Canal
or any part on it, though he dearly hoped, in Minto's words,
to "do something to save our 'amour propre.' " This was "in
deference to Canadian public opinion" and implied an expectation that something could be won at the southern end of
the Portland Channel where "American claims are not near
so strong." During the entire period under discussion, this
position of Laurier's held firm, and he would seem to have
been quite prepared to welcome the final decision had it not
been for the unexpected loss of two small islands.[43]

Lord Alverstone's inexplicable last-minute decision to
award two out of four islands at the mouth of the Portland
Channel to the United States prompted the Canadian commissioners to publish an angry minority report charging
Britain's chief justice with a craven surrender of principle to
politics. In fact, however, the disputed specks were utterly
insignificant relative to the overall package that Canada
received. The Canadians had themselves belittled the im-

portance of these islands in the course of the meetings, while
Roosevelt, insisting adamantly that all four belonged to the
United States, indicated a willingness to cede two for the
purpose of allowing Canada to save face. As it happened,
T.R. extended a rather generous hand, for the two which
went to Canada (Pearce and Wales) were valuable not only
for a set of supply depots erected by Americans in 1896, but
also because they measured eighteen and eight miles long
respectively. By contrast, the islets remaining in American
hands (Sitklan and Kannaghunut) averaged less than two
miles in length and were of doubtful value in controlling the
entrance to the Portland Channel (nearby Port Simpson was
then being proposed as the western terminus of a trans-
Canadian railroad). In the end, Canada's chief surveyor con-
ceded that the American case had been entirely correct all
along, and most British journalists refused to find fault
either with T.R.'s choice of commissioners or the decision
that had been reached. The crisis passed, and by 1908, Canada was well enough disposed to name one of her mountain
peaks after Lord Alverstone.[44]

What is interesting is that the betrayal most often
stressed by historians is Roosevelt's alleged sacrifice of
Canadian trust. According to Thomas Bailey, Roosevelt
"browbeat" the British. Alexander Campbell describes the
president as acting on the principle that might makes right
and compelling Britain to yield to *force majeure.* Tyler Dennett and Charles C. Campbell both stress T.R.'s eagerness
for the Republican nomination in 1904, and the latter sums
it all up as the "outbursts of a highly-strung, self-righteous
man sure of everything but his hold upon the presidency."[45]
Even Secretary Hay took exception to Roosevelt's methods
at the time, going so far as to threaten resignation.[46]

Unquestionably, the Canadians had a legitimate cause
for complaint when they found themselves sitting across the
table from the outspoken Henry Cabot Lodge, George
Turner, who, though a justice on the supreme court of the
state of Washington, had also represented his state in the

Senate, and Secretary of War Elihu Root.[47] Just as clearly, however, Roosevelt felt that his choice of commissioners did not vitiate the gentlemen's agreement on which the settlement was based, particularly in view of his alleged effort to appoint members of the United States Supreme Court and the constraint imposed upon him by a senate membership which felt even more strongly than he did about the justice of the American claim. He may have been naive to expect Lord Alverstone or President Marroquín to act as he fancied he himself would have acted in their positions. But he genuinely regarded both cases as matters of moral and gentlemanly obligation. As early as April of 1901, before he even reached the presidency, Roosevelt had written Lee that he did not see how the Alaskan issue could be arbitrated "except in some form of coming to an agreement among ourselves."[48] When the issue was finally settled, he wrote to Lee once again in much the same vein:

Every Canadian and British map thus officially submitted by the British and Canadian Commissioners, for sixty years after the signing of the treaty between the Russians and the British, in 1825, sustained the American case. Lord Alverstone could not have acted otherwise than he did and *the action of the Canadian commissioners, in my view, was outrageous alike from the standpoint of ethics and of professional decency....* I asked two judges of the Supreme Court, whom I thought most fit for the position to serve. They both declined; and as I now think, wisely. On this commission we needed to have jurists who were statesmen. If the decision had been rendered purely judicially, the Canadians would not have received the two islands which they did receive at the mouth of the Portland Canal; and one of the judges to whom I offered the appointment has told me that on that account he would have been unable to sign the award.[49] (Italics added.)

In 1907, after concluding what he characteristically termed a "Gentlemen's Agreement" with Japan, Roosevelt encountered what appeared to be still another case of bad faith. The agreement pledged good treatment of Japanese in the United States in return for voluntary Japanese restric-

tion of emigration to the United States, and T.R. carried out
his side of the contract by scolding his countrymen on the
west coast for their discriminatory practices, calling California officials to Washington for personal conferences and
raining letters and telegrams upon them until there were
definite signs of improvement.[50] Much to his dismay, he
soon discovered that Japan was not implementing her part
of the bargain. The agreement had been made in February
1907, but the number of Japanese immigrants to the United
States remained steady and even increased during the
months of March, April, and May. The June figures were
the highest of all, and it was in late June that he set in
motion the plans for a world cruise of the entire battlefleet—
sixteen battleships which eventually received an invitation
to visit Japan.[51]

By the time the ships reached the western Pacific en
route to their "good-will" visit, the Gentlemen's Agreement
was being implemented by both parties. In the meantime,
however, MacKenzie King, the Canadian commissioner of
labor and immigration, had come to the White House with a
story which confirmed what Roosevelt had long suspected.
In Roosevelt's words:

King struck me as a very capable, resolute fellow, and his decision
of character, coupled with his official position, had enabled him to
get hold of a number of Japanese documents such as we on this
side of the line had never seen. These documents he said fully bore
out what he has suspected but could not prove, namely, that the
Japanese government had deliberately overissued two or three
times the number of passports which they said they were issuing;
and he asserted that they showed that the immigration was really
completely under the control of their government. The papers he
seized were in the possession of an agent of the Japanese Immigration people, who had formerly been the Japanese Consul. They
contained many official papers from the Japanese Government
which as he stated showed its thoro [sic] understanding of all the
crooked work that was going on. Among other things, he told me
that in the first ten months of last year they received some 3500
Japanese who had passports to the United States—the Japanese

having arranged with us that the only Japanese who should come here were those who had passports direct to the United States and who were shipped direct to our shores. After the investigations were completed King states that a very curious touch was given to the proceeding by the fact that the Japanese ex-consul and other Japanese gave him a dinner in Japanese style, and that at this dinner the ex-consul made a speech the intent of which, inasmuch as he was an Oriental I cannot follow, but which in an Occidental would have been insolence; for he got up and to the intense and evident excitement of his countrymen repeated a dream that he had had to the effect that Japan had taken the mastery of the Pacific and pocketed the Island of Vancouver, and then had swallowed all America west of the Rocky Mountains.[52]

Roosevelt may have had more than one reason for sending the fleet, but his action followed a familiar pattern of Rooseveltian diplomacy: the use or threatened use of power in a situation where he felt a betrayal of trust. In the case of Colombia, he had ordered the navy to Colón and would probably have urged a direct intervention had events themselves not intervened. In the case of Canada, he had moved troops to the disputed area of Alaska and threatened to use them, if necessary, to vindicate his stated position. Where Japan was concerned, he had shown his determination through the most credible military means at his disposal. In all three instances, the central issue was charged with a moral overtone. In every case, he regarded himself as the injured party. And in each situation, he was willing to go to extremes to support what appeared to him to be justice.

Duplicity, a factor common to all three cases, was not something Roosevelt appreciated in the normal give-and-take of diplomatic exchange. Russia struck him as specially untrustworthy in this regard because Count Cassini, the czar's ambassador, not only lied, he lied to Roosevelt when he knew perfectly well Roosevelt knew he was lying. This, to the Rough Rider, was "brazen and contemptuous effrontery."[53] Count Lamsdorf, the Russian foreign minister, received a dose of the righteous Roosevelt when, after approving Washington as the site for American-sponsored peace talks between his country and Japan, he suddenly drew back and expressed a preference for the Hague. Roosevelt refused to hear of it and instructed George von Lengerke Meyer, American ambassador in St. Petersburg, to hold Lamsdorf right to the mark even if it meant appealing over his head to the czar. Meyer followed the president's instructions and told Lamsdorf that "in America, when we gave our word, we abided by it."[54] Needless to say, Lamsdorf was unaccustomed to such handling. He did, however, agree to abide by his original decision, and Roosevelt proceeded with his plan for bringing the belligerents to the peace table.

On occasion, T.R. seems to have been as much provoked by the kaiser as he was by the czar, and for the same reason. When Arthur Lee came to Washington in 1906, he was permitted to read portions of what he later described as a "unique and detailed 'diary' " which T.R. "kept for the national archives throughout his administration." According to Lee, it consisted of "official despatches, communications from foreign rulers and talks with Ambassadors which were quoted in full, linked up by a narrative of events and comments by the President himself. It was his custom to send extracts from this record to his Ambassadors abroad, so as to keep them exactly informed of the situation as he saw it." Among the "sensational" revelations Lee was allowed to observe in this diary was the information that Germany had backed Russia in the 1904 contest with Japan until the czar suffered his great reversal of fortune at Tsushima. The kaiser had then done a complete volte-face and begun to demand credit for the peace settlement: "The Kaiser particularly requested that his efforts should be acknowledged by the President and, having received a telegram which was sent confidentially, but in similar terms, to the heads of all states concerned, he alone proceeded to publish it and to seek to turn the incident to his own advantage."

Nor was this all. During the Algeciras Conference, Wilhelm had falsely assured Roosevelt that a critical last-minute proposal by Austria had been "approved by all the other powers including England." This maneuver "intensified the President's suspicions and, resenting what he considered a breach of faith on the Kaiser's part, he not only vetoed the Austrian proposal but threatened to publish the whole correspondence. Upon this the Kaiser surrendered precipitately, only stipulating that Roosevelt should publicly acknowledge Germany's magnanimity and sacrifices in the cause of peace." T.R. felt sorry for Specky, "who seemed 'heartily ashamed of the dirty work he was called upon by his master to do' ":

For some time after Algeciras, the Kaiser's personal intercourse with Roosevelt practically ceased. Before that he had been in the habit of writing or telegraphing several times a month, but now he assumed a pose of dignified aloofness, mitigated only by occasional personal messages such as that which he telegraphed when Alice Longworth visited him.[55]

T.R. appears almost gullible at times in his insistence on diplomatic candor and gentlemanly behavior. During the Algeciras Conference, he complained that the French and Germans had been less than frank with him, while his secretary of state described Germany's bargaining methods as "pettifoggery . . . unworthy of a great nation." We see the same attitude during the Russo-Japanese War, when Roosevelt was surprised to find each side asking for more than it expected to get. Characterizing Japan's maximum demands as "bluff," he found it incredible that men of noble Samurai lineage would insist on monetary indemnity, and he argued strongly that they would be disgraced if they stood out for their pound of flesh:

Ethically, it seems to me that Japan owes a duty to the world at this crisis. The civilized world looks to her to make peace; the nations believe in her; let her show her leadership in matters ethical no less than in matters military. The appeal is made to her in the name of all that is lofty and noble; and to this appeal I hope she will not be deaf.[56]

Naturally, there may have been ulterior motives
beneath such a stance. But this, in itself, would not offer
sufficient explanation, for there was an expansive side to
Roosevelt, one which preferred the advocacy of great causes
to the technical practice of law. In personal life, he had
shown himself loath to haggle; he had sunk large sums of inherited wealth into an unsuccessful ranching venture and
been driven in the end to borrow cash from a brother-in-law
rather than put his beloved Sagamore Hill up for sale.[57] It is
also well to remember, as suggested earlier, that we are dealing with an age, as well as with the principal exemplar of
that age, a man whose background was highly charged with
the moral imperative.

This is not to say that Roosevelt was soft as a statesman, or easily fooled. To conclude with a picture of him as
naive would be misleading in the extreme, for the remarkable thing about him was the degree to which his moral
instinct was tempered by *Realpolitik*. He was a man who
aimed at a logical, rather than sentimental, approach to
public issues, who used patronage skillfully, even ruth-
lessly, to eliminate party opposition. He could threaten Congress with an all-out fight for tariff reduction and then drop
it when he found that by doing so he might assure victory
for his first priority, a bill to regulate railroads. He implored
Congress for the money to build four battleships, knowing
full well this was the only way to procure two.

More specifically, he stressed the importance of power
in foreign relations. He did not think the rules of international morality applied to "savages" in the same way they
did to "civilized and cultured communities." Nor did he
believe that any nation "acts properly all the time." Public
officials were obliged "to compromise in order to do anything at all," and he continually preached the importance of
having "realizable ideals." The words inscribed near his
grave at Oyster Bay sum up a large part of his philosophy:
"Keep your eyes on the stars and your feet on the ground."[58]
Had he applied the code of honor to international diplomacy
without also dealing from strength, he might have been less

successful. Several years later, another "gentleman" leader would come to power who would apply an equally exalted moral standard to international relations. Like Roosevelt, Woodrow Wilson tried to hold other nations to a personal conception of righteousness. But unlike his predecessor, he tried to export the laws and traditions of American society, and he did so without the credibility or armament Roosevelt had been careful to build. The result was a high incidence of intervention, war, and bloodshed. It was Roosevelt's "realizable ideals" (the title of one of his books), along with a fair amount of luck, that brought him out on the good side of history and won for him the Nobel Peace Prize.

In sum, Roosevelt's policy toward Colombia, Canada, and Japan proceeded from a variety of motives. Self-interest and national interest were a clear part of the picture in all three instances. What is interesting, though, is the fact that the most pointed confrontations of his presidency arose, at least in part, from the kind of moral issue to which he was particularly sensitive. Felix Gilbert has written that "America has wavered in her foreign policy between Idealism and Realism, and her great historical moments have occurred when both were combined." Adrienne Koch attributes the success of the Founding Fathers to their reliance upon power as well as morals.[59] Perhaps Roosevelt, as the architect of America's role as world leader, deserves to be appreciated in like manner. In his Sixth Annual Message to Congress, he maintained that the United States should not disregard its interests or expect other nations to act unselfishly, but that it should nevertheless be "our steady aim to raise the ethical standard of national action just as we strive to raise the ethical standard of individual action."[60]

Notes

1. Philip C. Jessup, *Elihu Root,* 1:453.
2. Richard Hofstadter, *The American Political Tradition,* p. 209; Thomas A. Bailey, *A Diplomatic History of the American*

118 VELVET ON IRON

People, p. 527; Robert Endicott Osgood, *Ideals and Self-Interest in America's Foreign Relations,* p. 144; Merle Curti, *The Growth of American Thought,* pp. 557-58, 654.

3. See, for example, Alexander E. Campbell, *Great Britain and the United States,* p. 107; Eugene Trani, *The Treaty of Portsmouth: An Adventure in American Diplomacy,* p. 4; Charles S. Campbell, Jr., *Anglo-American Understanding, 1898-1903,* p. 326; G. Wallace Chessman, *Theodore Roosevelt and the Politics of Power,* p. 94; Thomas A. Bailey, *The Art of Diplomacy,* p. 230; Bradford Perkins, *The Great Rapprochement,* pp. 75, 173; Howard K. Beale, *Theodore Roosevelt and the Rise of America to World Power,* pp. 25, 34-35. Two recent accounts that are more sensitive than most to the prominence of a moral strain in T.R.'s diplomacy are David H. Burton, *Theodore Roosevelt,* pp. 18-19, 22, 46-48, 56-57, 168; and Theodore Roosevelt, *The Writings of Theodore Roosevelt,* ed. William H. Harbaugh, pp. xxii-xxvi.

4. Theodore Roosevelt, *An Autobiography,* p. 13; Roosevelt to Theodore Roosevelt, Sr., 22 October 1876; to Anna Roosevelt, 14 October 1877; to Martha Bulloch Roosevelt, 24 March 1878, *Letters,* 1:18, 29, 33; Chessman, *Theodore Roosevelt,* p. 15. Typical of the elder Theodore are the following excerpts from a letter which he wrote to his young daughter, Bamie: "A very good rule to follow is when doubtful whether it is right, not to do it. . . . I always believe in showing affection by doing what will please the one we love, not by talking, so I will expect to see an effort on your part [in the direction of better handwriting]." Theodore Roosevelt, Sr., to Anna Roosevelt, 31 July 1868, Theodore Roosevelt Collection, Houghton Library, Harvard University.

5. Mark A. DeWolfe Howe, *George von Lengerke Meyer, His Life and Public Services,* pp. 397, 409.

6. Roosevelt to Corinne Roosevelt, 5 February 1877, 22 November 1886, *Letters,* 1:23, 117.

7. Theodore Roosevelt, "Municipal Administration: The New York Police Force," *Atlantic Monthly* 80 (1897): 289-300; Carleton Putnam, *Theodore Roosevelt: The Formative Years, 1858-1886,* p. 225.

8. Roosevelt, *Autobiography,* pp. 470, 500.

9. Roosevelt to Corinne Roosevelt, 24 August 1881, 12 April 1886; to Martha Baker Dunn, 6 September 1902, *Letters,* 1:51, 96; 3:324-25. Roosevelt's interpretation of *Anna Karenina* may be more revealing of the critic than it is of the work. For his reference

to Tolstoi as a "moral pervert," see Lawrence F. Abbott, *Impressions of Theodore Roosevelt*, pp. 189–91.

10. Theodore Roosevelt, *Thomas Hart Benton*, in *Works*, ed. Hagedorn, 7:13, 27–28, 187; Roosevelt, *History of New York*, ibid., 10:383; Putnam, *The Formative Years*, p. 575; Roosevelt to Root, 18 February 1902, *Letters*, 3:232. In his presidential address to the American Historical Association, T.R. went on to say that "it is no proof of impartiality to treat wickedness and goodness as on the same level," and he concluded with the words, "Righteousness exalteth a nation." Roosevelt, *History as Literature and Other Essays* (1913; reprint ed., Port Washington, New York: Kennikat Press, 1967), pp. 19, 36.

11. Sir Claude M. MacDonald to Sir Edward Grey, 29 July 1905, FO 115/1356, PRO; Warren I. Cohen, *America's Response to China*, 70–77. Years earlier, Roosevelt had sided with President Harrison for defending Italian victims of mob abuse in New Orleans. Beale, *Roosevelt*, p. 41.

12. Robert W. Sellen, "Theodore Roosevelt: Historian with A Moral," *Mid-America* 41 (October 1959): 225, 228; David Barry, *Forty Years in Washington*, p. 283.

13. *Foreign Relations* (1905), p. xxx; *Outlook* 104 (1914): 633; Roosevelt, *The Strenuous Life*, in *Works*, ed. Hagedorn, 13:527; Roosevelt, *American Problems*, ibid., 16:311; Roosevelt to John R. Mott, 12 October 1908; Roosevelt to Frederick S. Oliver, 22 July 1915, *Letters*, 6:1282–83; 8:955–56. Roosevelt wrote Adelbert Moot on 13 February 1900 that "our only justification for keeping the islands [Puerto Rico] is that we intend to benefit them." Ibid., 2:1183. Max Beloff has written that Roosevelt's most original contribution to imperialist theory was the idea that the powers were trustees for the whole world, not just for themselves. Beloff, *The Great Powers*, p. 239.

14. J. Fred Rippy, "Antecedents of the Roosevelt Corollary," *Pacific Historical Review* 9 (September 1940): 267–79; Jessup, *Elihu Root*, 1:525; Warren G. Kneer, *Great Britain and the Caribbean, 1901–1913: A Study in Anglo-American Relations*, pp. x–xii. Lloyd Graybar, in a recent biography of Albert Shaw, has shown how closely Shaw's views on foreign policy paralleled those of his friend Roosevelt. Both men tended to view national diplomacy in terms of obligation; both "were moralists and expected the most elevated deportment from one another." Shaw conceived of imperialism as above all a duty; he rejoiced in the "moral jurisdiction"

the United States had assumed under the Monroe Doctrine and believed the policy had evolved from a negative to a positive concept under the guiding hand of Roosevelt. Lloyd J. Graybar, *Albert Shaw of the Review of Reviews: An Intellectual Biography*, pp. 113, 123.

15. Roosevelt to Bryce, 11 January 1913, James Bryce Papers, Bodleian Library, Oxford University; Roosevelt to Frederick S. Oliver, 22 July 1915, *Letters*, 8:954; Roosevelt, *Autobiography*, pp. 543, 545.

16. Samuel Flagg Bemis, *The Latin-American Policy of the United States*, p. 151; Richard W. Leopold, *Elihu Root and the Conservative Tradition*, p. 63; Bailey, *Diplomatic History*, pp. 494-95, 497.

17. Joseph B. Bishop, *Theodore Roosevelt and His Time Shown in His Letters*, and Willis Fletcher Johnson, *Four Centuries of the Panama Canal*. The only recent defense of Roosevelt's action in this connection is Robert A. Friedlander, "A Reassessment of Roosevelt's Role in the Panamanian Revolution of 1903," *Western Political Quarterly* 14 (June 1961): 535-43. Friedlander finds Roosevelt's course "morally straightforward and legally justified," p. 535.

18. Elihu Root, "The Ethics of the Panama Question," in Root, *Addresses on International Subjects by Elihu Root*, ed. Robert Bacon and James Brown Scott, pp. 190-97; *Review of Reviews* 29 (March 1904): 332.

19. U.S. Congress, House of Representatives, *The Story of Panama: Hearings on the Rainey Resolution Before the Committee on Foreign Affairs of the House of Representatives*, p. 186 (hereafter cited as *Story of Panama*); Root, "Ethics," in Root, *Addresses*, pp. 194-97. According to Thomas Favell, "The common Colombian assertion that the separation of Panama was the work of a small group of purchased traitors does not meet the facts. Bribery was used to obtain the important assistance of certain military commanders but the real revolutionary leaders, all civilians, neither sought nor received personal financial gain." Thomas Royden Favell, "The Antecedents of Panama's Separation from Colombia" (Ph.D. diss., Fletcher School of Law and Diplomacy, 1951), pp. 293-94.

20. U.S. Congress, Senate, *Diplomatic History of the Panama Canal, Senate Documents*, 63rd Cong., 2nd sess. (1 December 1913-24 October 1914), pp. 583-85 (hereafter cited as *Diplomatic*

History); Jessup, *Elihu Root*, 1:523; Friedlander, "Reassessment," pp. 538–39. E. Taylor Parks counted thirteen distinct United States interventions, Parks, *Colombia and the United States, 1765–1934*, p. 219.

21. Arthur M. Beaupré to John Hay, 4 May 1903, *Foreign Relations* (1903), p. 143; Dwight C. Miner, *The Fight for the Panama Route*, pp. 203, 218–22; *Story of Panama*, p. 321; Favell, "Antecedents," p. 220. Nicaragua was asking $6 million plus a $25,000 annuity as compared with the $10 million plus $250,000 annuity beginning in nine years that the United States agreed to pay Colombia. *Diplomatic History*, p. 572.

22. Hay to Beaupré, 9 June 1903; Hay to the Colombian Minister of Foreign Affairs, 13 June 1903, John Hay Papers, Special Correspondence, Library of Congress; Hay to Beaupré, 28 April 1903, *Foreign Relations* (1903), pp. 138–40. Colombia claimed the right to press the NPCC for a separate indemnity, while the United States insisted that she had waived this right (on moral grounds at least) in Concha's original draft of a treaty as well as in the Hay-Herrán Treaty itself. Washington rejected a pretreaty request on the part of Bogotá to have just such a right understood, but this did not stop Concha from trying to act upon it down to the last moment. Nor did it prevent the use of slightly ambiguous language in the treaty. Such ambiguity appears to have been deliberate on the part of Colombia and to have caused Roosevelt more than a little concern, even though he never admitted it. The United States was worried enough to give the NPCC an immediate conditional acceptance of its offer of sale in order, apparently to make Colombia's tacit acquiescence seem binding. *Story of Panama*, pp. 178–86, 253–54, 324, 329, 336; *Diplomatic History*, pp. 250–70.

23. C. Mallet [British minister to Colombia] to Lord Lansdowne, 20 January 1903, FO 55/415 PRO; George E. Welby to Lansdowne, 11 May 1903, FO 115/1274 PRO; Spenser S. Dickson [British vice-consul] Memorandum on the Bogotá Press, [?] July 1903, FO 115/1275 PRO; Beaupré to Hay, 30 March, 15 April 1903, *Foreign Relations* (1903), p. 134; Miner, *Fight*, pp. 246, 250; Dana Munro, *Intervention and Dollar Diplomacy in the Caribbean, 1900–1921*, p. 47; *Review of Reviews* 33 (January 1906): 67, 70; (May 1906): 566; Favell, "Antecedents," p. 227.

24. Beaupré to Hay, 15 April 1903, *Foreign Relations* (1903), pp. 134–35; Johnson, *Four Centuries*, pp. 161–62. One of the three

Panamanian representatives to the congress, José Arango, never bothered to attend, expecting the deliberations to be rigged. Another, José Domingo de Obaldia did attend and worked for the treaty, while the antitreaty delegate, Juan Pérez y Soto, is said to have opposed ratification on the basis of personal business interests which stood to be adversely affected. Favell, "Antecedents," p. 238.

25. See, for example, Munro, *Intervention*, p. 47, and Favell, "Antecedents," pp. 209, 217-18, 226, 237, 242, 261. This was also the view of the influential French engineer, organizer of revolution, and first Panamanian ambassador to the United States, Philippe Bunau-Varilla. Bunau-Varilla, *The Great Adventure of Panama*, p. 132.

26. Hay to the Colombian Minister of Foreign Affairs (marginal comment), 13 June 1903, Hay Papers, Special Correspondence, Library of Congress; Parks, *Colombia*, p. 407; Miner, *Fight*, pp. 242, 299-303, 308; Beaupré to Hay, 25 June, 9 July, 21 July 1903, *Foreign Relations* (1903), pp. 155, 163, 165. For additional evidence of how Marroquín stage-managed the congressional review process, see Beaupré to Hay, 23 June, 2 July, 5 July, 11 July, 5 August, 12 August, 21 October, 23 October 1903, ibid., pp. 155, 157-58, 163, 172, 180, 214, 217.

27. Beaupré to Hay, 5 August, 18 August, 26 August, 19 October 1903, *Foreign Relations* (1903), pp. 174, 187, 189, 213; Miner, *Fight*, pp. 300, 310.

28. John Bassett Moore, ed., *Digest of International Law*, 8 vols., 3:68; *Story of Panama*, p. 177; Friedlander, "Reassessment," p. 539 n.; Dr. Juan B. Pérez y Sota, senator from Panama, predicted as early as 11 May in *El Correo Nacional* that the treaty would be unanimously voted down. Beaupré to Hay, 12 May 1903, *Foreign Relations* (1903), p. 144.

29. Hay to Roosevelt, 13 September 1903, Hay Papers, General Correspondence, Library of Congress; Roosevelt to Joseph Cannon, 12 September 1904, *Letters*, 4:922; Beaupré to Hay, 6 November 1903, *Foreign Relations* (1903), p. 225. According to the British minister, there was "no doubt the movement for independence is popular with everybody, and the prospect of the early resumption of the canal works has created a profound feeling of satisfaction and joy amongst the people of all ranks on the Isthmus." C. Mallet to Lord Lansdowne, Panama, 3 December 1903, FO 115/1306 PRO.

30. Roosevelt, *Autobiography,* pp. 557–66 (esp. 561–62, 566); David H. Burton, "T.R.: Confident Imperialist," *Review of Politics* 23 (July 1961): p. 371; Beale, *Roosevelt,* p. 33; Gerstle Mack, *The Land Divided,* p. 454; Roosevelt to Kermit Roosevelt, 4 November and 5 December 1903, Theodore Roosevelt Collection, Houghton Library, Harvard University. Many in Congress would have preferred to see Roosevelt settle on a Nicaraguan route. But it is not at all certain that the slippery Zelaya would have been any easier to deal with than Marroquín. Munro, *Intervention,* p. 59; A. L. P. Dennis, *Adventures in American Diplomacy,* pp. 311–12; Johnson, *Four Centuries,* p. 131; Friedlander, "Reassessment," p. 542.

31. Hay also referred to Colombian leaders as "fools" and "hysterical jack rabbits." Hay to Roosevelt, 22 August, 23 August, 31 August, 3 September 1903; Hay to Alvey Adee, 23 September 1903, Hay Papers, General Correspondence, Library of Congress; Roosevelt to Hay, 19 August 1903, *Letters,* 3:566–67; Chester L. Jones, *The Caribbean Since 1900,* p. 303; Miner, *Fight,* pp. 350–51. Moore devoted his life to the study of international arbitration and wrote a six-volume *History of United States Arbitrations* (1898), an eight-volume *Digest of International Law* (1906), and a six-volume *History of International Adjudications* (1922–33). He also served as American justice on the World Court. The one doctoral dissertation which deals with this topic and utilizes Colombian sources holds that "Marroquín cannot escape from the moral responsibility of having acted in bad faith and the political responsibility for having played fast and loose with a great power . . . [he] contributed in an important degree to the rejection of the treaty." Favell, "Antecedents," p. 262. See also ibid., pp. 211–12, 215.

32. George E. Welby to Lord Lansdowne, 15 August 1903, FO 115/1276, PRO. See also Beaupré to Hay, 11 July, 21 October 1903, *Foreign Relations* (1903), pp. 164, 214.

33. Beaupré to Hay, 9 November 1903, *Foreign Relations* (1903), p. 227; Miner, *Fight,* pp. 165, 371; Parks, *Colombia,* pp. 388–89, 406; Miles P. Duval, *Cadiz to Cathay,* pp. 343, 356; *Diplomatic History,* p. 552. After a brief flurry of anti-American sentiment, leading journals of opinion also made it clear where they felt the burden of blame should rest. *El Relator,* a noted Conservative publication, insisted, "We made the Panamanians pariahs in their own land. We took away their rights and sup-

pressed their liberties. We took from them the most precious faculty of a free people—that of electing their own legislators, judges, and administrative officials. We made Panama into a virtual military territory." According to *El Comercio,* a prominent Liberal organ, "The separation of Panama was caused by our profound shortcomings. . . . it is a plain case of super-centralist suicide." And in the words of *El Correo Nacional,* a distinguished journal founded by Carlos Martínez Silva, "We have been completely lacking in common sense. . . . we are all to blame." Favell, "Antecedents," pp. 290–91. The London *Times* was equally exercised, referring to the conduct of Colombia as "wanton procrastination" and "blackmail" of both the United States and the NPCC; the *Times* (London), 5 November 1903, quoted in Ralph Weber, ed., *As Others See Us,* pp. 176–77.

34. Roosevelt to Hay, 10 July 1902, *Letters,* 3:287.

35. Roosevelt to Arthur Lee, 18 March, 24 April 1901, ibid., pp. 20, 66; Charles G. Washburn, ed., "Memoir of Henry Cabot Lodge," *Proceedings of the Massachusetts Historical Society* (April 1925): 339.

36. Lansdowne to Raikes, 16 July 1902; Laurier to Lansdowne, 12 August 1902, FO 5/2510, PRO; Joseph Choate to Hay, 5 July 1902, Hay Papers, Special Correspondence, Library of Congress; White to Hay, 28 June 1902, Henry White Papers, Box 4, Library of Congress. White gained the impression at this point that Laurier expected the arbitrators to decide in favor of Canada; but this is not the impression Laurier gave later, nor is it the one gained by Roosevelt and Hay. Beale, *Roosevelt,* pp. 114–16, 126, 126 n.

37. Roosevelt to Elihu Root, 8 August 1903, *Letters,* 3:546. Roosevelt received the same information from Ambassador Choate as he did from White. It should also be noted that Laurier visited Roosevelt at the White House on 7 December 1902, just before the signing of the treaty. Sir Wilfrid Laurier, *Life and Letters of Sir Wilfrid Laurier,* ed. Oscar Douglas Skelton, 2 vols., 2:142; Bradford Perkins, *Great Rapprochement,* p. 168.

38. Lansdowne to Herbert, 10 December 1902, FO 5/2510, PRO; Hay to White, 20 September 1903, White Papers, Special Correspondence, Library of Congress; Beale, *Roosevelt,* pp. 116–17, 119, 126. See also Durand to Lansdowne, 20 June 1904, Lansdowne Papers, FO 800/144, PRO. According to the *Review of Reviews* 28 (August 1903): 142–43, "The consent of the United States to allow this question to be opened at all is, so far as we are

aware, without precedent in history. . . . It is positively asserted on the highest authority that unless the Canadian claims are admitted by a majority of the present commissioners, they will have no further consideration on the part of the United States. In other words, if there should be a . . . disagreement of the commissioners, three to three, the United States would regard the case of the Canadian plaintiff as having failed and the question as being forever closed. . . . It is taken for granted, however, that a majority of the commissioners will decide that any new interpretation of the treaty of 1825 is now inadmissable."

39. Roosevelt to Hay, 10 July 1902, *Letters*, 3:288; Beale, *Roosevelt*, p. 122; Choate to Lansdowne, 5 August 1903, FO 414/174, PRO.

40. Beale, *Roosevelt*, pp. 113–14, 127; Roosevelt to Root, 8 August 1903, *Letters*, 3:546; Charles C. Tansill, *Canadian-American Relations, 1875-1911*, p. 252; *New York Times*, quoted in FO 5/2543, PRO.

41. Lansdowne to Herbert, 10 December 1902, FO 5/2510, PRO; Arthur H. Lee, *A Good Innings and A Great Partnership, Being the Life Story of Arthur and Ruth Lee*, 3 vols., 1:260.

42. Tansill, *Canadian-American Relations*, pp. 249–50, 251 n., 259, 261; Henry Cabot Lodge to Roosevelt, 12 October 1903, *Roosevelt-Lodge Correspondence*, 2:69.

43. "A Half Century of Service," film M 585, pp. 193–94, Joseph Pope Papers, PAC; Sir Wilfrid Laurier to Joseph Pope, 4 October 1903, MG 30 E 86, vol. 1, General Correspondence, ibid.; Lord Minto to Lord Lansdowne, 4 June, to Sir Michael Herbert, 21 October and 30 December 1902, Letterbook III, Lord Minto Papers, PAC; Clifford Sifton to the Hon. Arthur Elliot, M.P. (Minto's brother and editor of the *Edinburgh Review*), 18 October 1903; Lord Minto to Rt. Hon. A. Lyttleton, 23 October 1903, to Lord Alverstone, 9 December 1903, Letterbook IV, ibid.

44. Surveyor Klotz of Canada expressed his opinions to President Angell of the University of Michigan; Hay to Roosevelt, 31 October 1903, Hay Papers, General Correspondence, Library of Congress; Bradford Perkins, *Great Rapprochement*, pp. 171–72; Campbell, *Great Britain*, pp. 120–21. See also: John Anderson (British colonial official in charge of Canadian affairs) to Sir Wilfrid Laurier, 15 July 1902, MG 26 G, vol. 238, nos. 66547–66549, Wilfrid Laurier Papers, PAC; Lord Alverstone to Allen B. Aylesworth, 21 October 1903, MG 27 II D15, vol. 275, Clifford Sifton Papers, PAC; Alverstone Memorandum, 24 October 1903,

Alaskan Boundary Correspondence, MG 27 II, vol. 275, p. 15, ibid.; Lord Minto to Hon. Arthur Elliot, [?] October 1903, to Laurier, 22 October 1903, to Hon. A. Lyttleton, M.P., 23 October 1903, to Lord Alverstone, 9 December 1903, Letterbook IV, Minto Papers, PAC.

45. Thomas A. Bailey, "Theodore Roosevelt and the Alaska Boundary Settlement," in Alexander DeConde and Armin Rappaport, eds., *Essays Diplomatic and Undiplomatic of Thomas A. Bailey*, p. 154; Bailey, *Diplomatic History*, p. 509; Alexander Campbell, *Great Britain*, pp. 107, 122; Charles Campbell, *Anglo-American Understanding*, pp. 326, 332. Allan Nevins's appraisal is similar: "Roosevelt's threatening tactics were both improper and unnecessary." They left "in the breasts of Canadians a conviction that a powerful nation had used its strength to take advantage of a weaker neighbor." Allan Nevins, *Henry White; Thirty Years of American Diplomacy*, pp. 201-202.

46. Beale, *Roosevelt*, p. 124. At the same time, it should be realized that the two Canadian appointees were hardly nonpartisan. Both were known to be "in political sympathy" with the Laurier government, and one (Lieutenant Governor of Quebec Sir Louis Jetté) happened to be a personal friend of Laurier. As described by a high official on the Canadian side, one could "safely depend on them to interpret Canadian sentiment." Memorandum of a Conversation between Lord Alverstone and Joseph Pope, 13 September 1903, MG 26 G, vol. 758, nos. 216540-216547, Laurier Papers, PAC.

47. Hay had originally held out hope that the United States would be represented by the chief justice of the Supreme Court, along with two associate justices. Herbert to Lansdowne, 19 December 1902, Lord Lansdowne Papers, FO 800/144, PRO.

48. Roosevelt to Arthur Lee, 24 April 1901, *Letters*, 3:66. The Senate refused to consider the use of even the *word* "arbitral" and insisted on its excision in the preamble to the convention as well as in the main body of the text. Bradford Perkins, *Great Rapprochement*, p. 168.

49. Roosevelt to Lee, 7 December 1903, Arthur Lee Papers, Courtauld Institute, Portman Square, London.

50. Thomas A. Bailey, *Theodore Roosevelt and the Japanese-American Crises*, pp. 316, 324.

51. Roosevelt to Root, 13 July 1907, *Letters*, 5:717-18; Bailey, *Japanese-American Crises*, pp. 233-34; Oscar Straus,

Under Four Administrations: From Cleveland to Taft, pp. 225–26, 228. Charles Neu emphasizes that a recurrence of mob violence against the Japanese in California (20–21 May 1907) placed the American side of the Gentlemen's Agreement in jeopardy; only later in his narrative does he refer to Japanese violations. Neu, *An Uncertain Friendship: Theodore Roosevelt and Japan, 1906–1909,* pp. 79, 168–69.

52. King gave precisely the same account to Sir Edward Grey when the two met in London. Grey to Bryce [April] 1908; Roosevelt to Arthur Lee, 2 February 1908, Lee Papers, Courtauld Institute.

53. Raymond A. Esthus, *Theodore Roosevelt and the International Rivalries,* pp. 19–20.

54. Meyer to Roosevelt, 18 June 1905, quoted in Howe, *Meyer,* p. 168. The hard-working Meyer was a man after Roosevelt's heart, judging from the latter's remarks in a letter dated 26 December 1904: "You come in the category of public servants who desire to do public work, as distinguished from those whose desire is merely to occupy public place—a class for whom I have no particular respect." Too many people, Roosevelt wrote, "seem to think that the life-work of an ambassador is a kind of glorified pink tea-party." Ibid., pp. 110–11.

55. Lee, *Good Innings,* 1:329–30, 332–33. The "diary" to which Lee alludes has not been found among Roosevelt's surviving papers.

56. Durand to the Foreign Office, 1 September 1905, RA Add G/9, Windsor Castle; John St. Loe Strachey to Roosevelt, 16 October 1905, John St. Loe Strachey Papers, House of Lords Library, London; Roosevelt, *Autobiography,* p. 586; Roosevelt to Spring Rice, 24 July 1905; Roosevelt to Trevelyan, 12 September 1905, to Henry White, 30 April 1906, *Letters,* 4:1285; 5:22, 252; Sternburg to Foreign Office, 18 March 1906, E. T. S. Dugdale, ed., *German Diplomatic Documents, 1871–1914,* 4 vols., 3:247; Trani, *Portsmouth,* p. 148; Esthus, *Rivalries,* pp. 106–107; Beale, *Roosevelt,* p. 386. Roosevelt admitted that Russia might not have ceded South Sakhalin if Japan had not "bluffed" on the question of indemnity. But he still regarded the bluff as an act of folly. Roosevelt to Spring Rice, 1 November 1905, *Letters,* 5:62.

57. For references in Roosevelt's writings to the idea of gentlemanliness, see Roosevelt to Corinne Roosevelt, 5 February 1877 and 15 April 1886, *Letters,* 1:23, 97.

58. Roosevelt, *Autobiography,* p. 575; Roosevelt to Frederick W. Oliver, 22 July 1915, *Letters,* 8:956; Howard C. Hill, *Roosevelt and the Caribbean,* p. 207.

59. Adrienne Koch, *Power, Morals, and the Founding Fathers: Essays in the Interpretation of the American Enlightenment* (Ithaca: Cornell University Press, 1961); Felix Gilbert, *To the Farewell Address: Ideas of Early American Foreign Policy* (Princeton: Princeton University Press, 1961), p. 136.

60. Osgood, *Ideals and Self-Interest,* p. 89.

CHAPTER 4

The Man and the Myth

W E come, finally, to the question of what cautionary
principles, if any, lay at the root of "Big Stick" diplomacy. One of the stranger paradoxes of American history is
the sharp contrast between Roosevelt's impressive diplomatic record and the standard conception of him as reckless,
bellicose, and overbearing. Broadway's popular *Arsenic and
Old Lace* told the story of two maiden aunts who poisoned
lonely old men as an act of mercy. In their spare time, they
took care of an insane brother who imagined himself to be
Theodore Roosevelt. He appeared on stage in the garb of a
Rough Rider, began every other sentence with the word
"Bully," and liked to bolt up a flight of stairs with sword
drawn, shouting "Charge!" More recently, a motion picture
based on the Perdicaris incident depicted Roosevelt as a
man who spent much time at his rifle range and took more
interest in a stuffed bear than he did in Morocco—a cautious
elder statesman by the name of John Hay had to explain to
him patiently that the Moroccan situation should not be
taken lightly, that it might even lead to war.[1]

Scholarly appraisals of the Rough Rider are replete with
such terms as "megalomania" and "militarism." He is said
to have had a "trigger-like willingness to use troops" and
an "adolescent love of war." One account calls him a "born
bully," another a "sophomoric" adventurer. His tactics
have been labeled "impetuous." And Howard Beale, the
leading student of his diplomacy, has written that he "ro-
manticized war," "gloried" in it, and "craved" its
excitement—it was "such fun to have a big navy." Beale

concludes that "in the sense of power that ordering ships about gave him he found exhilaration and perhaps compensation for unfulfilled yearnings of a sickly boy whose boyish urges had been unsatisfied."[2]

Some historians have allowed that Roosevelt mellowed beneath the weight of age and experience. Others have recognized his flare for *Realpolitik*. But few approach his record without sharp reservation.[3] According to Beale, he was a shrewd tactician whose conduct of foreign relations was marred by racial arrogance and a taste for imperialism; he refused "to take seriously other methods than armed force in establishing international stability" and, in the end, "failed in his most important objectives." Dexter Perkins credits him with a rare grasp of the role of power in international relations but finds his view of war "juvenile and romantic." Robert Osgood admires his realism, yet faults him for being, at heart, a "romantic militarist, an aggressive national egoist."[4]

At first sight, one is tempted to bridge the gap between Roosevelt's reputed bellicosity and his record of peace by attributing his success to the conservative influence of two fine secretaries of state.[5] While it is not easy to measure the subtle effect of one personality upon another, Hay and Root were gentler than Roosevelt and more given to legal solutions. They were also far more cautious in their emotional makeup. Either of them could be viewed as the carrot to Roosevelt's stick, and the president may well have chosen them with this very idea in mind.

On the other hand, Roosevelt took firm charge of foreign policy from the moment he entered the White House. He sent troops to Alaska in the spring of 1902 against the advice of Secretary Hay and in October ordered Hay to adopt a harder line in negotiations with Cuba. When Hay fell ill during the critical interval 1903–1905, T.R. assumed complete responsibility for the talks leading to Portsmouth and Algeciras.[6] Furthermore, when Hay offered his resignation in July 1903, because he objected to the sending of troops to Alaska and disapproved of the tremendous pres-

sure Roosevelt was bringing to bear on Britain, the chief
had his way, and the cabinet remained in tact.[7]

On another occasion, Hay pushed for a harder line than
the Rough Rider was willing to grant in regard to Russian
control of Manchuria: "If we give them [the Japanese] a
wink, they will fly at the throat of Russia in a moment."
Roosevelt, who had earlier said he wished to go to extremes
with Russia, demurred when it came to an actual showdown,
assuring Hay that continued patience would eventually be
rewarded.[8] T.R.'s later reference to Hay as a "fine figurehead" may have been somewhat harsh. Yet, in all three of
the major crises of the period, not to mention the talks
leading to peace in the Far East and a settlement in western
Europe, Hay played a distinctly minor role. Even on the
question of Panama, while Hay may have been optimistic
about a treaty with Nicaragua, there is no evidence that he
acted as a brake upon Roosevelt. Both he and Root were
quite comfortable with the course finally taken.[9]

No one is likely to forget what Root is supposed to have
said during a cabinet meeting when Roosevelt demanded to
know if he had not ably defended himself against all charges
of wrongdoing in connection with Panama: "You have
shown that you were accused of seduction and you have con-
clusively proved that you were guilty of rape."[10] Unfortu-
nately, the anecdote is as misleading as it is entertaining.
Root was obviously speaking in jest, and his relationship
with Roosevelt as secretary of state turns out to have been
very much the same as Hay's. T.R. praised him for his
statesmanlike qualities, credited him with important help
on speeches, and claimed that when it came to Latin America, he had been given carte blanche.[11] Root managed the
American position at the second Hague Peace Conference as
well as the campaign for arbitration treaties and a Central
American court of justice. He followed Roosevelt's example
of winning a Nobel Peace Prize. But this hardly warrants
the conclusion that he was a significant "restraining" influence. Interestingly enough, when he first accepted the
post of secretary, at least one commentator supposed Roo-

sevelt to be the one who would exercise the restraining influence: *Le Matin* of Paris commented that when Root ran
wild, there would be a strong hand to hold him in check.[12]
Only two serious crises remained to be settled after 1905.
In the clinch with Japan, Roosevelt acted on his own; and
during the initial stages of the Cuban crisis (20 September
to 1 October 1906) Root was away on a good-will tour. Like
Hay, Root argued unsuccessfully for a harder line on Russian occupation of Manchuria and exerted minimal influence
on American Far East policy in general. If his counsel
served as something of a check in connection with one or
two incidents in the Caribbean, Roosevelt was equally in-
hibited by public opinion, for as he later wrote, with
customary vehemence, the nation refrained from war "merely because our people declined to be irritated by the actions
of a weak opponent."[13]

The more closely one examines the record, the more apparent it becomes that the real controls on Roosevelt's
policy are to be found within the man himself. Careful exam-
ination reveals a complex character with a wide range of
ideas often obscured by the popular image.

There is, for example, the Roosevelt who hated war with
its attendant suffering, who waxed melancholy over the
Boer conflict, who considered it a tragedy that Napoleon
had to engage France in a foreign war in order to avoid war
at home, and who took genuine delight in Browning's anti-
war poem, "Love Among the Ruins." This is the Roosevelt
who criticized those "who would lightly undergo the chance
of war in a spirit of mere frivolity, or of mere truculence"
and who, when faced with the closest approximation of a
war scare during his presidency, fairly exploded with indignation at "prize jingo fools" on both sides of the Atlantic.
The wars of 1812 and 1861 he regarded either as a result of
poor preparation or the fruit of appeasement; both were
avoidable, as was the war of 1898.[14]

T.R. was as fast to condemn fire-eaters as he was to
heap scorn on pacifists. Treitschke, Carlyle, and Homer Lea

he classed with Norman Angell. Nor did he accept Bismarck's doctrine of blood and iron. Such a policy could succeed only if one's opponent responded with a policy of milk and water. He did believe that the United States had erred more on the side of too little preparedness than too much. But he was quick to brand militarism "a curse" when it appeared in other cultures; and, although he was far from regarding war as the ultimate tragedy, he did regard it as an evil and "a vice."[15] Placing justice above peace in his hierarchy of values, he was proud that Europe had used its strength to resist the scourge of the Turk. The suffering endured by Cubans under Spain and by Armenians under the Turkish yoke were evils that cried out for remedy, even if this meant intervention by the United States or, as in the case of Armenia, by some other foreign power. But he could also write without feeling inconsistent that "I loathe war," that "unjust war is dreadful," and that peace "is the aim of the greatest statesmen."[16]

There is no doubt of his fascination with bodily strength. He was enthralled by the battle scenes in Carlyle's *Frederick the Great,* and he returned more than once to Thucydides' graphic account of the Athenians who marched to crushing defeat in Sicily.[17] In *Hero Tales,* which he coauthored with Henry Cabot Lodge, we find Lodge writing of Francis Parkman, Abraham Lincoln, and John Quincy Adams, while Roosevelt concentrates almost exclusively on men of war. Beyond question, he prized the strenuous life and performed the most daring feats on horse and foot as a way of testing his mettle and gaining respect from his peers. With something of the wolf in his blood, he was not slow to put up his fists, whether this meant knocking down an intruder on the premises of his Harvard fraternity or shooting a rampant dog whose owner had received fair warning. Nor was he afraid to point out that war brings out the best in man, as well as the worst, and that "no triumph of peace is quite so great as the supreme triumphs of war."[18] Temperamentally impatient, there was little room in his system of

values for the "patient Griselda" or for those whom he liked
to call the "timid good."[19]

One might add that he was intrigued by "the affairs of
war," if by this is meant equipment and operations. He took
as much pride in a first-class cruiser as a fireman would take
in a brand-new hook and ladder. He corresponded regularly
with army and naval officers, offering advice on every subject from grand strategy to the proper design for a
uniform.[20] It is well known that he did more than any other
president to build the fleet into a first-class weapon.

Yet to infer from this, as some have done, that he
"gloried in war" or was in some way trigger-happy would
hardly be fair. He may have been more willing than others
to enter the lists, but he was no more anxious to precipitate
war than a professional fire-fighter is anxious to kindle a
flame. Everything he did as police commissioner, governor,
and president was expressly calculated to *avoid* the clash of
arms.

Preparedness was a cardinal principle of his philosophy,
because he believed that weakness would invite attack, and
that any nation as rich and potentially powerful as the
United States would not remain long at peace while other
nations were waging war unless it was prepared to defend
its vital interests. One could not rely on world opinion or
any other international tribunal for the defense of vital
rights, because an aggressor nation would brush public
opinion aside and achieve legitimacy by sheer dint of force.
Of all attitudes that could be held by foreigners in regard to
the United States, contempt was the most dangerous. China
seemed to him the example par excellence of a great nation
which, through long inattention to martial matters, had
become not only a bloody ground of civil war but "the
plaything" of foreign powers. Indeed, he coined the word
"chinafy" to describe the process of rendering a group or
nation impotent.[21]

He was never willing to concede that power, when properly exercised, was provocative. On the contrary—the

United States Navy struck him as "an infinitely more po-
tent factor for peace than all the peace societies of every
kind and sort." When the Turkish minister to the United
States complained that the sending of an American fleet to
Turkish waters implied sympathy for a group of insurgents,
Roosevelt reminded him that the fleet was supporting legitimate demands and that any false impression regarding
American sympathy would be dispelled the moment the
Turkish government complied with its obligations.[22] The
same attitude is evident in two incidents drawn from the
domestic scene. As New York City police commissioner, he
had sent men to protect a taxicab company from potential
damage at the hands of striking drivers. The strikers complained that the presence of police officers would "provoke
them to violence," and Roosevelt replied as follows:

If the strikers are law abiding and peaceable they can have no possible objection to the presence of the police, who will interfere only
with the disorderly and lawless, and if any man is incited to violence by the presence of an officer of the law, the very fact affords
proof that he is of disorderly and vicious character, and that there
is urgent need of the presence of the officers of the law to sustain
him.[23]

When dockworkers struck in Buffalo during his term as
New York governor, he made swift preparations to meet any
violence that might occur. He did not intend to use the
militia except at the mayor's request; but he was determined to have his men close enough to the danger area and
sufficiently alert as to be available the moment such request
might be made. Labor leaders insisted that the proximity of
troops tended to intimidate the strikers. But again, Roosevelt responded predictably: "It would intimidate no one unless he was anxious to commit lawlessness, and that in that
case it would be my especial care to see that he *was* intimidated."[24] In the end, state intervention was avoided.

To put Roosevelt's position in more positive terms, he
believed that power was of primary importance in the search

for peace. Without it, even benevolence and magnanimity would appear suspect in the eyes of the world, and the most statesmanlike advice would be apt to fall upon deaf ears. Whatever influence the United States had exercised at the first Hague Peace Conference was due to the fact that she had come in "as strong man and not as a weakling." Likewise, whatever respect the kaiser accorded her was due to his belief that "we have a pretty good navy with which to fight."[25]

Not that power was sufficient in and of itself to deter war. One could not remain immune from attack merely by sitting behind a wall of battleships. Peace, in Roosevelt's opinion, had to be sought actively in a variety of ways. Righteousness weighed heavily in the balance, as did good faith, international law, and particularly the principle of national sovereignty.[26] Since the country was large and powerful, it had an obligation to take part in a collective world effort to avoid Armageddon. The day would come when a supranational police organization would permit individual nations to relegate their armies to domestic police duty. But the world, as he saw it, was not ready for so drastic a scheme. Until such time as it was, he refused to support disarmament, believing that it would only cause civilized powers to disarm and leave mankind to the government of a military despot. It was thus the limitation of armaments, rather than their reduction, that he had in mind when he initiated the movement for a second international peace conference at the Hague.[27]

He was a great believer in the principle of arbitration, except in cases of national honor or vital interest, where he felt the principle would prove unworkable. As the first world leader to submit a foreign dispute to the Hague Court of Arbitration (the Pious Fund Case involving Mexico), he called for an upgrading of the court to provide an adequate salary for permanent judges. He also allowed Secretary Root to sign twenty-four bilateral arbitration treaties ending with an agreement in January 1909 to arbitrate

Anglo-American differences on the fisheries and Great Lakes. As we have seen, he backed Britain's demand for arbitration on the question of Panama tolls and worked hard for American compliance with an unfavorable Hague ruling on the fisheries and Great Lakes.[28]

Whenever he could prevail upon the powers to resolve their differences without resort to war, he stood ready to be of service. It was in this spirit that he branded German fear of an attack by England in 1905 as "utter nonsense," while advising the British to attach less importance to German naval preparations, as they were "not so unfriendly" as imagined. It was thus that he assumed the role of peacemaker in controversies ranging from the Far East to Europe and the Americas. In Central America, he succeeded in erecting judicial machinery designed to halt the recurrent cycle of revolution and war. During the Russo-Japanese War he sought to limit the number of belligerents and restrict the area of fighting, as well as to end the conflict before either contestant won an all-out victory. By establishing a position of "balanced antagonisms," he hoped to ensure a more stable and lasting peace. A similar strategy prompted him to foster informal alliances between the United States and Britain, between the United States and Japan, and, as the possibility of world war loomed ever larger, between Britain and France.[29]

He was no less willing to lead the way toward compromise when the interests of his own country were involved. He felt, for example, that a reduction in the tariff could be defended on the supposition that greater trade between nations, and hence more economic interdependence, would increase the likelihood of world peace. In response to the Chinese boycott of American goods, he promised greater federal protection for Chinese nationals plus the remission of a large portion of the Boxer indemnity. When a diplomatic impasse occurred in 1907 with Japan, he was willing to offer Tokyo greater proection for its visitors to the United States as well as an effort to secure legislation from

Congress which would increase the opportunity for natural-
ization of Japanese immigrants. Even where he felt the
course followed by the United States to be totally justified,
as in the case of Colombia and the Panama Revolt, he sustained a thirty-one-month post-mortem effort to satisfy the
grievances of all parties concerned. In sum, one might say
that, apart from disarmament, there was hardly a single
peace initiative which Roosevelt did not support by some
practical expedient. He had tremendous confidence in the
future and shared the widely held belief in history as a story
of man's progress.[30]

Where he parted company with what he labeled the
"world gush creatures" was in his fear that the peace movement would lull Americans into a false sense of security and
cause them to regard a set of genuinely helpful tactics as an
alternative to "the fighting edge." A situation might arise
at any time which contained the seeds of irreconcilable conflict, either in terms of national interest or moral principle,
and the nation must be prepared to meet it. It is interesting
to read his address to the Nobel Prize committee, wherein he
supports arbitration, a world court, and a league of nations,
but prefaces his remarks with the warning that righteousness must come before peace and that there is no substitute
for a readiness to employ physical force. Throughout his life,
he railed at "maudlin sentimentalists," "flubdubs and flap-
doodle mollycoddles"—the "peace at any price boys," who
were always ready to belittle the importance of the military.
These individuals were as dangerous as the militarists, since
weakness, timidity, and sentimentality would, in the end, do
more harm than violence and injustice. Sentimentality, he
once wrote, is "the most broken reed on which righteousness can lean."[31]

This is why he proposed an eleventh commandment,
"Thou shalt not slop over," which held it the greatest folly
to rely on an atmosphere of good will for reconciling basic
differences of national interest. Despite a personal and informal approach to diplomacy, he left no room for partiality

or the display of emotion, taking it upon himself on occasion to warn Lord Bryce against gushing and responding to the warm good wishes of Edward VII with the admonition that "we need judgement and moderation no less than . . . good will itself." This may seem a rather curious reversal in the normal pattern of Anglo-American exchange, particularly if one recalls the standard image of T.R. Yet it was a definite facet of his style. When Alice Roosevelt visited the German naval base at Kiel, the kaiser was prompted to write T.R. that she "has an unstinted admiration for her Pappa as I have." According to Arthur Lee, the president reacted with "an almost comic terror lest this should fall into the hands of the press and remarked whimsically: 'The Kaiser evidently thinks I shall be flattered if he treats me as a social equal!' " Roosevelt did indeed abhor the emperor's compromising tone and always strove in his own correspondence to be "entirely dignified."[32]

Another means by which Roosevelt sought to keep the United States at peace was by tailoring policy to power. He was anxious to obtain a power base sufficient to implement foreign policy goals; but he was equally adamant about matching the pretensions of American policy to the size of the military force at his disposal. He recoiled from the Open Door policy in its broadest form because he believed that any effort in China beyond the customary protection of American commerce would require an army the size of Germany's and a fleet of the caliber of the Royal Navy. He acquiesced in Japanese control of the Korean peninsula because the Korean nationalists could not lift a finger in their own defense. Always wary of acquiring distant military bases, he substituted Pearl Harbor for Subic Bay (the Philippines) as the farthest fortified outpost consonant with congressional defense appropriations. By this time, the Philippines had begun to assume the shape of an Achilles' heel, and he looked forward to the earliest possible withdrawal in keeping with the honorable discharge of imperial responsibility.

If he is justly remembered for his effort to increase the size of the fleet, he deserves similar recognition for the regularity with which he restricted American overseas commitments. When he said that he was no more anxious to annex the Dominican Republic "than a gorged boa constrictor would be to swallow a porcupine wrong-end-to," he was summarizing his view of expansion in general. Beyond the expectation shared by many contemporaries that Canada would some day belong to the United States and aside from his decision to hold a limited number of naval bases for the protection of an isthmian canal, he cannot be styled an ardent imperialist. While he admired enlightened imperial rule and defended it for the benefits of peace and progress that it might confer upon less developed regions of the world, he did not, as a rule, recommend it to Americans.[33] Prior to 1898, he showed no particular interest in Cuba or the Philippines. Furthermore, as a judge of American history, he had condemned the annexation of Texas and portrayed the more forward pioneers as ruthless "Vikings."[34]

Once in the White House, he failed to satisfy the navy's desire for bases in China, Haiti, and the Dominican Republic. In addition, while all factions in Santo Domingo preferred to be on the same footing with the United States as Cuba, he was no more interested in such a scheme than he was in Colombia's offer of offshore islands.[35] He allowed Secretaries Hay and Root to yield two out of four of the Cuban military bases gained by Leonard Wood under the Platt Amendment. He showed no interest in Cuba's Isle of Pines, nor did he even ensure that Guantanamo Naval Base would be large enough to supply its own water.[36] On balance, the size of the nation actually shrank during the years of his stewardship if one weighs the acquisition of the Canal Zone against his cession of Alaskan panhandle fringe plus the two islands at the mouth of the Portland Canal.[37]

In only two countries did he initiate prolonged intervention: Cuba and the Dominican Republic. Both nations were caught up in the coils of civil strife and threatened by European intervention. Both actions, moreover, were preceded by a thorough investigation and carried out with extreme reluctance.[38] "I loathe the thought" of military involvement, he wrote. In neither case was there loss of life or any decline in American popularity, since Roosevelt refused to take sides. He was so eager, in fact, to avoid even the appearance of partisanship that he allowed all factions in the Dominican war to fight to the death outside those towns where foreign life and property were concentrated, with the understanding that he would cheerfully hand over the urban areas to whatever side emerged victorious.[39] His agreement to establish an American customs receivership was popular with most groups on the island since it removed the incentive for civil war and seemed the best alternative to military intervention by a more predatory European power. There was opposition, to be sure, but chiefly among chronic enemies of law and order. As the British consul general observed:

No coercion seems to have been used although there was some discussion over minor points. The Dominican government was unanimously in favor of the American proposals, speaking in a general point of view. . . . The Dominican Minister of Finance . . . has the reputation of being a man of undoubted integrity and patriotism, and he expressed himself . . . as being well satisfied with the agreement, fully realizing that something of the kind could not be avoided.[40]

In Cuba, American troops were landed so deftly that no one on the island knew whether or not Roosevelt was intervening, and if so, on which side. Charles Magoon, the genial midwesterner who governed the island from 1906 to 1908, ended his term without issuing a single death sentence and was actually criticized for granting too many pardons. The marines thus marched out of Cuba to the tune of friendly bands and cheering crowds—in marked contrast, one might add, to subsequent landings under Presidents Taft and Wilson. Taft took a decidedly partisan position in several Caribbean upheavals, one of them implicating Americans in the death of a hundred natives, while Wilson's record was bloodier still.[41]

In line with Roosevelt's reluctance to engage in sustained intervention, one can cite numerous examples of his refusal to become involved at all when it might have been warranted by the facts of the situation. He was less ready than his predecessors to resort to gunboat diplomacy in China, and he never considered Japanese or Russian encroachments on Chinese sovereignty serious enough to justify a military response. Commenting on the explosive Chinese boycott of American goods in September 1905, William Rockhill, American minister to Peking, wrote: "I think I understand the views of the Department [of State] concerning the use of our naval forces sufficiently well to believe that it does not approve of our consular officers asking for the presence of a man-of-war except when conditions absolutely require it." There was to be no more of "the old gunboat policy of twenty years ago."[42] T.R. resisted the temptation to land troops in Haiti and Honduras despite serious consideration of such action by the State Department. In another case, he refused a request by Senator Lodge to send a cruiser to Newfoundland in defense of alleged American fishing rights. It was suggested on one occasion that he send troops to fight Turkish raiders in Armenia, on another that he strike at Moro insurrectionists in the Philippines. The answer in both cases was again no.[43]

Not that this restraint was always self-imposed. He was highly sensitive to currents of public opinion even as he tried, wherever possible, to bend them to his will. It was only because of congressional recalcitrance in 1907 that he remained calm under stinging provocation by the ruler of Venezuela. President Castro had flatly refused to arbitrate American claims and, within a few years, confiscated or destroyed nearly all property belonging to American residents. Some of the confiscation was ordered in accordance with the law; much of it was not. As a symbol of Castro's insolence, the official mailbag of the United States legation had been twice cut open on its way from La Guaira harbor to American headquarters in Caracas.[44] Roosevelt was predictably furious, but his thwarted intention in this particular instance does not negate the record of opposition to most forms of intervention.

Even in domestic policy, it is interesting to note that he intervened in labor-management disputes with extreme diffidence and only after a searching investigation. As governor of New York, he sent troops into action only once—for a strike at Croton Reservoir. A mediation board had handed down a verdict favorable to labor and one which Roosevelt was prepared to support. Before he could do so, however, violence erupted, causing him to move troops at the request of the local sheriff. We have seen that he was prepared to use troops in the Buffalo dock strike, and one might add that he readied the militia in 1899 to back up the New York police during a Brooklyn trolley strike. Neither of these actions, however, justifies the familiar charge that he exhibited a "trigger-like willingness to use troops" in industrial and labor disturbances.[45] Such instances merely illustrate his firm belief that the best way to avoid the use of troops was to have them on hand in time of crisis.

As president, Roosevelt resisted more than one local call for the National Guard. He refused troops for strike duty when Governor Peabody of Colorado requested them in 1903 and again in 1904. In 1907, Governor Sparks of Nevada wanted the aid of the Guard to police a miners' strike. This time, he reluctantly complied. He soon became convinced, though, on the basis of his usual careful investigation, that Sparks was relying on the Guard "to do his work for him." Consequently, he gave the governor five days to call a meeting of the legislature with a view to establishing an equivalent of the Texas Rangers:

If within five days from receipt of this telegram you shall have issued the necessary notice to convene the Legislature of Nevada, I shall continue the troops during a period of three weeks. If when the term of five days has elapsed the notice has not been issued, the troops will be immediately returned to their former stations.[46]

The governor did summon the legislature, it voted the necessary funds, and Roosevelt was able to pull his men out without clashing with either labor or management. It was another typical performance.[47] National Guard units were dispatched to the territory of Arizona in 1903; and in 1906, when Idaho was faced with mob disorder, T.R. ordered two cavalry troops into the area on a "practice march" from nearby Walla Walla, Washington.[48] But in neither case was there any fighting.

Thus, while Roosevelt could claim, at the end of seven and a half years as president, that not a single shot had been fired at a foreign foe, he could claim with equal justice that none of the forces at his command had ever taken the life of an American.[49]

Charges of impetuosity and boyish behavior dogged him all through his life and continued to tarnish his reputation after death, nor will there ever be an end to them as long as critics mistake the personality for the man.[50] But if anything can be said to have been a touchstone of the Roosevelt style, it was caution. From the time he arrived in Cambridge as a college freshman and asked his mother to provide him with the name of a reliable doctor "in case of accidents," the conservative strain in his character never failed to assert itself. It was not out of character for him to warn his son Kermit in 1909 that in hunting big game "we must be very cautious."[51] As a historian, he described certain Dutch governors of New York as "rash" and judged the British provocative in their efforts to enforce the Stamp Act. Likewise, in his account of General "Mad Anthony" Wayne, he was at pains to show that Wayne had not been as foolhardy as the name would suggest, but rather "a vigilant and cautious leader" who happened also to be a "born fighter."[52] He considered Polk reckless in regard to both the Oregon and Texas questions since he had courted war, in contrast to Calhoun's policy of "masterly inactivity."[53]

Admittedly, words do not always afford a reliable guide to action. But in the case of Roosevelt, word and deed were remarkably well matched. He made sure, for example, that the world cruise of the battlefleet was accompanied by every conceivable precaution. Six torpedo boats traveled a week in

advance to scout possible danger; commanding officers were
carefully chosen for their prudence; and shore patrol was invented to guard against any untoward incident on the part
of roaming sailors. At first, T.R. was highly dubious about a
fleet visit to Japan lest "some desperado" do "something
that will have very bad effects." Only when informed that
the Tokyo leadership insisted adamantly on the acceptance
of its invitation did he feel obliged to comply.[54] During the
Cuban occupation of 1906, all orders issued by field commanders were relayed to the State Department, and a civilian commanded American troops on the ground.[55] Under
pressure throughout the Venezuelan blockade crisis, Roosevelt ordered his captains to do nothing without specific
authorization from him. Later, when Admiral Dewey, Admiral Taylor, and General MacArthur overstepped their
bounds by making statements with political overtones, we
have seen how quickly he called them to account. A similar
rebuke was administered to General Chaffee for speaking ill
of Russia while the United States sought to occupy neutral
ground in the Russo-Japanese War.[56]

Of all T.R.'s diplomatic messages, the one which seems
most rash is the famous "We want Perdicaris alive or
Raisuli dead," fired off to Morocco during a lackluster
Republican nominating convention in the summer of 1904.
Again, though, it is hard to avoid the conclusion that
appearances are in conflict with reality. Five weeks had
elapsed since Raisuli's kidnapping of Perdicaris (18 May). In
the interim, Roosevelt had sought the victim's release
through British and French diplomatic channels. Furthermore, his sharp note included a less well known but equally
important clause to the effect that no American troops were
to be landed without clearance from the Department of
State (meaning the White House). When he wrote Hay on 15
June that "our position must now be to demand the death of
those that harm him if he is harmed," the armed intervention which he contemplated would have been carried out
with French and British troops. One day later, the ranking
American naval officer at Tangier asked for the return of a

British battleship which had just weighed anchor, and his request was promptly granted. Roosevelt is said to have conveniently ignored information that Perdicaris was not really an American citizen. His information on this point was inconclusive, however, and he had already committed the United States to a positive course of action. Critics have suggested that he sent a shrill message merely to gain support for his nomination. Hay's sensational phrase did bring the delegates to their feet, and all the arrangements for the release of Perdicaris had been made by the time the note was dispatched. On the other hand, the release itself had not been accomplished—certainly Roosevelt was not aware of it—and he was contemplating immediate military intervention with other interested parties. In short, there is no evidence that in the absence of a nominating convention the note would not have gone out exactly as it did, for by 22 June, Roosevelt had exhausted every rational expedient in his effort to deal with the Moroccan government.[57]

Another T.R. pronouncement frequently cited as evidence of a desire to jump headlong into the fray is his corollary to the Monroe Doctrine, whereby the world was given to understand that Washington would undertake hemispheric police duty in case of flagrant "wrongdoing or impotence." But here again there is another side to the story. The country had just emerged from an explosive confrontation with Britain and Germany over their blockade of Venezuela. The specter of European intervention seemed ready to rear its ugly head a second time on the coast of Santo Domingo, and Roosevelt clearly aimed to forestall any such eventuality. Some historians have called the corollary a new policy, a perversion of the Monroe Doctrine. They assume that Roosevelt sought to use the doctrine as a cover for imperial designs on Latin America. The reverse, however, is more nearly true. Under strong pressure from foreign chancelleries, Whitehall in particular, he volunteered American action to justify the doctrine. It was neither fair nor realistic, in his opinion, to expect Europe to keep "hands off" the

Western Hemisphere when there were so many situations in
which intervention would be both legal and moral, as well as
a standing invitation to acquire a naval base athwart vital
sea lanes. The only alternative to the corollary was the
Drago Doctrine, which would have bound major powers to
abjure force in the collection of debts and which received
strong support both from Roosevelt in his Annual Message
of 1905 and at the second Hague Peace Conference.[58] But
even this was not really an alternative to the corollary since
it ignored the question of claims other than debts.

In a surprising number of instances, it is the man of caution rather than the volatile personality which attracts our
attention. In 1906, there occurred the unpleasant incident
regarding seal poachers on St. Paul Island (see note 49).
Five Japanese were killed and two wounded. T.R.'s immediate response, in light of the lethal consequences of
Russia's recent decision to divide her battlefleet, was to
move his Pacific-based battleships to a safe haven in the
Atlantic. At the first hint that Germany might occupy
Venezuela's Margarita Island in 1901, he not only reiterated
the Monroe Doctrine in a public address, but also went
directly to the German consul in New York and spelled out
his warning in person. Later, when Germany appeared to
cast a proprietary eye in the direction of the Galápagos
Islands, he made similar on-the-spot representations.
Perhaps the best example of all of precautionary action on
Roosevelt's part was his role in the Algeciras and Portsmouth conferences, for by preserving a Far Eastern balance
of power he sought to protect American commerce, and by
helping arrange a settlement of the Moroccan crisis he
hoped to avert a world war certain in the long run to involve
the United States. Nor is this surprising, since he regularly
criticized others for moving too slowly to head off an impending crisis, whether Canada for not guarding against the
outbreak of race riots in Vancouver or President Cleveland
for failing to impress the British clearly enough with the
urgency of his stand on Venezuela.[59]

The Portsmouth Conference illustrates still another quality rarely associated with Roosevelt, namely, patience. Six weeks elapsed between Japan's initial request for his good offices and the time when he formally proposed peace talks based on the belligerents' prearranged acceptance. By this time, he had prepared the ground by canvassing each of the major powers, making certain of the support of all. When it appeared that Tokyo and St. Petersburg were each waiting for the other to appoint plenipotentiaries, he asked to see both sides' confidential list of names so that he could notify each of the other's choice, again confidentially, in case either wished to make a change. This done, he announced the final selections simultaneously so as to avoid any embarrassment. Finally, he had to spend many additional weeks poring over questions of time and place before concluding the preliminary phase of the journey toward peace.[60]

Even the case of Panama, frequently cited as evidence of Roosevelt's impatience, was viewed at the time from quite a different perspective. *Le Temps* of Paris marveled on 8 November 1903 at the "serenity and dignity" maintained by the American government "following the recent vote of the Congress of Bogotá."[61] After waiting two years before concluding negotiations with Colombia for a canal treaty, T.R. did nothing during the six-week interval between Colombia's rejection of the treaty and the outbreak of revolution.

Restraint is implicit in the very maxim for which the Rough Rider is most famous: "Speak softly and carry a big stick."[62] Too often, historians have concentrated on the second phrase to the virtual exclusion of the first, even though Roosevelt was as steadfast in avoiding bluster as he was in building the fleet. His public boast in 1911 that he had "taken" the Canal Zone has been worn threadbare by successive generations of scholars as an example of supposed indiscretion. In fact, the remark is curiously out of character when placed alongside his studied silence during the Venezuela blockade, the Alaskan boundary dispute, the negotia-

tions for Panama, the Portsmouth Conference, the Algeciras Conference, and the world cruise of the battlefleet. Much
has been said about his mobilization of power, his warnings
to rival nations, and, in one case, his claim to have delivered
a striking ultimatum to Germany. But what is most remarkable is the fact that all the warnings were given sub rosa.[63]

Two rather amusing anecdotes relating to his earlier career in New York indicate the development of a soft-spoken
style long before he ever became president. As sponsor of an
Assembly bill to expand certain railway terminal facilities,
he was seeking to win over the majority of a committee of
which he was chairman. As he tells it in his *Autobiography:*

The crooked members of the committee held the bill up, refusing
to report it either favorably or unfavorably. There were one or two
members of the committee who were pretty rough characters, and
when I decided to force matters I was not sure that we would not
have trouble. There was a broken chair in the room, and I got a leg
of it loose and put it down beside me where it was not visible, but
where I might get at it in a hurry if necessary. I moved that the
bill be reported favorably. This was voted down . . . I then put the
bill in my pocket and announced that I would report it anyhow.
This almost precipitated a riot. . . . The riot did not come off;
partly, I think, because the opportune production of the chair-leg
had a sedative effect, and partly owing to wise counsels from one
or two of my opponents.[64]

More than ten years later, as New York City police commissioner, he sought to protect a peaceful parade of Protestant
Irish:

The other day there was an Irish riot against the Orange parade in
Boston. Friday was the anniversary of the Boyne battle, and the
Orangemen paraded here. There had been some uneasiness because of the Boston riot; so I had all the reserves in the stations
with their night sticks, and sent a double number with the parade,
under Inspector McCullough, who is of protestant Irish blood; and
instructed him that the word was to be "clubs" if there was the
slightest disturbance or attempt to interfere with the procession.
It went off as quietly as a Sunday school meeting![65]

The first commandment, then, of "Big Stick" diplomacy was to speak softly. But there was a second: never allow a vanquished opponent to lose face. The Rough Rider went out of his way to wrap his military demonstrations in verbal disguise, referring to the unprecedented Caribbean buildup of 1902 as "fleet exercises," labeling the dispatch of additional troops to Alaska in the spring of 1902 a "police action," and dubbing the world cruise a "practice voyage" on the part of sixteen "messengers of peace." We have had occasion to refer to his repeated use of the words "tact" and "courtesy." Typically, he recommended Leonard Wood as governor of Cuba not only because his firmness commanded respect, but also because he was "a born diplomat" who would pay deference to local "prejudices" and sensitivity. "Scrupulously courteous and polite," he would understand the Cuban "spirit of punctilio."[66]

Only once, in the case of a Russian threat to American commerce in Manchuria, did Roosevelt come close to cornering an adversary by resort to public diplomacy—and then the circumstances were extraordinary. First, he was dealing with statesmen whose word meant nothing. Second, the issue itself did not provide him with sufficient congressional support to allow the kind of quiet but firm response he might have preferred. He therefore decided on a public reaffirmation of the Open Door policy, coupled with the sending of a powerful naval squadron to Chefoo Bay (anchorage of the Russian fleet). He also made clever use of a petition drawn by American citizens to protest the shocking Kishineff pogrom. But instead of presenting the petition directly to Russian authorities, he addressed a formal inquiry to St. Petersburg asking *if* such a petition would be received and in the process outlining its contents. He knew the answer would be no, but he thus succeeded in mobilizing world opinion and bringing maximum diplomatic pressure to bear without risking a breach of relations. The result was that the Russians changed their policy on Manchuria and took action against the governor of Kishineff, while Roosevelt continued to "show his confidence" in the czar by asking him to select judges for the important arbitration case involving Germany, Britain, Italy, and Venezuela, as well as the United States.[67]

One is reminded of his solution to a similar problem during his New York police commissionership. An anti-Semitic preacher by the name of Rector Ahlwardt had come from Berlin to preach a crusade against the Jews. As Roosevelt tells it:

Many of the New York Jews were much excited and asked me to prevent him from speaking and not to give him police protection. This, I told them, was impossible; and if possible would have been undesirable because it would have made him a martyr. The proper thing to do was to make him ridiculous. Accordingly, I detailed for his protection a Jew sergeant and a score or two of Jew policemen. He made his harangue against the Jews under the active protection of some forty policemen, every one of them a Jew![68]

The scathing epithets which he hurled at certain foreigners were invariably uttered in private, for he considered good manners as much a prerequisite for successful relations between nations as between individuals. This helps to explain why he became so furious when his countrymen administered rude treatment to Oriental immigrants. It accounts in part for the concern he voiced while traveling in Uruguay that American manners were "not as good as theirs." Good-natured roughhouse was something he relished to the end of his life, but he drew a clear line between roughhouse and ruffianism. As a student he had been disgusted by the violent hazing tradition at Yale, and not simply because he was a Harvard man. He generally opposed exhibitions of unbridled power, whether on the part of the American pioneer or the Brazilian gaucho.[69] Repeatedly, in private correspondence, he expressed his taste for refined and gentlemanly behavior. Once, when Secretary Hay threatened the Turkish ambassador with an American naval squadron unless certain demands were met, Hay reported to

the White House: "I was not brutal. I was very friendly and
polite." This was vintage Hay; yet nothing could have been
more quintessentially Roosevelt.[70]

A third cautionary principle of the administration was
"Never draw unless you intend to shoot."[71] Bluff was "the
one unpardonable sin" since it destroyed that most precious
of all national attributes next to power: credibility. Believing that the Open Door policy would remain viable only as
long as it could be maintained by general diplomatic agreement and that it would evaporate the moment a powerful
nation chose to ignore it, Roosevelt naturally objected when
President Taft tried to deny Japan her natural sphere of
influence in China. Before he left the White House, he
reviewed some of the diplomatic crises of his presidency, including the Venezuela blockade and the world cruise, and
reached the following conclusion: "I have never yet failed to
do what I said I would do if called upon to do it!"[72] So far as
the record would seem to indicate, he never did.

Still another tenet of "Big Stick" diplomacy—actually
an adjunct to the cardinal rule of preparedness—was the notion that one must never strike "unless one is prepared to
strike hard."[73] One might be strong and yet commit the
fatal error of intervening in some part of the world with only
a fraction of the power required to bring the issue to a swift
and certain conclusion. Roosevelt advised the British to
handle the Boers of South Africa by throwing in "at least
fifty thousand more men" than they felt "could possibly be
needed." When President McKinley was asked to send a
warship to the eastern Mediterranean as a symbol of American concern over conditions in the Ottoman Empire, Roosevelt counseled against dispatching a lone warship. Three
were eventually sent. Likewise, after the battleship *Maine*
exploded in Havana harbor, he rejected the idea of sending
another vessel in its place because "in point of force, it is
either too great or too small."[74]

In 1900, he warned against an invasion of the Turkish
port of Smyrna since he doubted the commitment could be

maintained with sufficient strength. The Turkish navy might be impotent, but the Ottoman army was another matter; there were no better ground forces in Europe, including those of Germany and Russia. Turkey had fielded two hundred thousand men against the Greeks and gone through them "like a hot knife through butter." What would lie in store for the American invaders, he predicted, would make the British experience in South Africa seem pleasant by comparison.[75]

As president, he put his words into action by keeping American troops out of Turkey. He was unwilling to involve the government in efforts to ransom a female American missionary who had been kidnapped near Salonika. He was equally slow to use force in pressing American claims on the sultan. By the same token, when he did use force it was impressive. On 6 August 1904, a powerful naval squadron under Admiral Jewell was ordered to Smyrna, while another one at Gibraltar, under the command of Admiral Barker, was ordered to stand by for action. Some of the largest and most powerful ships in the navy were included in this demonstration, which, within a week, convinced the sultan to grant the American minister a long-sought interview and led ultimately to the satisfaction of substantial American demands. Again, when the Chinese threatened serious harm to American life and property in 1906 and the army planned to send between three and five thousand troops, Roosevelt wanted the figure raised to fifteen thousand, for "it would be an act of utter folly to underestimate our foe who would beyond comparison be more formidable than they showed themselves in 1900."[76]

This was the Roosevelt who, at the time of the Venezuelan blockade, marshaled every battleship and torpedo boat in the fleet within short sailing distance of the allied operations. This was the man who, once having decided to force Moroccan authorities to avenge the Perdicaris kidnapping, sent not one warship, as requested by the American consul, but the entire Mediterranean squadron, followed by the

South Atlantic squadron. Prior to his reoccupation of Cuba in 1906, he made a strong effort to maneuver native politicians into a settlement that would obviate the need for American intervention. At the same time, he signaled his determination by sending three battleships and two cruisers to Havana, followed by two more cruisers with eight hundred battle-ready troops. In 1908, he dispatched over twelve hundred marines to Panama to help monitor an election on the assumption that "the larger the force the less chance there is of bloodshed."[77]

Interestingly enough, his handling of power on the domestic front is again on an exact parallel with his approach to foreign policy. During the Croton Dam strike, he wrote to General Roe:

I am glad you ordered out plenty of troops. I need not say that I trust you have a discreet and firm man in charge. No disorder must be permitted and rioters must not be allowed for a moment to gain the upper hand. On the other hand, discretion is of course just as much needed as firmness, and I earnestly hope that a collision can be avoided.[78]

His advice to the commander of federal troops in Nevada during the great strike of 1907 ran along much the same lines: it would be "better to avoid conflict by sending too many troops than, by sending too few, to run the risk of inviting bloodshed." It would also be advisable, however,

to use utmost caution and good judgement in the very delicate and responsible situation which confronts you. Firmness and good nature are equally necessary. Anything rash or impulsive is to be avoided. . . . You should be especially conservative in speech and say nothing whatever which is not absolutely necessary in fulfilling and carrying out your duty.[79]

In both cases, he concerned himself with two things: sufficiency of power and its tactful application.

Finally, we come to an axiom which cuts to the very core of Roosevelt's philosophy. This is the notion that power and diplomacy work best when they work together. Just as he made certain in 1903 that his representations to the czar were buttressed by the guns of an American squadron as well as by the solicitous might of Britain and Japan, so, too, did he expect that the use of overwhelming force against Aguinaldo's guerrillas would prove ineffective without a provision for civilian government.[80] Nor is either of these cases as revealing as the way in which he marshaled diplomatic support for the naval demonstration against Japan in 1907. He not only conferred with Canadian officials in an effort to underline the similarity between immigration problems in British Columbia and California, but also sent Taft, who had replaced Root as secretary of war, to Moscow, St. Petersburg, and Berlin so that he might consult with such figures as Admiral Rozhdestvenski. Several Russians in the United States and a good many more in St. Petersburg actually approached American authorities to volunteer for military service in anticipation of war with Japan. Secretary Root traveled to Mexico and managed to arouse speculation over the possibility of a Mexican-American alliance. At the same time, the British ambassador to Mexico City heard rumors that Magdalena Bay would be used as a coaling base by the United States navy and that Germany had promised to defend the American east coast against the possibility of British attack.[81] The fact that the British ambassador attached a certain credibility to these rumors raises the question of how Roosevelt created the appearance of a German-American combination.

Going out of his way to foster the impression of an actual or impending alliance between Berlin and Washington, Roosevelt called Ambassador Sternburg to the White House to look over war plans and told him that the arrival of the American fleet in the Far East would present an excellent occasion for announcing a new German-American relationship. The kaiser, much encouraged, wrote "Bravo!" on Sternburg's report and leaked his hopes to the press. He had long been trying to engineer a Sino-American-German alliance, and it now seemed as if he might be on the verge of success. The Wilhelmstrasse began to moderate its tariff policy on American exports. American visitors to Berlin received unusual attention; Specky suddenly replaced Jusserand as T.R.'s most favored tennis partner; and the French ambassador began to notice that T.R. looked and talked just like the kaiser! Nor was this all, for while Wilhelm had a tooth pulled by Berlin's most fashionable American dentist, elements of the French press began to discuss the possibility of war between France and the United States. A French editor wanted to know, "Is there or is there not a secret United States-German Alliance?" Most striking of all, American and German cruisers rendezvoused in Samoa, and sixteen German warships emerged from the Baltic on their maiden voyage outside home waters just as Roosevelt's battlefleet was steaming for the Orient.[82]

No diplomatic silence could have spoken more loudly. The British, bound to fight on the side of Japan in any war involving the United States and Germany, responded by working out a new war plan designed to cope with the latest threat of cross-channel invasion. Beginning on 27 November 1907 and ending on 3 March 1908, the Committee of Imperial Defence held eight meetings in order to review the danger of overseas attack.[83] As late as March, we find a military memorandum drafted for the eye of the Foreign Office raising the question: "Is a German invasion as 'a bolt from the blue' during normal peacetime diplomatic negotiations reasonably conceivable?" Answer: "In certain circumstances, yes."[84] By this time, Roosevelt's armored ambassadors had, of course, reached the Pacific, and the diplomatic crisis had begun to abate by virtue of timely concessions on the part of Japan. England and the United States breathed a sigh of relief. Germany and China, to whom Roosevelt had held out the hope of alliance, were just as naturally disappointed. But this was all a part of international politics, the world's most dangerous game, and one in which T.R. well knew how to hold his own.

That Roosevelt proved himself no mean player in the thrust and parry of diplomatic combat is a fact far better known than the explanation behind it. One will search many a page without encountering the cautious strategist who figures so prominently in the foregoing chapter. Historians have made a notable effort of late to separate the man from the myth.[85] Yet there is much work still to be done.

So it is that we return to the paradoxical contrast between the man's record and his reputation. T.R.'s boyish enthusiasm caused Spring Rice to liken him to a six-year-old child; and an embittered quondam friend by the name of Maria Storer published a posthumous tract entitled *Roosevelt, The Child*.[86] Although his closest associates testified that he frequently sought counsel and was eminently advisable, those less close to him gained the impression that he was impulsive.[87] To John Davis Long, he was a "bull in a china shop." Lord Bryce feared his impetuosity during the Japanese war scare. The British foreign minister, Lord Lansdowne, expressed even less confidence: "[he] terrifies me almost as much as the German emperor"—while Sir Mortimer Durand paid tribute to Hay's "restraining influence."[88]

Neither Durand nor Lansdowne knew Roosevelt well. Neither of them ever gained his confidence. Still, their impression of him is the one that, in the main, has endured to this day, and it is difficult to find in this image the man who believed that force must be wielded with restraint and applied with courtesy, the man who reserved his greatest admiration, not for the plain warrior, but for the "just man armed who wishes to keep the peace."[89] Somehow, the comic cartoon showing huge white teeth and a spiked club is what remains most vivid. Across the years, it is a personality which is remembered rather than a philosophy. The "Big Stick" is still viewed by many as a policy of unvarnished power, when, in fact, it was a series of cautionary principles. Roosevelt may well have flashed his teeth and waved his arms on the rostrum, and his prose undoubtedly owed much

to the Old Testament; but juvenile he was not, reckless and
bellicose he was not. In thought and action he was sufficiently cautious to merit the untrammeled peace which
crowned his efforts both at home and abroad.

NOTES

1. Among the many misrepresentations in *The Wind and the
Lion* (1975) is the substitution of Mrs. Perdicaris and her two
young children for Mr. Perdicaris and his stepson. The film is an
entertaining tissue of historical nonsense.

2. See, for example, William E. Leuchtenburg, "Progressiv-
ism and Imperialism: The Progressive Movement and American
Foreign Policy, 1898–1916," *Mississippi Valley Historical Review*
39 (December 1952): 490; Richard Hofstadter, *The American
Political Tradition*, p. 209; Harold and Margaret Sprout, *The Rise
of American Naval Power*, p. 230; Howard K. Beale, *Theodore
Roosevelt and the Rise of America to World Power*, p. 36; Arthur
Ekirch, *The Civilian and the Military: A History of the American
Antimilitarist Tradition*, pp. 141, 164; Foster Rhea Dulles,
America's Rise to World Power, pp. 68, 73–74, 76; and G. Wallace
Chessman, *Theodore Roosevelt and the Politics of Power*, pp. 31,
62, 64. According to George Mowry, T.R. was "cautious" in
domestic but "bold" in foreign affairs. Mowry, *The Era of
Theodore Roosevelt*, p. 163. In the opinion of Louis Halle, he was
"both an ungoverned child who should not have been entrusted
with a toy pistol, and a statesman whose vision might have
averted much of the grief that has come upon us in this century."
Halle, *Dream and Reality*, p. 260.

3. Dulles, *America's Rise*, p. 70; William H. Harbaugh, *The
Life and Times of Theodore Roosevelt*, p. 260; Henry Pringle,
Theodore Roosevelt, p. 196; Richard D. Challener, *Admirals,
Generals, and American Foreign Policy, 1898–1914*, p. 177.

4. Beale, *Roosevelt*, pp. 26–27, 456, 458; Dexter Perkins,
Yield of the Years, p. 178; Robert Endicott Osgood, *Ideals and
Self-Interest in America's Foreign Relations*, pp. 28, 47, 85, 144.
Raymond A. Esthus, in *Theodore Roosevelt and Japan*, assumes
that T.R. was far more cautious and restrained in the Far East
than he was in the Caribbean (p. 7). For other recent interpreta-
tions on this order, see note 89.

5. For accounts that portray his secretaries as a significant braking influence, see Tyler Dennett, *John Hay: From Poetry to Politics,* pp. 345, 349; Foster Rhea Dulles, "John Hay," in Norman A. Graebner, ed., *An Uncertain Tradition: American Secretaries of State in the Twentieth Century,* p. 25; Charles W. Toth, "Elihu Root," ibid., pp. 45–46; Raymond A. Esthus, *Theodore Roosevelt and the International Rivalries,* p. 8; Richard W. Leopold, *Elihu Root and the Conservative Tradition,* pp. 51, 67–68; Charles Campbell, *Anglo-American Understanding, 1898-1903,* p. 286; Mowry, *Roosevelt,* p. 161; J. Fred Rippy, *The Caribbean Danger Zone,* p. 204; Eugene Trani, *The Treaty of Portsmouth: An Adventure in American Diplomacy,* pp. 10, 21 ("Hay was a tower of moderation for the president"). Philip C. Jessup speaks of Root's "metier of curbing the fiery TR" and assumes that Roosevelt's restraint with regard to Cuba in 1906, while Root was away, must have been due to "the attitude of Bacon" (Robert Bacon, assistant secretary of state). Jessup, *Elihu Root,* 2 vols., 1:450, 453, 531.

6. See, for example, Roosevelt to Lodge, 28 January 1909, *Letters,* 6:1490–96; Roosevelt to Lodge, 5 June 1905, *Roosevelt-Lodge Correspondence,* 2:131; John Hay, *Life and Letters of John Hay,* ed. William R. Thayer, 2 vols., 2:297.

7. Dennett, *Hay,* pp. 359–60; Charles C. Tansill, *Canadian-American Relations, 1875-1911,* p. 244.

8. Beale, *Roosevelt,* p. 195.

9. Hay to Roosevelt, 13 September 1903, John Hay Papers, General Correspondence, Library of Congress; Dennett, *Hay,* pp. 375–80. Actually, Roosevelt's use of the term "figurehead" occurred in a letter which was generally complimentary to Hay, emphasizing the secretary's gift for language and the respect he commanded from others. Roosevelt to Lodge, 28 January 1909, *Letters,* 6:1490.

10. Quoted in Esthus, *Rivalries,* p. 8; Jessup, *Elihu Root,* 1:404–405.

11. He gladly acknowledged Root's editing of his speeches: "Sometimes I would not recognize my own child and sometimes I was very thankful I could not." Esthus, *Rivalries,* p. 9.

12. Lodge to Roosevelt, 8 July 1905, *Roosevelt-Lodge Correspondence,* 2:163.

13. Roosevelt to Root, 29 February 1908, 29 March 1908, *Letters,* 6:957, 957 n., 984; Charles Neu, *An Uncertain Friendship:*

Theodore Roosevelt and Japan, 1906-1909, p. 281; Howard C. Hill, *Roosevelt and the Caribbean,* p. 208; Mowry, *Era,* p. 161; Esthus, *Roosevelt and Japan,* p. 306. According to his principal biographer, Root suffered at least two physical breakdowns from overwork as secretary of state. Jessup, *Elihu Root,* 1:526.

14. Roosevelt to Bradley Tyler Johnson, 7 March 1898; to Frederick Selous, 7 February 1900; to Cecil Spring Rice, 2 and 12 March 1900; to John St. Loe Strachey, 8 March 1901, *Letters,* 1:789; 2:1176, 1208-1209, 1217; 3:9; Theodore Roosevelt, *Gouverneur Morris,* in Hagedorn, ed., *Works,* 7:427; Harbaugh, *Roosevelt,* p. 280; Carleton Putnam, *Theodore Roosevelt: The Formative Years, 1858-1886,* p. 224; Chessman, *Theodore Roosevelt,* p. 121.

15. Theodore Roosevelt, *An Autobiography,* p. 245; Roosevelt to Anna Roosevelt, 19 June 1886; to St. Loe Strachey, 22 February 1907; to Frederick Scott Oliver, 22 July 1915, *Letters,* 1:103; 5:596; 8:949; Joseph B. Bishop, *Theodore Roosevelt and His Time Shown in His Letters,* 2 vols., 1:40-41; John P. Mallan, "Roosevelt, Brooks Adams, and Lea: The Warrior Critique of the Business Civilization," *American Quarterly* 8 (Fall 1956): 228-29; Robert W. Sellen, "Theodore Roosevelt: Historian with a Moral," *Mid-America* 41 (October 1959): 235. On 16 August 1903, T.R. wrote to his sister-in-law, Emily Carow, that the newly arrived German ambassador had come to present his credentials in "a very striking costume, that of a hussar. As soon as the ceremony was over I told him to put on civilized raiment." Roosevelt, *Theodore Roosevelt's Letters to His Children,* in Hagedorn, ed., *Works,* 19:441.

16. Roosevelt to William W. Kimball, 19 November 1897; to Brooks Adams, 21 March 1898; to Mrs. John G. Graham, 5 March 1915, *Letters,* 1:717, 798; 8:907; Roosevelt, *Autobiography,* p. 590; Roosevelt, *Oliver Cromwell,* in Hagedorn, ed., *Works,* 10:198. To his friend Strachey he explained that his "unspeakable contempt" for professional peace agitators was balanced by "a sincere horror of war." Roosevelt to Strachey, 18 August 1906, John St. Loe Strachey Papers, House of Lords Library, London. To his son Kermit, he confided that he "would be loathe to see it [the United States] forced into a war in which it was wrong." 27 October 1906, Theodore Roosevelt Collection, Houghton Library, Harvard University.

17. Bishop, *Roosevelt*, 1:266. Other martial favorites included Longfellow's "Saga of King Olaf"; Browning's "Prospice" and "Childe Roland"; and the "Battle Hymn of the Republic," which he wanted to have as the national anthem. Edward C. Wagenknecht, *The Seven Worlds of Theodore Roosevelt*, pp. 52, 59.

18. Roosevelt, Address to the Naval War College, June 1897, quoted in Theodore Roosevelt, *American Ideals and Other Essays*, p. 251. See also Wagenknecht, *Seven Worlds*, pp. 247–53.

19. He used the terms frequently in reference to people of wealth and superior education. See, for example, Roosevelt, *American Ideals*, p. 242.

20. Roosevelt to Root, 27 December 1902, Box 162, Elihu Root Papers, Library of Congress.

21. Roosevelt to Theodore Burton, 23 February 1904; to Spring Rice, 27 December 1904; to William Rockhill, 22 August 1905; to George Otto Trevelyan, 1 October 1911; to Frederick S. Oliver, 22 July 1915, *Letters*, 4:736–37, 1087, 1310; 7:352; 8:949–58; Tyler Dennett, *Roosevelt and the Russo-Japanese War*, p. 154.

22. Hay to Roosevelt, 31 August 1903, John Hay Papers, Library of Congress; Harbaugh, *Roosevelt*, pp. 280–81.

23. Roosevelt to Jacob E. Bausch, 12 January 1897, *Letters*, 1:576.

24. Roosevelt to Thomas Collier Platt, 8 May 1899, ibid., 2:1005.

25. Beale, *Roosevelt*, p. 337; Gordon C. O'Gara, *Theodore Roosevelt and the Rise of the Modern Navy*, pp. 7–8; Roosevelt to Kermit Roosevelt, 8 March 1908, Roosevelt Collection, Harvard University.

26. Hill, *Roosevelt*, p. 172; Roosevelt, *The Strenuous Life*, in Hagedorn, ed., *Works*, 13:501, 503.

27. David H. Burton, "T.R.: Confident Imperialist," *Review of Politics* 23 (July 1961): 365; Roosevelt to Sir Edward Grey, 28 February 1907, *Letters*, 5: 600–601; Toth, "Root," in Graebner, ed., *Uncertain Tradition*, p. 53.

28. Roosevelt, *Autobiography*, pp. 581–82; Roosevelt to Paul Estournelles de Constant, 1 September 1903; to Carnegie, 5 April 1907; to Wilhelm II, 6 May 1908; to Lodge, 12 September 1911; to Spring Rice, 31 December 1912; to Frederick S. Oliver, 22 July 1915, *Letters*, 3:584; 5:641; 6:1023; 7:343, 680–81; 8:954.

29. Beale, *Roosevelt*, pp. 151, 154; Dana Munro, *The United States and the Caribbean Area*, chap. 5; Durand to Lansdowne, 10 March 1905, Lord Lansdowne Papers, FO 800/144, PRO; Frank C. Lascelles to Lansdowne, 11 February 1904, FO 115/1307, PRO; Lansdowne to Durand, 23 March 1904, 14 January 1905, FO 115/1350, PRO.

30 Roosevelt to Hugo Munsterberg, 8 August 1914; to Frederick S. Oliver, 22 July 1915, *Letters*, 7:795-96; 8:955; Roosevelt, *Autobiography*, p. 576; Beale, *Roosevelt*, pp. 393-94.

31. Lawrence F. Abbott, *Impressions of Theodore Roosevelt*, p. 150.

32. Roosevelt to John Ireland, 31 July 1903, *Letters*, 3:537; Beale, *Roosevelt*, pp. 93 n., 138; Arthur H. Lee, *A Good Innings and a Great Partnership, Being the Life Story of Arthur and Ruth Lee*, 1:333; David H. Burton, "Theodore Roosevelt and His English Correspondents: The Intellectual Roots of the Anglo-American Alliance," *Mid-America* 53 (January 1971): 18, 29. As suggested in chap. 1, T.R.'s eleventh commandment answered the needs of domestic as well as foreign politics.

33. For his doubts on the export value of democracy, see his *Gouverneur Morris*, in Hagedorn, ed., *Works*, 7:322. He favored the acquisition of Hawaii, Samoa, and the Virgin Islands for the security of the canal.

34. Roosevelt, *Thomas Hart Benton*, in Hagedorn, ed., *Works*, 7:13, 37, 115-16, 186; Roosevelt to Captain Mahan, 3 May 1897; to Robert Bacon, 8 April 1898, *Letters*, 1:607; 2:814. His only interest in Cuba prior to 1898 was to drive Spain out, and he looked forward to withdrawing from the Philippines "whenever the islands can stand alone." As he wrote to Frederic René Coudert on 3 July 1901, "We do not want to expand over another people capable of self-government unless that people desires to go in with us—and not necessarily even then. . . . Barring the possible necessity of fortifying the Isthmian canal or getting a naval station, I hope it will not become our duty to take a foot of soil south of us." Ibid., 3:105. See also Roosevelt to Charles William Eliot, 14 November 1900, ibid., 2:1415.

35. J. Fred Rippy, "The Initiation of the Customs Receivership in the Dominican Republic," *Hispanic American Historical Review* 17 (November 1937): 438-39, 442-43, 446-48; Roosevelt to President Rafael Reyes of Colombia, 20 February 1905, *Letters*, 4:1124.

36. Roosevelt to Root, 6 November 1905, *Letters*, 5:69; Russell H. Fitzgibbon, *Cuba and the United States, 1900–1935*, p. 106. Chester L. Jones, *The Caribbean Since 1900*, pp. 36–37. Roosevelt chafed a bit at Hay's indecisive negotiations with the Cuban government, but he does not appear to have exerted much personal pressure. Roosevelt to Hay, 23 October 1902 and 13 May 1903, *Letters*, 3:367, 474; Challener, *Admirals*, pp. 97, 99.

37. The difference between what the United States first claimed in Alaska and what it eventually settled for under Roosevelt was an area larger than the state of Rhode Island and considerably more than the 600-square-mile Canal Zone.

38. Roosevelt to Dewey, 20 February 1904, *Letters*, 4:734; Allan Reed Millett, *The Politics of Intervention: The Military Occupation of Cuba, 1906–1909*, p. 67.

39. Roosevelt to Taft, 28 September 1906, *Letters*, 5:432. On 25 November 1905, Secretary of the Navy Bonaparte cabled Commander Bradford at Santo Domingo City: "The President says do not interfere with coastwise shipment arms and ammunition between ports." Office of Naval Intelligence MSS, Santo Domingo Correspondence, vol. 2, National Archives.

40. A. G. Vansittart to Lansdowne, 13 February 1905; H. H. Gosling to Vansittart (British consul general), 27 January 1905, FO 115/1351, PRO.

41. Samuel Flagg Bemis, *The Latin-American Policy of the United States*, p. 164; Osgood, *Ideals and Self-Interest*, p. 105; Millett, *Politics of Intervention*, p. 81; David A. Lockmiller, *Magoon in Cuba: A History of the Second Intervention, 1906–1909*, p. 197.

42. William Rockhill to Root, 18 September 1905, Record Group 59, Microfilm 92, Reel 129, National Archives.

43. Roosevelt to Col. W. C. Sanger, 20 April 1902; to Lodge, 19 August 1905, *Letters*, 3:253; 4:958 n., 1306. He did finally threaten to send a cruiser to Newfoundland, but the threat did not have to be carried out. Tansill, *Canadian-American Relations*, pp. 99, 108. See also Millett, *Politics of Intervention*, pp. 97–101 (T.R. refused two of Taft's requests that he land troops in Cuba).

44. Outram Bax-Ironside to Edward Grey, Caracas, 8 May 1907, FO 115/1431, PRO; Hill, *Roosevelt*, p. 208.

45. Howard Hurwitz, *Theodore Roosevelt and Labor in New York State, 1880–1900*, pp. 255, 296.

46. Roosevelt, *Autobiography*, p. 411.

47. *Letters*, 5:863 n.

48. Ibid., 5:214 n. The term "practice march" is, of course, a forerunner of the term that he would use a year later to describe his world cruise.

49. Roosevelt, *Autobiography*, p. 602. The Aguinaldan rebels who laid down their arms soon after T.R. took office were not included in the designation "foreign foe," since the Philippines was a United States territory at the time. Neither were the Japanese seal poachers who had been shot as private trespassers by the authorities of St. Paul Island (16 and 17 July 1906). See Roosevelt to Harrison Gray Otis, 8 January 1907, *Letters*, 5:542; Thomas A. Bailey, *Theodore Roosevelt and the Japanese-American Crises*, pp. 24–26.

50. Typical was Mark Hanna's alleged comment on the prospect of T.R.'s vice-presidential nomination: "Don't you realize that there's only one life between this madman and the White House?" John Morton Blum, *The Republican Roosevelt*, p. 22. Also, a magazine reference to Roosevelt in 1899: "He's only a boy—don't take him too seriously." Frank Luther Mott, *A History of American Magazines, 1885-1905*, 5 vols., 4:170.

51. Roosevelt to Martha Bulloch Roosevelt, 23 October 1876; to Kermit Roosevelt, 6 June 1908, *Letters*, 1:19; 6:1060. In the same letter to Kermit, he continued: "We must always be ready to back one another up, and probably we ought each to have a spare rifle when we move in to the attack." Not surprisingly, Kermit later recalled how meticulous his father had been in preparing every detail of an upcoming trip. Nothing was left to chance. See also Nicholas Roosevelt, *Theodore Roosevelt: The Man as I Knew Him*, p. 16. T.R. was cautious even as a trustbuster in the sense that his choice of trusts was so carefully limited.

52. Theodore Roosevelt, *Hero Tales* and *History of New York*, in Hagedorn, ed., *Works*, 10:41, 378, 382, 458–59.

53. He also regarded Benton, a leading champion of Polk's policy, as "rash and headstrong." Roosevelt, *Benton*, in ibid., 7:182.

54. Robert A. Hart, *The Great White Fleet*, pp. 46–49, 51, 56, 80, 221; Esthus, *Roosevelt and Japan*, p. 246. This was the origin of the expression "Join the Navy and See the World."

55. Roosevelt to Bacon, 13 September 1906; to Taft, 2 October 1906, *Letters*, 5:409, 437; Challener, *Admirals*, pp. 164–66.

56. Roosevelt passed judgment on General Miles, and Root

upbraided an insubordinate naval commander for similar reasons. Challener, *Admirals*, p. 172; Roosevelt to Root, 19 March 1902; to Taft, 7 March 1904, *Letters*, 3:244–47; 4:744; Paul S. Holbo, "Perilous Obscurity: Public Diplomacy and the Press in the Venezuela Crisis, 1902–1903," *The Historian* 32 (May 1970): 434–35. The president would brook no infringement on the principle of civilian control, not only because he believed in it, but also because he took a personal interest in the military and was anxious to synchronize military and diplomatic movements. He insisted on being informed of the slightest changes of fleet itinerary and on several occasions overruled his military advisers. He rejected the General Staff plan for a Cuban landing in 1906 because he felt it called for too few mounted troops, just as he later overruled naval objections to sending the battlefleet on around the world with destroyers in the lead. Roosevelt to Hay, 2 May 1903, *Letters*, 3:473; Seward Livermore, "The American Navy as a Factor in World Politics, 1903–1913," *American Historical Review* 51 (April 1946): 866 n.; Millett, *Politics of Intervention*, pp. 89–90; O'Gara, *Theodore Roosevelt*, p. 79; Challener, *Admirals*, p. 224. See also Roosevelt, *American Ideals*, p. 346.

57. Roosevelt to Hay, 15 June 1904, Hay Papers, Special Correspondence, Library of Congress Microfilm, Reel 9; Charles Darling to John Hay, 16 June 1904, Department of State MSS, Record Group 45, Confidential Letters Sent, vol. 4, National Archives; Harold E. Davis, "The Citizenship of Jon Perdicaris," *Journal of Modern History* 13 (December 1941): 517–26. For a popular account, see Barbara W. Tuchman, "Perdicaris Alive or Raisuli Dead," *American Heritage* 10 (August 1959). For references to magazine articles of the period, see Luella Hall, *The United States and Morocco, 1776–1956*, p. 383. For details on what Raisuli demanded and what he got, see *Review of Reviews* 30 (1904): 24, 147; Thomas H. Etzold, "Protection or Politics? 'Perdicaris Alive or Raisuli Dead,' " *The Historian* 37 (February 1975): 297–304.

58. Roosevelt to Root, 7 June 1904, *Letters*, 4:821; Balfour to Carnegie, 18 December 1902, Arthur James Balfour Papers, No. 49742, British Museum, London; Cabinet Report to Edward VII, 4 May 1904, CAB 41/29, PRO; Rippy, *Caribbean Danger Zone*, chap. 3; Munro, *Intervention*, p. 7. For the view that the corollary was "a completely new policy," see Thomas A. Bailey, *A Diplomatic History of the American People*, p. 505.

59. Roosevelt to Lodge, 11 September 1907, *Letters*, 5:790;

Beale, *Roosevelt,* pp. 403–404; E. Taylor Parks and J. Fred Rippy, "The Galápagos Islands, A Neglected Phase of American Strategy and Diplomacy," *Pacific Historical Review* 9 (March 1940): 43.

60. Lansdowne to Durand, 25 June 1905, FO 115/1353, PRO. The series of painstaking moves which finally produced a peaceful settlement of the anthracite coal strike required a similar degree of self-control.

61. Ralph E. Weber, *As Others See Us,* p. 180.

62. His first public use of the phrase seems to have occurred 2 September 1901; see pp. 60 and 84 (note 90). He used the expression again on 2 April 1903 with reference to his tactics in the Venezuelan blockade crisis.

63. This was particularly evident in his handling of congressional opinion during the Venezuela crisis. See also his letter to Richard Pearson Hobson, in which he said that "to be 'brutally frank' is the surest way to bring about trouble and is an exceedingly poor way of preparing for it." *Letters,* 6:1142.

64. Roosevelt, *Autobiography,* pp. 82–83.

65. Roosevelt to Lodge, 14 July 1895, *Letters,* 1:467.

66. Roosevelt to Hay, 1 July 1899, ibid., 2:1025.

67. *Review of Reviews* 28 (1903): 140–41, 156; Moody to Hay, 30 June 1903, Department of State, Miscellaneous Letters, Microfilm M179, Reel 1176, National Archives.

68. Roosevelt, *Autobiography,* pp. 205–206.

69. Roosevelt to Lodge, 1 October 1906 and 10 July 1907, *Roosevelt-Lodge Correspondence,* 2:238, 275; Beale, *Roosevelt,* p. 173; Warren I. Cohen, *America's Response to China,* pp. 71, 73; Edward B. Parsons, "Roosevelt's Containment of the Russo-Japanese War," *Pacific Historical Review* 38 (February 1969): 21; Roosevelt, *Benton,* in Hagedorn, ed., *Works,* 7:25–26; *Outlook* 106 (1914): 475.

70. Hay to Roosevelt, 3 September 1903, Hay Papers, General Correspondence, Library of Congress. For Roosevelt's sensitivity, refinement, and extraordinary tenderness toward children, see Roosevelt to Anna Roosevelt, 15 October 1876; to Theodore Roosevelt, Sr., 22 October 1876; to Corinne Roosevelt, 5 February, 3 June 1877; to Henry Davis Minot, 20 February 1878; to Corinne Roosevelt, 15 April 1886; to Anna Roosevelt, 15 May 1886; to Gertrude Carow, 18 October 1890; to Arthur Lee, 26 September 1899; to Edward Sanford Martin, 26 November 1900; to Kermit Roosevelt, 8 and 17 January 1903; to Theodore Roosevelt, Jr., 20 Jan-

uary 1903; to Kermit Roosevelt, 1 February 1903, *Letters*, 1:17, 18, 23, 28, 31, 97, 100, 233–34; 2:1079 (love for his wife), 1443; 3:401, 406, 408, 414.

71. "Don't bluster, don't flourish your revolver, and never draw unless you intend to shoot." Roosevelt to Lodge, 27 March 1901, *Letters*, 3:32. Also typical is what he wrote to Hay on 22 May 1903: "I hate being in the position of seeming to bluster without backing it up." Ibid., 3:478.

72. Roosevelt, *Autobiography*, p. 586; Roosevelt to Root, 30 April 1900; to Trevelyan, 12 September 1905; to Reid, 4 December 1908; to Taft, 22 December 1910, *Letters*, 2:1275; 5:22; 6:1410; 7:190. Will power was valued as highly as gunpowder, and it had to be demonstrated on occasion. Thus, while children could generally be managed with a combination of firmness and mercy, parental credibility called for spanking at some point along the way. Appeasement, whether of children or nations, would only invite insult and, in the long run, the very violence it was intended to avert. Roosevelt to Granville Stanley Hall, 29 November 1899, ibid., 2:1100.

73. Roosevelt to Albert Lenoir Key, 6 July 1901, ibid., 3:111.

74. Roosevelt to President McKinley, 26 April 1897; to John Davis Long, 16 February 1898; to St. Loe Strachey, 27 January 1900, ibid., 1:602, 773–74; 2:1145.

75. Roosevelt to Root, 20 April 1900, ibid., 2:1268–69.

76. The European squadron had been sent to Beirut in August 1903, but only after urgent request by the American minister as well as the supposed assassination of an American vice-consul. As for Miss Stone, the missionary, Roosevelt believed that men went into "wild lands" at their own risk and that women had no business going at all. *Review of Reviews* 30 (September 1904): 275, 282; Roosevelt to Alvey Adee, 2 October 1901; to Hay, 1 March 1902; to Leishman, 12 August 1904; to Taft, 11 January 1906, *Letters*, 3:156–57, 156 n., 237; 4:891; 5:133; A. L. P. Dennis, "John Hay" in Samuel Flagg Bemis, ed., *American Secretaries of State and their Diplomacy, 1776–1925*, 9:180–82.

77. Roosevelt to Truman H. Newberry, 17 June 1908, *Letters*, 6:1082; Millett, *Politics of Intervention*, p. 91.

78. Quoted in G. Wallace Chessman, *Governor Theodore Roosevelt*, p. 221.

79. Bennett Milton Rich, *The Presidents and Civil Disorder*, p. 127.

80. Roosevelt to Hay, 1 July 1899, *Letters*, 2:1027. He like-

wise wrote, as governor of New York: "If there should be a disaster at the Croton Dam strike, I'd order out the militia in a minute. But I'd sign an employer's liability law, too." Quoted in Hurwitz, *Roosevelt and Labor,* p. 251.

81. Reginald Tower to Edward Grey, 8 October 1907, FO 414/195, PRO; Lord Bryce to Grey, [?] January 1908; Grey to Bryce, 28 February 1908, Bryce Papers, FO 800/331, PRO; Roosevelt to Arthur Lee, 2 February, 8 April 1908, Lee Papers, Courtauld Institute, Portman Square, London.

82. Clippings from the *New York Sun,* 4 December 1906, 6 January 1907, FO 800/106, FO 800/81, PRO; Hart, *Great White Fleet,* pp. 38–40, 55. Charles Neu emphasizes Roosevelt's abortive effort to enlist the active diplomatic support of Canada and Britain, without ever mentioning Roosevelt's far more successful effort to woo Germany. Neu, *Uncertain Friendship,* p. 314.

83. "Invasion Plan," items 47–48, Arthur James Balfour Papers, Whittinghame, Scotland. The third of March was several weeks after the cementing of the Japanese-American Gentlemen's Agreement and two weeks before Roosevelt received a formal invitation from Tokyo for an official fleet visit. It was also the day that the American ambassador, Whitelaw Reid, was invited to Buckingham Palace. After prolonged social ostracism, Reid now had the king take him by the arm to seek his advice on how best to improve relations between the United States, Britain, and Japan. Hart, *Great White Fleet,* p. 155.

84. FO 800/92, PRO. See also Spencer Wilkinson to Sir Edward Grey, 14 January 1908, FO 800/112, PRO.

85. Esthus, *Roosevelt and Japan,* preface, 298–300; Neu, *Uncertain Friendship,* pp. 11, 319; David H. Burton, *Theodore Roosevelt,* preface, 109, 207; Challener, *Admirals,* p. 248; Bradford Perkins, *The Great Rapprochement,* p. 103.

86. David H. Burton, "Theodore Roosevelt and His Correspondents: A Special Relationship," *Transactions of the American Philosophical Society,* n.s. 63, pt. 2 (1973): 9; Perkins, *Great Rapprochement,* p. 109. According to Mrs. Storer, Roosevelt was "like a child" in loving contention for its own sake and, with "child-like caprice," he "went on waving his big stick and quarreling with his best friends." Maria Storer, *Roosevelt, The Child,* pp. 5, 6, 8–9. Other historians who have perpetuated the image include Henry Pringle, Louis Halle, Wilfrid Callcott (who refers to Roosevelt's "boyish enthusiasm" and "bullying of the adolescent"), and the

Sprouts (who speak of his "perpetual adolescence"). Halle, *Dream and Reality*, p. 260; Wilfrid H. Callcott, *The Caribbean Policy of the United States*, p. 116; Harold and Margaret Sprout, *Rise of American Naval Power*, p. 225.

87. Among those who remarked on Roosevelt's patience and openness to a wide range of opinion were Lawrence Abbott, James Amos (Roosevelt's valet), Charles Willis Thompson (of the *New York Times*), Eugene Hale, Albert Beveridge, John Hay, Oscar Straus, Henry Cabot Lodge, and Elihu Root. Wagenknecht, *Seven Worlds*, p. 162; Oscar Straus, *Under Four Administrations: From Cleveland to Taft*, pp. 182, 208; Abbott, *Impressions*, pp. 22-23; James E. Pollard, *The Presidents and the Press*, pp. 570-71, 579; William Bayard Hale, *A Week in the White House with Theodore Roosevelt*, pp. 54-55; James Ford Rhodes, *The McKinley and Roosevelt Administrations, 1897-1909*, p. 398; Roosevelt, *Works*, ed., Hagedorn, 7:xvi, xvii; *Review of Reviews* 30 (1904): 598.

88. A. Whitney Griswold, *The Far Eastern Policy of the United States*, p. 13; Rich, *Presidents and Civil Disorder*, p. 121; Esthus, *Rivalries*, pp. 58, 118, 123; Sir Percey M. Sykes, *The Right Honorable Sir Mortimer Durand*, p. 275. Bryce was unusual in differentiating between Roosevelt's astuteness in action and his impetuosity in speech. The normal opinion among those who did not know him was expressed by the Colombian chargé, Tomás Herrán, who warned his government of T.R.'s "impetuous and violent disposition." *Story of Panama*, p. 317. Jutaro Komura found T.R. "excitable" and at times "bombastic." Claude M. Mac-Donald to Lansdowne, 30 December 1904, FO 115/1350, PRO. See also Durand to Lansdowne, 29 November 1904 and 23 October 1905; Lansdowne to Durand, 11 December 1904 and 4 February 1905, Lansdowne Papers, FO 800/144, PRO.

89. Roosevelt to Theodore E. Burton, 23 February 1904, *Letters*, 4:737. For a good example of the vitality of the Roosevelt myth, see Gerald Markowitz, "Progressivism and Imperialism: A Return to First Principles," *The Historian* 37 (February 1975): 274. According to Markowitz, "Most progressives rejected the crassness and jingoism that characterized Theodore Roosevelt's 'Big Stick' approach." For further reference, see the listings provided in footnote 2 of this chapter; also, Kenton J. Clymer, *John Hay: The Gentleman as Diplomat*, pp. 114-15, 189-95; Hart, *Great White Fleet*, pp. viii, ix, 232-36; Trani, *Portsmouth*, p. 10. Depending on which account one reads, T.R. is apt to be called an

"arch expansionist," a man of "bristling militancy" and "jingois-
tic nationalism," or a "headstrong and romantic belligerent" with
a "love of violence." One is likely to read that "his pugnacity and
bellicosity were almost pathological." Robert Beisner, *Twelve
against Empire*, pp. 226, 230; Thomas A. Bailey, *Presidential
Greatness*, pp. 306–307; Chessman, *Theodore Roosevelt*, pp. 62,
64, 67.

CHAPTER 5

The Cosmopolitan Roosevelt

THIS concluding essay will suggest something of the nature of T.R.'s reputation abroad as well as some of the reaons for it. "Big Stick" diplomacy and childlike ebullience might not seem the normal ingredients of international prestige and popularity. Yet Roosevelt's name was given to a river in Brazil; his portrait was hung in Japan beside that of the emperor; he received the highest academic honors at Oxford; and a conference of Latin peoples voted him a commendation in 1906. It was Roosevelt who assumed the role of mediator in disputes between Colombia and Venezuela, Guatemala and Salvador, Nicaragua and Honduras, as well as between Russia and Japan, France and Germany. His work at the Portsmouth Conference and elsewhere earned him the Nobel Peace Prize, while his aid to American states led to a revised standard of political legitimacy and a Central American Court of Justice.

For the first time, America was taken into account by world leaders, not only in questions affecting the Western Hemisphere, but in all major diplomatic decisions. To the sultan of Muscat, whose people had not set eyes on an American warship since the days of Andrew Jackson, the United States appeared to be the holder of the world's balance of power. Italian leaders expressed admiration for the president's straightforward ways and looked to him for a lead on their China policy. The Japanese not only consulted Roosevelt before renewing their treaty with Britain, they offered him a direct alliance. And the English, also eager for some formal tie, took American naval officers into their confidence and twice in 1905 invited the United States fleet to join in Mediterranean maneuvers.[1]

German statesmen seem to have been particularly awed by the Rough Rider, whom they envisioned as speaking for a "mighty rising power with a tremendous fleet." After confronting American battleships in 1902, they tried to anticipate Roosevelt's reaction to a contemplated neutralization of the Baltic Sea. Later, when they considered extending citizenship to all people of German descent anywhere in the world, including Brazil and the United States, they gave up the idea when their embassy in Washington warned of "the American danger," the consequences of which could "not be foreseen." Even more significant, Friedrich von Holstein warned Chancellor von Bülow in 1903: "I find the greatest drawback of going with Russia in the fact that we would draw further away from America, which could revenge itself on us in some way or other, even without war." What Holstein had in mind, as well he might, was a possible Anglo-American entente. Although Roosevelt does not seem to have considered this a real option in view of adverse congressional opinion, he was certainly receptive to the idea and maintained the illusion so successfully that even a historian as astute as Howard Beale spoke of an entente as if it had been a reality. What actually existed was less an entente than a balancing act so evenhanded that Whitehall entertained serious concern in 1907 that Roosevelt might accept a formal offer of alliance from Berlin.[2]

The kaiser and his advisers alternated between fear of an Anglo-American entente and satisfaction in Anglo-American friction. They were convinced that the "fear of Roosevelt" was "visibly increasing in England" and that the British would "never venture to do anything against America." At the time of the Venezuelan blockade, Count Metternich, the German ambassador in London, had written Bülow that if Roosevelt should decide to take his case on the blockade to the yellow press, the British government would surely fall. Later, it seemed certain that England would not work out an understanding with Russia "because

America has taken an anti-Russian stand, and England will and must remain on the same side as America." The British would refrain, likewise, from giving France "any further assistance on the Morocco question in the face of the entry of President Roosevelt on the scene." And in 1907, Berlin was sure that John Bull intended "to use the Hague Conference for improving Anglo-American relations at the cost of German-American," having instructed Lord Bryce to ascertain "American wishes."[3]

Certain officials at the Wilhelmstrasse even began to imitate Roosevelt's manner of speaking. Bülow described Germany, in typical Roosevelt style, as the "strong, silent man who without heroic verbiage defends himself and his family." Holstein used the phrase "Big Stick" to describe what he feared would be the probable impression of the kaiser's sudden visit to Tangier in 1905. From the German ambassador to the Court of St. James's, there came this remarkable comment in January, 1903: "Lord Lansdowne asked me whether we might not be riding for a fall in calling on President Roosevelt to decide our differences with Bowen over the Venezuela issue." The entire telegram is in German except for the expression "riding for a fall," which was one of T.R.'s favorites and which appears in English.[4]

Paradoxically, Roosevelt's grip on German leaders bore no relation to his rapport with the German people. He struck no sympathetic chord when he visited Berlin in 1910, even though he became the first civilian ever to review a parade of imperial troops. Moreover, the muted public response to his coming merely reflected an ambivalence in his own personal feeling. As a youth, he had passed several months in the home of a Dresden family and had come to admire the Germans for their literature, *gemütlichkeit*, hard work, and toughness. On the other hand, he had always been inclined to want to "damn the Dutch." He once described Carl Schurz's two-volume biography of Henry Clay as the kind of belaboring one might expect from "that Dutchman"; and he found it something of an imposition to entertain the kaiser's brother, Prince Henry, on his good-will trip to America in 1902. Perhaps it was not accidental that the only German officials whom he liked, Speck von Sternburg and the kaiser, were both half-English.[5]

Nor were his feelings about the kaiser unmixed. The two resembled each other in many ways. Both had overcome physical handicaps stemming from birth. Both possessed a broad range of interests and exuded immense magnetism. Both expressed themselves in colorful language, Wilhelm's "unmitigated noodles!" (in reference to British officials) matching Theodore's "sublimated sweetbreads!" The kaiser liked to consider himself "intimate" with the president, corresponding with him as often as he did with his cousin the czar. And he was apt to exclaim, when he heard mention of Roosevelt's name, "That's my man!" The feeling was not entirely mutual, however. Roosevelt regarded his host as "a big man and on the whole a good man" and told him that "in America we think . . . you would carry your ward"; but he also felt that he was inclined to be "jumpy" and hence a threat to world peace. He shared the widely held opinion that Germany's appetite for imperial conquest had yet to be satisfied, especially in the region of the Panama Canal. Furthermore, when he spoke at the University of Berlin, he lectured an audience which included the kaiser himself on the world movement toward arbitration, limitation of armaments, and democracy, as contrasted with the concept of divine right of kings. Men did "not need a rule of absolutism imposed upon them by the unfathomable decrees of heaven."[6]

The Berlin visit was only one stop on a whirlwind tour of Europe which took in nearly every court and capital between Russia and Spain. In all of these places, Roosevelt was greeted with high enthusiasm. Rome gave him a victor's welcome, and he was warmly entertained by King Victor Emmanuel, whom he imagined to be as capable as "Bill the Kaiser" of "carrying his ward." When he entered the northern village of Porto Maurizio, home of his sister-in-law, he found it placarded with posters proclaiming him "the promoter of international peace" and "champion of human fraternity." Villagers rained bouquets upon him from third-story windows until they literally covered his open carriage with flowers. It was the same spirit which caused an Italian sergeant in 1917 to respond to the name Roosevelt by exclaiming *"Il gran Americano!"*—the same spirit which warmed his way through most of Europe.[7] Specially gratifying were the invitations he received to address prestigious forums in Berlin, Cairo, Oxford, and finally Christiania, Norway, where he accepted the Nobel Prize.

Two of his European speeches are of particular significance, not only for his manner of speaking, but also for the audience he addressed and the way in which his words were taken. The first of these was delivered in France. Five years earlier, Premier Rouvier, along with members of his cabinet, had returned the body of John Paul Jones to the United States and followed the coffin on foot as a mark of appreciation for the role T.R. was expected to play in negotiations leading to the Algeciras Conference. Roosevelt never betrayed this French confidence, and he was still popular in 1910 as he addressed a select audience at the Sorbonne. By this time, however, Paris was riding a wave of radical socialism, with large street demonstrations planned for May Day to embarrass the government. Roosevelt spoke to the issue with characteristic bluntness—and tact. After commending his listeners for their brilliance and paying "all homage" to things of the mind, after making sure as well to affirm his concurrence with certain planks in the socialist platform, he assailed the leftist cause unreservedly and castigated demagogic appeals to class conflict. Although this was but a small portion of the total speech, its effect was electric. One of the leading dailies, *Le Temps*, printed fifty-seven thousand copies of the speech and distributed them without charge to every schoolteacher in the country. In addition, the government of M. Briand resolved to suppress the street demonstrations and did so easily with the aid of the Paris gendarmerie, which, for the first time in fifteen years, was ordered to use its weapons in self-defense.[8]

A few weeks later, Roosevelt addressed another distinguished audience at London's famed Guildhall. Again he confronted a current issue and spoke frankly. Radical nationalists had assassinated the Egyptian prime minister, Boutros Pasha, and T.R. had been stunned during his recent visit to Cairo by the vacillation of Crown policy. Although warned at the time not to condemn the assassins publicly, he accepted an invitation to speak at the University of Cairo and did just this, only to have his words cheered to the echo. Sir Eldon Orst, British consul general, was not exhibiting the firmness that civil and military officials had come to expect from his predecessor, Lord Cromer. These officials had therefore asked Roosevelt to relay their desire for a stronger stand to the authorities in London. It was with this in mind that he spoke out at the Guildhall, praising the British record in South Africa but indicating the need for a harder line in Egypt. "Either it is or it is not your duty to establish and keep order," he insisted. "If you feel that you have not the right to be in Egypt, if you do not wish to establish and to keep order there, why then by all means get out." Clearly, though, he was urging the British to stay, and stay they did. A Liberal, antiimperialist ministry appointed Lord Kitchener consul general. He, in turn, proceeded to restore British authority with customary vigor.[9]

This Guildhall address, approved before delivery by Balfour, Grey, and Cromer, was afterwards praised by the London *Times* for its "substantial truth." The *Daily Telegraph* agreed that Britain must "govern or go," thus coining the phrase which came to be regarded as the speech's title; the *Pall Mall Gazette* called Roosevelt's effort "great and memorable," while the *London Spectator* recognized it as "one of the greatest compliments ever paid to a people by a statesman of another country"—something "useful and practical."[10] According to Arthur Lee:

The whole occasion, whilst traditional and familiar in its setting, was unusually impressive on account of the distinction of the audience and the atmosphere of tense anticipation, but the effect of the speech, as it proceeded, was electrifying and almost volcanic. Such uncompromising straight from the shoulder talk had never before been heard in those hallowed precincts from a foreign statesman, and the City Fathers fairly gasped although they applauded vociferously. Ruth and I were on the däis next to Balfour and Edward Grey, and the latter whispered to me "this will cause the devil of a row—although I hope a healthy one!" Balfour was frankly delighted and said to us afterwards "I just *love* that man. There is no use, you've simply got to go Nap with him!" Ruth, in her diary commented: "TR moved and spoke with great dignity and with astonishing courage and reality! He looked so young too, and so tously-headed in spite of the fact that Arthur had brushed his hair most carefully for him before starting from Chesterfield Street!"[11]

Londoners were positively charmed by T.R.'s presence, turning out en masse to greet him at every turn. James Garvin, editor of the influential *Observer* and a former critic of the president, found him "wonderful and amusing. . . . he makes me sigh terribly for a Roosevelt of our own." Leo Maxse of the *National Review,* who, by comparison with Garvin, had been ferociously critical, now wished to see Britain's Downing Street "mandarins" relegated to the scrap heap and "replaced by a Roosevelt Dictatorship." The lion was hosted by such luminaries as George Otto Trevelyan, Lewis Harcourt, Lord Curzon, and Sir Edward Grey. But it was with his best friends, the Arthur Lees, that he spent most of his time, first at their home on Chesterfield Street and then at their country estate, Chequers, where, on the weekend of its housewarming, he was introduced to Arthur Balfour and Lord Roberts. As Lee recalled the meeting:

TR was so entirely different to anything that A.J.B. had either imagined or experienced and their two minds almost fizzed chemically when brought into contact for the first time. . . . It was, on Balfour's side, at any rate, almost a case of love at first sight. Both were at the top of their form, and in the almost ceaseless play of coruscating talk which illumined the weekend like summer lightning, Lord Roberts seemed a little silent and outgunned. But TR who was steeped in *Forty-One Years in India* and all "Bob's" campaigns, treated him with a deference and almost boyish hero-worship which greatly touched the "Little Man's" heart.[12]

Roosevelt also went up to Oxford, where he gave the celebrated Romanes Lecture for 1910. Not to be outdone, the Cambridge dons awarded him their highest honorary degree and added a precious bit of humor when, at the appropriate moment in the ceremony, they lowered a teddy bear (Darwin had gotten a monkey, and Kitchener a Mahdi!).

When it comes to the question of Roosevelt's reputation in other parts of the world, the Orient suggests itself as an area of prime importance. There is little to be said of China during this period except that its people were struggling to maintain their national identity and holding all foreigners under suspicion. Roosevelt made no great contribution to the well-being of the Chinese, but neither did he treat them roughly when they tried his patience by boycotting American goods and assassinating American citizens. As pointed out in chapter three, he stood ready to defend the national interest, yet behaved with restraint and offered to remit the unpaid half of the Boxer indemnity as a token of American good will. Liang Ch'eng, Chinese ambassador to the United States during most of T.R.'s administration, regarded the president as "upright and principled" as well as highly knowledgeable on the subject of world affairs. This was probably an accurate estimate since the president had acquired a vast fund of information on the Chinese from such sources as Sternburg, the two Adamses, and William Rockhill.[13] On the other hand, his effort in 1907 to dispel the war scare between Washington and Tokyo placed a decided strain on Sino-American friendship. Diplomatic leverage with Japan was obtained by first encouraging and then discouraging China's hope for an American-Chinese-German coalition; also by having the American battlefleet cancel one scheduled appearance after another at Chinese ports and then arrive with only a fraction of its total complement.

Needless to say, Roosevelt's main goal in the Far East was to keep relations with Japan on a stable footing—a purpose which suited his personal taste as much as it did the precarious nature of America's presence in the Philippines.

Long before the Japanese humbled Russia on the field of battle, he respected them for their industry and cleverness. "What people those Japs are!" he once exclaimed in admiration of some poetry which they had translated into English. Not that he was alone in this feeling. Americans had played a major part since the time of Commodore Perry in helping Nippon rise to the rank of a world power. Roosevelt, however, was especially positive. He insisted that the inferiority usually associated in the Western mind with yellow skin meant nothing in this case. Did history not show that people of fair complexion had once been the ones regarded as barbarians? Although he suspected Japan of feeling superior to the West, distrusting and resenting its overlordship, he had no trouble understanding that the United States would have reacted the same way "if the circumstances were reversed." During the Russo-Japanese War, he advised Japanese envoys that their paramount interest in areas surrounding the Yellow Sea entitled them to a Monroe Doctrine of their own. As pointed out earlier, he used his Annual Message of 1906 as well as a speech given at the Jamestown Exposition to lecture his countrymen on their scandalous treatment of Oriental immigrants. "We have as much to learn from Japan as Japan has to learn from us," he exclaimed. Small wonder that Baron Kaneko hailed these words as the "greatest utterance of an American president since Washington's Farewell Address," or that Count Itō, one of Japan's leading statesmen, placed a portrait of Roosevelt alongside that of the Meiji emperor.[14]

It has been thought that because Roosevelt responded to the immigration crisis of 1907 by sending a battlefleet to the Pacific, his reputation in Tokyo must have suffered. This is not confirmed by the evidence, however, nor is there any valid basis for the assumption that he incited lasting hostility when he opposed the more extreme Japanese war aims at Portsmouth. Although anti-American riots erupted along the Tokaido, this did not reflect the general mood of Japan, then or later.[15] Interestingly enough, the Japanese defense budget actually declined the year after the visit of the American fleet. Several treaties were signed; the Gentlemen's Agreement of 1907 was given effective implementation; and American naval officers were welcomed with unexpected good will. In this way, American relations with Japan ended under Roosevelt as they had begun, amicably.

Much the same can be said of Roosevelt's experience with Latin America. There was the same sense of what Americans could learn from a foreign people, especially in such matters as courtesy, taste, and refinement; there was the same unwillingness to generalize about diverse elements within a single ethnic group. Not that traditional fears, suspicions, jealousies, and misconceptions suddenly evaporated in 1901. Having originated long before Roosevelt entered the White House, they would remain long after he left.[16] A certain amount of ill feeling is likely to dampen any relationship between parties as unequal in wealth and power as the United States and its neighbors to the south. What is remarkable, though, is that tension and misunderstanding were at a minimum during the early years of the century and that the president won such a large measure of respect for his style and policy.

Historians have generally assumed that T.R. was unpopular with Latin Americans because of his alleged "rape" of Colombia and the corollary to the Monroe Doctrine whereby he claimed the role of hemispheric policeman. In the words of W. H. Calcott, "Latin-American nations sympathized with Colombia [on the question of the Panamanian revolt] but were unable to do anything about it beyond sending expressions of friendship." Charles W. Toth and G. Wallace Chessman have suggested that the president's "condescending" attitude, along with the corollary, "added greatly" to Latin "suspicion, distrust, and hostility." And according to Henry Pringle, "The 'Dagos' of Latin America, as Roosevelt had referred to them in a less formal moment, continued to view the United States with distrust and alarm."[17]

In fact, American prestige south of the border was exceptionally high under Roosevelt. The United States had just defeated Spain in a war for the liberation of Cuba. Leonard Wood, short-term military governor of Cuba, enjoyed unprecedented success and popularity. Roosevelt forced Germany and Britain in 1902 to agree to arbitrate their differences with Venezuela, and he surprised the world by honoring the American pledge to withdraw from Cuba in 1903. His famous corollary, far from causing resentment in Latin America, received solid support. Nor was his handling of the Panamanian revolt widely criticized. Venezuela sympathized openly with the rebels; Guatemala urged Roosevelt to annex Panama outright; and opinion in the chief nations of South America generally applauded the course of events on the isthmus.[18]

Even Colombia and Venezuela, two countries whose policy aggravated Roosevelt in the extreme, came to adopt a cooperative line by 1909. Colombian leaders, who had faced the prospect of Venezuelan intervention in their civil strife of 1901 and 1903, were again threatened by that bellicose neighbor in 1905. They were also confronted by a serious threat on the part of their coastal provinces to secede and join newly independent Panama. Not surprisingly, they met the crisis by resuming diplomatic relations with Washington, offering offshore naval bases, and inviting Roosevelt's good offices. Secretary Root visited Colombia, as well as Panama, on his good-will tour of Latin America the following year; and Bogotá officials went so far as to urge American intervention in Venezuela. They were on the verge of accepting a series of treaty arrangements in 1909 which would have drawn Panama, the United States, and Colombia into an agreed settlement of the Panamanian revolt when President Reyes was ousted from office.[19] At the same time, Cipriano Castro of Venezuela, one of the world's leading scapegraces and a personal irritant to Roosevelt, was overthrown by Juan Vicente Gómez, who immediately resumed friendly relations with the United States.[20]

Root found the atmosphere decidedly enthusiastic when he visited Argentina, Brazil, Chile, and Uruguay. An assembly hall, specially erected in Rio de Janeiro for the third Con-

ference of American Republics, had been named the Palacio
de Monroe, and the conference itself voted a formal resolution of commendation for the president of the United States.
Root, in turn, made a famous statement, later quoted by
Roosevelt in his Annual Address.

We wish for no victories but those of peace; for no territory except
our own; for no sovereignty except the sovereignty over ourselves.
We deem the independence and equal rights of the smallest and
weakest member of the family of nations entitled to as much
respect as those of the greatest empire, and we deem the obser-
vance of that respect the chief guarantee of the weak against the
oppression of the strong.

Enthusiastic students had to be dissuaded from unhar-
nessing the horses pulling Root's carriage so that they
themselves might draw it through the streets of Rio. In
Buenos Aires, despite a terrific downpour, large crowds
lined the avenues in anticipation of his arrival.[21]
    When he stopped in Peru on his way home, he heard "vi-
vas" and "hurrahs" from the mass of people gathered
everywhere along his path—on the wharves of Callao, at the
town square of Lima, at railroad stations high in the Andes.
His short, graceful speeches were continually interrupted by
applause—seven times in the town hall of Lima, eleven
times at San Marcos University. In addition, President José
Pardo remarked in one of his addresses that the United
States had placed "before the great powers of the world the
pillars of Hercules of the Monroe Doctrine"; it had excited
"the admiration of the whole world by its grandeur" and
reestablished "on the one hand peace between the empires
of Europe and Asia and, on the other hand, between the
republics of Central America." Most impressive, it had
obtained invitations for the Latin countries to attend the
second Hague Peace Conference; it had even delayed the
opening of the Hague convention in order that the Pan-
American Congress in Rio might complete its sessions. According to Pardo, the Hague invitation meant that Latin
rights of sovereign equality were at last to be recognized:

"This will be the world's formal and final declaration that no part of the American continents is to be deemed subject to colonization."[22]

American battleships, on their way from Norfolk, Virginia, to the Pacific in 1907, encountered friendly demonstrations at every South American port of call. Rio buzzed with the rumor of an approaching United States–Brazil alliance; President Peña hosted a galaxy of receptions for Admiral Evans and spoke glowingly of the Monroe Doctrine. Officers received passes to all the city's clubs, and Evans recalled that the "extreme warmth" of the people had surpassed anything in his memory. Requests by Ecuador and Argentina for a fleet visit were gracefully declined, although a persistent Argentina obtained permission to entertain the torpedo boat squadron and nearly fired its minister in Washington when this small privilege seemed in doubt! Peru, still grateful for American diplomatic support in a long round of border disputes, extended a splendid welcome, with President Pardo outdoing Peña in his praise of the Monroe Doctrine and Foreign Minister Polo gracing the wall of his office with a portrait of James Blaine, originator of Pan-Americanism.[23]

Roosevelt himself visited Latin America in 1913, at a time when anti-American sentiment was on the rise, only to be toasted by Uruguay's president as the defender of the Monroe Doctrine. Not everyone understood or approved his interpretation of the doctrine, and he reported "much misconception." On one occasion he was even booed by partisans shouting "Viva Mexico! Viva Colombia!" But the majority of people seemed in accord with the attitude shown by their officials, and on the issue of Panama there was no question whatever. He was invited by the "big three," Argentina, Brazil, and Chile, to make formal speeches and welcomed so enthusiastically by the people of Buenos Aires that he was twice moved to speak impromptu in the street. Later, by charting the course of an unmapped tributary to the Amazon known only as the River of Doubt, he caused it to be rechristened Rio Teodoro.[24]

Throughout the trip, he hammered away at two major themes: first, that he regarded each of the big three as the equal of the United States and in no way on a par with the unstable governments of the Caribbean; second, that the three had every right to regard themselves as coguarantors of the Monroe Doctrine. "If Santo Domingo had been in the Pacific," he told an audience in Santiago, "I should have asked the Chilean government to undertake the task which we were undertaking," and "as soon as the Chilean ships appeared off the island, ours would retire." He praised his hosts for their rapid progress in industry and urban development, predicted still greater strides for the future, and, in a series of articles published in *Outlook* magazine, encouraged American businessmen to look to South America for investment opportunity of real promise. Brazil, he pointed out, offered as many opportunities for settlement as the Mississippi Valley sixty years earlier; its climate was "better than our own western cattle country." Rio seemed "as progressive" as any city of the United States and "ahead of us" in such things as municipal theater and public parks. Slum districts did not exist, and living quarters for the poor were superior to what one found in the United States. "Nowhere in any nation of the world," he concluded, "has a more enlightened policy been pursued than that pursued by the statesmen who have had the control of Brazilian affairs during the past fifteen or twenty years."[25]

He believed that Latin America had handled "the whole question of slavery" far better than the United States, and he was equally impressed with the tolerance of interracial marriage. Blacks could claim their rightful place in society, and Indian blood had "added a good and not a bad element." He found it remarkable that persons of different social class mixed so easily at public celebrations with a "curious democracy in enjoyment which we of the North find it so difficult to achieve in spite of our more genuine political democracy." There was also an "innate refinement" and courtesy about the people that he found perfectly delightful. More than once, he marveled at women who spoke French and English as well as Spanish, dressed attractively, conversed with intelligence, and still found time to raise large families. Latin-American education seemed to be doing everything for women that was being done in the United States without any of the ill effects.[26]

He was equally frank, of course, when it came to ways in which the host country appeared less advanced. Certain traits of "national character and temperament" struck him as deficient, though remediable by education. The common practice of gambling on horses grated on his puritan conscience, and he pointed out in no uncertain language that Chile's attempt to nationalize its railways had proven a disastrous failure. He believed that although San Martín, liberator of the Argentine, had demonstrated unquestionable military genius, he had lacked Washington's power to gather people behind him and achieve that unity and order "without which the liberty of the United States would have been of so little worth." These were minor points, however. In general, he stressed the similarities between the people of North and South America more than their differences.[27]

The factors that explain Roosevelt's popularity in Latin America are diverse. But it can be stated with certainty that, despite his direct methods of thought and action, he exhibited gentleness, tact, and a powerful regard for Latin *amour-propre*. Nowhere is this better illustrated than in his instructions to Secretary of State Hay on American participation in the International Conference of American States to be held in the fall of 1901.

It is not . . . opportune for the delegates of the United States to assume the part of leadership in the Conference, either in its official organization or in its discussions—a position which naturally belongs to Mexico, the inviting nation and host of the occasion. It is desirable that the plans and propositions of the Latin-American states should be solicited, received with consideration, and if possible brought to fruition, if this can be done in consonance with our national interests and without offense to other powers. Great care should be taken not to wound the sensibilities of any of the republics, or to take sides upon issues between them, but to treat them with frankness, equity, and generosity and to disabuse their minds of any false impressions, if such exist, regarding the attitude and purposes of the United States.

Nothing, Roosevelt continued, could be "of greater importance, from a political point of view, than that the United States should be understood to be the friend of all the Latin-American republics" and "support only such measures as have the weight of general acceptance." Peru and Chile, for example, should not be pressured into an arbitration of their border dispute, no matter how much we might favor it. The American preference might be made known in this regard; but nothing should be decided without the full consent of the parties involved. On commercial matters, the American delegates were to "avoid even the semblance of an attempt to obtain unfair advantage for ourselves. The true interest of our people, it is being more and more generally admitted, lies in helping the Latin-American countries with our more advanced industries . . . and not in seeking to aggrandize ourselves at their expense."[28]

With regard to a court for Central America on the order of the Hague, Roosevelt thought it better to establish a special arbitral tribunal with modifications appropriate for the area. He warned Hay against calling such an agency a Court of Claims, since certain domestic courts went by this name and the name, as applied internationally, might "easily give rise to misapprehension." A better designation, he suggested, would be the Tribunal of International Equity. He felt, too, that "projects upon this subject should come from the other American states," for we must "be most careful of their autonomy." Above all, the American delegates were to "cultivate a sympathetic spirit" so as to "remove any prejudices that may exist against us as a people." They should not fail to convey to the president and government of Mexico "the pleasure felt by this Government in accepting the hospitality generously extended to the representatives of the United States, and the gratification afforded by the relations of amity and cordial intercourse now existing between the two republics."[29]

Similar sensitivity caused him to fear a senate amendment to the treaty with Santo Domingo which would require American extraterritorial control and thus place that country in the same category as China, Turkey, and Morocco. Likewise, when he intervened in partnership with Mexico to restore peace between the Central American states in 1906 and 1907, he wanted to "have it appear as if we were backing up Mexico rather than taking the initiative and being backed up by Mexico," even though the initiative had come from him and a peace treaty was signed aboard the U.S.S. *Marblehead.*[30]

In 1906, when American troops returned to Cuba at the request of both sides in the civil war, Roosevelt reminded Foreign Minister Quesada of his "affectionate admiration and regard" for the "beautiful Queen of the Antilles" as well as his pride in having been the one to withdraw American troops a short time earlier. He also dispatched William Howard Taft and Robert Bacon with orders to effect a settlement between the native factions at any cost. Although the mission failed, thousands of grateful natives lined the Havana shoreline to see Taft and Bacon off, pressing every available boat into festive escort service. Subsequently, the provisional American governor received orders from Roosevelt to fly the Cuban flag, avoid the word "intervention," issue a minimum of proclamations, and be "as gentle as possible." Cuba was permitted to maintain the outward appearance of diplomatic relations, including an exchange of ministers with the United States. At the same time, American soldiers were confined to a few inconspicuous stations and kept out of Havana altogether, as there was no wish to appear to be taking over the island. Violence gave way to peace as the weeks passed, and Roosevelt's forces returned home without causing the slightest damage to life or property.[31]

The president also knew how to be generous. When a dispute arose in the Canal Zone over ports of entry, customs houses, tariffs, and post offices, the Panamanians received less than they hoped for but more than they expected. In addition, the man who negotiated the settlement, Mr. Taft again, was heartily cheered whenever he spoke. The self-same spirit prompted T.R. to break pan-American precedents and transform international law by referring a dispute with Mexico to the Hague Court of Arbitration.[32] There is the fact that he fought long and hard to secure reciprocal trade privileges for Cuba. He became the champion of Latin countries at the second Hague Peace Conference, securing them invitations and mounting an effective campaign for approval of the Drago Doctrine. This, too, was a significant gain for Latin governments, even though they balked at compulsory arbitration and would have preferred the principle of absolute nonintervention.

Finally, Roosevelt would have been the first to admit that he had been fortunate in his choice of Elihu Root for secretary of state. Son of a college professor, Root understood the Latin people and acted as their spokesman on a wide range of issues. He felt strongly, as he once told Senator Tillman, that the best way to secure their friendship "is by treating them like gentlemen. . . . I really like them and intend to show it." And show it he did, by appearing at diplomatic receptions never before attended by an American secretary, socializing with the Brazilian minister and his wife, and insisting that his own wife and daughter accompany him on trips to Latin America. When the popular Enrique Creel resigned as Mexican minister to the United States, Root's wife wrote Mrs. Creel a personal note. It was Root who decided that the United States should send a minister to each of the Central American countries instead of relying on two envoys with responsibility for the whole area (Brazil and the United States raised their respective legations to embassies in 1905). Root engineered the judicial machinery for Central America whereby each government agreed not to grant asylum to revolutionary leaders or recognize any regime which had not won a popular mandate based on the principle of free elections. It was also Root who prevailed upon Andrew Carnegie to donate land for the construction of the majestic Pan-American Building in Washington—an edifice which still stands as an enduring symbol of his unbending effort to strengthen hemispheric cooperation.[33]

To suggest reasons for Roosevelt's rapport with Latin America is not, of course, to account for the respect he enjoyed elsewhere. Of all American presidents, he was undoubtedly the most internationally popular, and any explanation of his broad appeal would have to include a variety of other factors, such as his reputation for wielding every power at his command. The king of Denmark considered him more powerful than a monarch, as indeed he was. He refused to summon Congress "Buchanan-like" at every minor crisis; he flew directly in the face of recalcitrant lawmakers in the case of both the world cruise and the Dominican customs receivership, and he outflanked the legislature by means of executive agreements and secret understandings, as witness the Taft-Katsura Memorandum. When obliged to reject overtures for a share in the Anglo-Japanese alliance, he characteristically volunteered parallel action wherever possible.[34] This was a president who made it clear by word and deed that he considered national honor a fighting matter rather than something to be conveniently shelved or entrusted to the care of professional arbitrators. For the first time in American history, international prestige became a sticking point, with Roosevelt showing as much concern for the rank of an American naval officer representing his country abroad as for avoiding the impression of national "infirmity" in the building of a navy. The collapse of American railway construction in China, described by Ambassador Rockhill as the worst blow to American prestige ever suffered in China, was especially mortifying to Roosevelt, believing as he did that Hay could have moved earlier to prevail upon the American company to do its proper job and China to back it.[35] All of which was consistent with the firm stand he had taken on such questions as the Alaskan boundary and the Panama Canal. If he appeared to be something of a *caudillo* in the eyes of his fellow presidents to the south, the impression was fully justified.

Still another factor in America's rising influence was the phenomenal growth of the fleet from the rank of fifth in the world (1901) to a position second only to Britain (1909). If Roosevelt had been asked to prescribe a formula for success in foreign relations, he would have enjoined upright conduct and an unremitting effort on behalf of world peace; but he would have insisted equally on the need for power, since he was absolutely convinced that nations "despise weakness even more than they prize justice." Without strength and a well-advertised readiness to use it, there would be no respect; and without respect, there would be no peace. This was one of the reasons why he believed that British indecision in Egypt and South Africa would prove ruinous in the long run, and why he moved vigorously in the opening phase of his own presidency to vindicate American interests in Panama, Alaska, and Venezuela.[36] Tested by Germany and England, he demonstrated within two short years that he lacked nothing in the way of nerve or finesse. Even in private life, he acted on the theory that if one wanted to remain morally upright and still command respect, one must remain strong. At Harvard, he caught the attention of his peers by challenging the lightweight boxing champion, just as in Albany he countered the common reference to himself as a city "dude" by flooring a fellow assemblyman in a tavern brawl. Both times, he acted on the assumption that respect was denied to the weak more quickly than it was withheld from the strong, and that the display of power would alone permit him to practice a superior brand of ethics. Once this principle had been established on the individual level, it required little imagination to apply it to nations.[37]

Added to his insistence on power and prestige, and fully as important in explaining his success as an international peacemaker, was his ability to appreciate diverse points of view without sacrificing patriotism or principles. Because he believed that "two nations with violently conflicting interests" might "each be entirely right from its standpoint," he could not make the kind of snap judgment on the Boxer affair that Mark Twain and Edwin L. Godkin had made. During the Boer War, he read accounts from observers on both sides, and although he favored the English, it was not because he felt they had a better case in equity, but rather because their triumph would better serve the long-range interests of all parties concerned, as of humanity in general. His capacity to identify with the aspirations of Japan and Latin America is of a single piece with his tolerance for Canadian bumptiousness: "In Canada they are now much as we were fifty years ago; they pull the tail feathers out of the eagle in a way that gives me an admiring remembrance of the old days when our people, and especially the Irish-Americans, used to work themselves into a fine frenzy twisting the lion's tail." The Canadian parliament was spending so much time berating American foreign policy and pointing out the defects of the American character that Sir Edward Grey rose in London to offer an apology. He need not have done so, though, for Roosevelt responded, very simply and from the heart, that "the Canadians are our own brothers! That is just exactly what Congress would have done if the British Prime Minister, or some prince of the blood royal, happened to come over here. It is a sure proof of the kinship of the two peoples."[38]

If we stop to examine Roosevelt's view of imperialism and democracy we discover still another sample of generous and cosmopolitan thought. To be sure, he held imperialism to be a temporary phase in the march of civilization, one which had lost its relevance for such places as Ireland and South Africa. He favored it, nonetheless, in areas like the Sudan, where a British withdrawal had led to the slaughter of two-thirds of the native population. Some parts of eastern Europe seemed to him ripe for independence, but he felt that Turkestan continued to benefit from Russian rule, and he would gladly have seen Bosnia and Herzegovina under Austria-Hungary. In the same way, though he tended to be

optimistic about the benefits of imperialism for the occu-
pying power, he regarded this as a function of time and
place. To the humorist Peter Finley Dunne ("Mr. Dooley"),
he once remarked: "As you know, I am an Expansionist, but
your delicious phrase about 'take up the white man's burden
and put it on the coon' exactly hit off the weak spot in my
own theory—though, mind you, I am by no means willing to
give up the theory yet." On the domestic front, he accepted
democracy as the finest form of government for the United
States. Still, there were some people who required a dictator, some who flourished better under a king, still
others whose brightest future lay in temporary submission
to the rule of an outside power. Democracy, he never tired of
saying, required a relatively high level of education, a certain popular spirit, and, in the case of the United States,
centuries of experience. It was unsuited to Turkey, and it
had positively ruined Haiti. It could not be taken by France
in the same dosage as England, nor was there the slightest
chance of its developing in China as it had in the West.
Even in America, 51 percent of the people might be the
voice of God in a majority of cases, but in the rest it was
"quite as likely to be the voice of the devil, or, what is still
worse, the voice of a fool."[39]

T.R.'s independence of mind should not come as any
surprise to those familiar with his lifelong tendency to shun
party loyalty. He remained a Republican for most of his life,
but nothing had been harder for him in 1884 than to back
the regular GOP candidate for president when he much preferred to support Senator Edmunds of Vermont. Shortly
thereafter, he again showed his true colors by serving in a
bipartisan capacity as police commissioner of New York and
United States civil service commissioner. In the executive
office, he was known to support such progressive Demo-
crats as Joseph Folk of Missouri and Tom Johnson of Cleveland. And four years after leaving the White House, he led
one of the most dramatic bolts of American political history.
Opinionated as he was, it is surprising how consistently he
recognized good qualities in members of the opposite camp.
He remained on close terms with Grover Cleveland and

found praise for such rivals as Boss Platt, Nelson Aldrich, and Mark Hanna.[40] Nor does the parallel between domestic and foreign policy end here.

The same mentality which won him an invitation to act as mediator between many different countries prompted him to step into the anthracite coal strike at home and become the first president to mediate a labor-management dispute. The same balance which produced mixed views on imperialism and democracy produced a position on domestic issues that again sought to reconcile extremes. While he believed that large corporations might be a cancer on the economy, he considered most of them benign. Railroads should be brought under federal control, but one had to remember that they could not pay proper wages or render good service unless they made money. Labor unions were needed to counterbalance the power of organized capital. At the same time, they must not be permitted to do so at the cost of law and order. In short, he had "an almost Greek horror of extremes" and knew "plenty of honest fanatics on each side."[41]

His professional writing reflects a similar sense of balance. He went beyond the call of duty to write the life of Oliver Cromwell, an Englishman, and he penned an account of the War of 1812 so scrupulously fair to the enemy that he was invited to contribute to a British history of the Royal Navy. Some years later, he found it necessary, in biographies of Thomas Hart Benton and Gouverneur Morris, to condemn the former individual for "ignorant pride in and love of country" while commending the latter for not allowing himself to "intrude his national prejudices" on France as the American minister.[42] We are made to see the courage and brilliance of Morris as a youth without glossing over his debauchery or missing the eccentric reaction which gripped him in old age. Cromwell, for whom Roosevelt had great respect, comes across to us as impatient, censorious, and, above all, self-righteous. It is interesting, too, that of the three subjects whose lives he chose to sketch, one was a Jacksonian Democrat, one an arch-Federalist, the third a foreigner. Herein lies the charm of his work. His *Winning of the West* is brought to life by the heroic pioneer, who lacks even a rudimentary respect for private property, and the narrow, gloomy Presbyterian preacher, who represents a definite force for good.[43]

Naturally, there were limits to Roosevelt's equanimity, and it evaporated altogether in a fight. During World War I, he subscribed to the whole range of anti-German sentiment that swept the country, labeling his former friend the kaiser "one of the leading conspirators" and joining a call for elimination of the German language from classroom study. Wherever he perceived an issue to be one of morality—and patriotism fell distinctly in this category—he was apt to become unyielding. Thus, he branded Jefferson Davis "an unhung traitor," Eugene Hale a "physical coward" for his vote against defense spending, and Thomas Paine a "filthy little atheist." He reserved some of his choicest epithets for Woodrow Wilson, who reminded him by turns of "an apothecary clerk" and an "early Victorian maiden aunt." As for Wilson's peace plan, it appeared to invite the country to "float to heaven on one wide slushy sea of universal mush."[44]

One can also detect a strain of chauvinism in his ceaseless insistence on "one hundred percent Americanism." He castigated parents who sent their children abroad for an education, and he scorned the expatriate writer as a man of "delicate effeminate sensitiveness" who "finds that he cannot play a man's part among men, and so goes where he will be sheltered from the winds that harden stouter souls." Such cosmopolitanism was of the "milk-and-water" variety, for a person of this type did not really become a European; he merely ceased being an American and became nothing. Roosevelt also believed, in good Jacksonian fashion, that great wealth and a high level of education tended to subvert one's love of country. As evidence he pointed to the "northeastern provincial spirit of admiration for things foreign."[45]

Beyond this, however, he did not go. He was far more in character when seeking to broaden national horizons, as when he insisted that it was "mere folly to refuse to profit by whatever is good in the examples of Manchester and Berlin because these cities are foreign, exactly as it is mere folly blindly to copy their examples without reference to our own totally different conditions." His reaction to reports of sexual misconduct on the part of Japanese residents in California could not have been more instructive: "Every nation is always peculiarly susceptible to horror over forms of wickedness which it, tho equally wicked, happens not to possess." In the same manner, he frowned upon self-proclaimed patriots who liked to denounce civil service reform as "Chinese" simply because written examinations had been used in China: it would have been "quite as wise," in his opinion, "to declaim against gunpowder because it was first utilized by the same people." Generally, he was delighted to find "less of this parochial spirit than there was formerly."[46]

One cannot help wondering what could possibly account for Roosevelt's ability to reach across such a broad spectrum of ideas and culture. Was it, perhaps, the presence of two highly disparate points of view within his own family? On his mother's side were relatives who had fought gallantly in the front ranks of the Confederacy, while his father worked just as closely with Lincoln. As a child, he had thrilled to firsthand war stories told him by Uncle James Dunwoodie Bulloch, head of the Confederate shipbuilding mission to England. According to the *Autobiography:*

My mother's two brothers, James Dunwoodie Bulloch and Irvine Bulloch, came to visit us shortly after the close of the war. Both came under assumed names, as they were among the Confederates who were at that time exempted from the amnesty. "Uncle Jimmy" Bulloch was a dear old retired sea-captain, utterly unable to "get on" in the worldly sense of that phrase, as valiant and simple and upright a soul as ever lived, a veritable Colonel Newcome. He was an Admiral in the Confederate navy, and was the builder of the famous Confederate war vessel *Alabama.* My uncle Irvine Bulloch was a midshipman on the *Alabama,* and fired the last gun discharged from her batteries in the fight with the *Kearsarge.* Both of these uncles lived in Liverpool after the war.[47]

Roosevelt's wide-open mind may also have owed something to an extraordinary range of friends and interests. Although he did not come to the White House, as some of his predecessors did, with ambassadorial experience, his exposure to faraway places began early and must have made a deep imprint upon his youthful mind. At the age of fourteen he had traveled through Palestine on horseback and shot game birds along the Nile. Repeated and extended travel afforded him the opportunity to live with a German family and study under foreign tutelage. In addition, two lengthy honeymoons drew him back to Europe and reintroduced him to a favorite aunt and uncle (the Bullochs) who made their home in Liverpool. It was in London that he married Edith Carow—London, too, where he enjoyed a wide circle of socially prominent friends. This in itself was something few other American presidents could claim. He was the only chief executive to select a foreigner as his best man, the only one to count among his personal friends the diplomats of other nations, and the only one to have a son enlisted in the armed service of another government. Appropriately enough, he also became the first president to leave the country while in office, and he would most likely have led the American delegation to the second Hague Peace Conference if tradition had permitted.[48]

A multiplicity of interests gave him something in common with nearly everyone. If the person spoke German, French, or English, T.R. could discourse with him on most phases of world history, to say nothing of ornithology, natural science, art, sport, politics, and ancient, medieval, or modern literature. His scholarly contributions to journals of science while president were taken as a matter of course; he was internationally recognized as an expert on certain species of deer and bear; and the list of reading which he devoured in his first two years as president would redound to the credit of any university professor then or now.[49] It was as easy for him to scan the pages of *Anna Karenina* while floating down the ice-choked Little Missouri River in pursuit of outlaws as it was for him to bury himself in Thucydides during the roar of the 1900 Republican nominating convention. Never at a loss for words, he could regale his hosts in Cairo by recalling passages from Ibn Batuta, the Marco Polo of Islam, or create a sensation in Budapest by displaying his knowledge of the Arpád Dynasty and the Golden Bull. Both Jules Jusserand and Baron Kaneko of Japan gave him books about their respective countries, which he read, as well as suggestions for further study, which he followed. Indeed, he became so absorbed in the French epic, *Chanson de Roland*, that his mastery of its detail quickly exceeded that of the scholarly Jusserand. It was said of him that he could give points on historical synchronism to the great Macaulay. And his literary output, in excess of thirty volumes, led to his election as president of the American Historical Association.[50]

Close friends he did not have in large number, for he was totally devoted to his public career, family, and hobbies.[51] Henry Adams correctly referred to him as "pure act," and the little spare time that remained went into an ambitious regimen of reading, writing, and exercise. To the degree, though, that he did cultivate friendship, he was apt to seek out foreigners. As civil service commissioner in Washington, he often dined at the British legation and regularly found English partners for tennis and rowing. He entertained the British ambassador and his wife on more than one occasion and considered himself "quite devoted" to them. Spring Rice, who became his best man as well as a trusted lifelong correspondent, was a young member of this very embassy. Other friends among the British, as we have already seen, included Lord Bryce, whose classic, *The American Commonwealth*, he read in manuscript form; Arthur Balfour, who visited Oyster Bay in 1917 and was said to have come away completely refreshed; the historian George Otto Trevelyan, to whom T.R. wrote a famous fifty-page letter; Arthur Lee, known in parliament as "the member for America"; and John St. Loe Strachey. He remained on familiar terms with Rudyard Kipling, King Edward, and Sir Edward Grey. Even Lord Lansdowne found him "a very attractive personality," albeit "awkward to handle in certain contingencies." In sum, one might say that he was as much appreciated in Britain as he was in America. It was there

that he received the greatest acclaim after each of his trips
into the wilderness (Africa and Brazil), and there also that
he was accorded the honor of a memorial service in West-
minster Abbey on the occasion of his death in 1919.[52]

Outside the Anglo-Saxon circle, but just as high in his
estimation, stood the French and German ambassadors,
Jusserand and Sternburg. With the former he hiked, played
tennis, and discussed history and literature. Specky became
his frequent riding companion. And he looked to both men
for advice on foreign affairs, particularly to Jusserand.[53]
Here again, he appears unique among the presidents. John
Quincy Adams may have strolled the banks of the Neva
River beside Czar Alexander, but his friendships were
generally of the domestic variety, as was his preference for
the turkey over the eagle as the national bird.[54]

Actually, the comparison between Roosevelt and
Adams is most revealing for what the two men had in common. Both came to power with an impressive set of cosmopolitan credentials; both were ideologically flexible. Both of
them presided over a phase of Anglo-American rapprochement, and they both advanced the national interest in
dramatic fashion, Adams laying claim to the Pacific coast
by treaty with Spain, Roosevelt fusing east and west by
means of an isthmian canal. Each, in his own way, propelled
the nation far into the stream of world politics, as far as its
position at the time would allow. And each man attained
peace from a position of strength, thereby enhancing the
image of the United States in the eyes of the world.

One major difference lies in the degree of international
influence they enjoyed. Adams could never have been as
popular as Roosevelt, apart from any factor of personality,
because the country in 1823 was still relatively weak, a
republic in the midst of hostile monarchs. Roosevelt took
office at a time when the democratic cause seemed about to
control the destiny of the world—one reason, possibly, why
he sought to abandon the isolationist tradition so eloquently defended by Adams. Above all, however, Roosevelt
stands in a class by himself for that blend of statesmanlike

qualities which might best be described as velvet on iron. In this respect, no other occupant of the White House to date, not even an Adams, can quite come even.

Notes

1. Sir Edward Grey to Arthur Lee, 24 October 1906, Arthur H. Lee, ed., *Letters That Remain (Friendly and Otherwise) From the Postbag of Arthur and Ruth Lee, 1891-1941,* p. 188; Roosevelt to Arthur Lee, 21 September 1905, Arthur H. Lee Papers, Courtauld Institute, Portman Square, London; J. Colwell to Secretary of the Navy, 11 November 1902, Naval Records Collection of the Office of Naval Records and Library, Microfilm 625, Reel 393, frames 48-49, National Archives; George von Lengerke Meyer to Roosevelt, 20 January and 5 March 1905; Meyer to his wife, 16 January 1907; Mark A. DeWolfe Howe, *George von Lengerke Meyer, His Life and Public Services,* pp. 113, 127, 328; William R. Braisted, *The United States Navy in the Pacific, 1897-1909,* p. 183; Howard K. Beale, *Theodore Roosevelt and the Rise of America to World Power,* pp. 156-58; Raymond A. Esthus, *Theodore Roosevelt and Japan,* preface, pp. 298-99. In Japan, Roosevelt was said to be greater than Lincoln or Grant; in Italy, he was ranked on a par with Washington; and the Dutch were said to be more interested in him than in anyone except their own queen; *Review of Reviews* 27 (April 1903): 387; Louis E. Van Norman, "President Roosevelt as Europe Sees Him," ibid. 30 (September 1904): 299-305; 30 (November 1904): 505; 31 (February 1905): 238; 31 (March 1905): 344-45; 33 (May 1906): 634.

2. Holstein to Bülow, 17 January 1904 and 3 September 1908, Holstein, *Holstein Papers,* 4:278, 560-61; Bülow to Baron von Schoen [German minister to Denmark], 13 November 1903; Bülow to Count von Metternich, 21 December 1903, Bernhard von Bülow, *Letters of Prince von Bülow,* pp. 19, 21 (see also pp. 25, 38, 40); Beale, *Roosevelt,* pp. 159-60; Sir Sidney Lee, *King Edward VII,* 2 vols., 2:438; Kaiser Wilhelm to Czar Nicholas, 3 May 1905, Wilhelm II, *Letters from the Kaiser to the Czar,* pp. 183-90.

3. Metternich to Bülow, 4 February 1903, *Grosse Politik,* 17:289; Bülow to Kaiser Wilhelm, 4 April 1905; Wilhelm to Bülow, 4 April 1905 and 30 December 1907, Bülow, *Letters,* pp. 121, 228; Holstein to Bülow, 17 January 1904, Holstein, *Holstein Papers,* 4:278; Lee, *Edward VII,* 2:438.

4. Bernhard von Bülow, *Memoirs of Prince von Bülow*, 1:688; Metternich to Foreign Office, 30 January 1903, *Grosse Politik*, 17:284; Holstein to Hugo von Radolin, 31 January 1906, Holstein, *Holstein Papers*, 4:391. Arthur Lee was thought to have affected a kind of bluff heartiness originating from his company with T.R., Alan Clark, ed., *'A Good Innings': The Private Papers of Viscount Lee of Fareham*, p. 7.

5. Roosevelt to Henry Cabot Lodge, 20 August 1886; Roosevelt to William Archer, 31 August 1899 ("I wish them well where they do not conflict with the English-speaking peoples"); Roosevelt to Hay, 18 January and 15 February 1902; Roosevelt to George Otto Trevelyan, 1 October 1911, *Letters*, 1:109; 2:1064; 3:219, 230; 7:391. Wilhelm's mother was so English that, according to Bülow, she asked that when she died her body be wrapped in a British flag and sent for burial to England. Bülow, *Memoirs*, 1:614-15. Sternburg not only had an English mother, he was married to an American, like so many other "foreign" friends of T.R., including Jusserand, Kipling, Lee, and Curzon.

6. Roosevelt to Spring Rice, 13 August 1897; Roosevelt to Trevelyan, 1 October 1911, *Letters*, 1:646; 7:395; Lee, *Edward VII*, 2:119; Howe, *Meyer*, p. 383; Beale, *Roosevelt*, pp. 442-44; Bülow, *Memoirs*, 1:658-60. The kaiser's letters to the czar have been published. Those to T.R. have not.

7. Lawrence F. Abbott, *Impressions of Theodore Roosevelt*, p. 230; Isaac F. Marcosson, *Adventures in Interviewing*, p. 93.

8. General Horace Porter [American ambassador to France] to Secretary of State, 6 July 1905, *Foreign Relations* (1905), pp. 440, 442; Abbott, *Impressions*, pp. 162-66.

9. Abbott, *Impressions*, pp. 148-57; Arthur H. Lee, *A Good Innings and a Great Partnership, Being the Life Story of Arthur and Ruth Lee*, 1:424-25.

10. Abbott, *Impressions*, pp. 157-62. The king and Grey actually urged T.R. to speak as he did. Every word of the address was carefully weighed in the presence of Arthur Lee and Spring Rice. Asquith Morley later objected. But this had been foreseen. Letters of appreciation came from Kitchener, Beresford, Wingate, and Kipling. Roosevelt to David Gray, 5 October 1911, *Letters*, 7:401-404.

11. Lee, *Good Innings*, 1:425.

12. Clark, ed., *'Good Innings'*, pp. 108-109; Lee, *Good Innings*, 1:418-21, 427; James Garvin to Arthur Lee, 6 October

1910; Lee, ed., *Letters That Remain*, p. 146. The Curzons also wanted to entertain T.R., but they were unable to prevail upon Lee to give up his precious guest.

13. Liang to the Chinese Foreign Minister, quoted in Michael H. Hunt, *Frontier Defense and the Open Door*, p. 128; Beale, *Roosevelt*, p. 181.

14. Roosevelt's Annual Message to Congress, December 1906, *Foreign Relations* (1906), pt. 1, xlii; Roosevelt to Lodge, 15 June 1903, *Roosevelt-Lodge Correspondence*, 2:29; Roosevelt to Meyer, 26 December 1904; Roosevelt to Spring Rice, 27 December 1904; Roosevelt to David B. Schneder, 19 June 1905, *Letters*, 4:1078, 1087, 1240; Amy Simpson Strachey, *St. Loe Strachey: His Life and His Paper*, pp. 181–82; Roosevelt, *The Writings of Theodore Roosevelt*, ed. William H. Harbaugh, p. xxxviii; Esthus, *Roosevelt and Japan*, preface, pp. 41, 101; Beale, *Roosevelt*, pp. 266–69; Edward C. Wagenknecht, *The Seven Worlds of Theodore Roosevelt*, p. 237; Thomas A. Bailey, *Theodore Roosevelt and the Japanese-American Crises*, pp. 90, 95. Kaneko was a former cabinet minister, professor of law at Tokyo University, a graduate of Harvard Law School, and a special envoy of Japan to the United States. Count Itō was one of the four elder statesmen (genro) of Japan. He had served as consul general of Korea and founded the Sei-yu-kai (Model Party) in 1903 to convert the Japanese House of Representatives to western ideas of party vs. clan organization. His success is reflected in the fact that by 1906 the Sei-yu-kai controlled 130 votes in the lower house out of a total of 300. See also Roosevelt to Robert Grant, 14 March 1905, Theodore Roosevelt Collection, Houghton Library, Harvard University.

15. Esthus, *Roosevelt and Japan*, pp. 96, 298–300.

16. For a sampling of Latin American editorial opinion critical of the Monroe Doctrine (mostly opposition newspapers), see *Foreign Relations* (1903), pp. 24–27. For Root's sense of Latin hostility, see Philip C. Jessup, *Elihu Root*, 1:469, 483. For other indications of the same, see ibid., 1:500–501; *Review of Reviews* 31 (April 1905): 399; Gerard Lowther to Lansdowne, 29 May 1904, FO 115/1308, PRO; Reginald Tower to Sir Edward Grey, 6 September 1906, FO 115/1393, PRO.

17. Wilfrid H. Callcott, *The Caribbean Policy of the United States, 1890–1920*, p. 161; G. Wallace Chessman, *Theodore Roosevelt and the Politics of Power*, p. 97; Charles W. Toth, "Elihu

Root," in Norman Graebner, ed., *An Uncertain Tradition: American Secretaries of State in the Twentieth Century*, p. 45; Henry Pringle, *Theodore Roosevelt*, p. 211.

18. Lionel Carden to F. H. Villiers, 2 April 1902, FO 5/2496, PRO; Gerard Lowther to Lord Lansdowne, Santiago, Chile, 23 November 1903, FO 115/1306, PRO; Dexter Perkins, *A History of the Monroe Doctrine*, p. 246; *Review of Reviews* 29 (February 1904): 247; Paul Holbo, "Perilous Obscurity: Public Diplomacy and the Press in the Venezuela Crisis, 1902-1903," *The Historian* 32 (May 1970): 440, 440 n.; John Patterson, "Latin-American Reactions to the Panama Revolution of 1903," *Hispanic American Historical Review* 24 (May 1944): 342-51. Patterson has been too often ignored in recent appraisals of Roosevelt. His article is exceedingly important for its research in Latin sources. It shows that only Ecuador and a few clerical groups in Mexico withheld support from American policy. To this should be added Bemis's opinion that Roosevelt's Dominican receivership did not awaken "any appreciable resentment or distrust" in Latin America, and that Yankeephobia was something which "flamed up later." Samuel Flagg Bemis, *The Latin-American Policy of the United States*, p. 158.

19. C. Mallett to Lansdowne, 26 December 1904, FO 115/1350, PRO; Jessup, *Elihu Root*, 1:518-22; Callcott, *Caribbean Policy*, p. 241. The Colombian foreign minister wrote Root in 1907: "I have great pleasure to express my satisfaction at the course you consider acceptable for the United States to follow in the matter of the relations between my country, the United States, and Panama. Your proposed letter to Mr. Obaldia is a fair and unbiased exposition of the question at issue, doing honor to the government of the United States." Quoted in *Senate Documents*, 63rd Cong., 2nd sess. (December 1913-24 October 1914), p. 151. In the proposed treaty of 1909 between Panama and Colombia, Panama agreed to transfer to Colombia the first ten United States payments of $250,000 each as its unpaid share of the old Colombian debt. There was also an agreement to submit a boundary dispute to arbitration. Jessup, *Elihu Root*, 1:527.

20. Roosevelt to Rafael Reyes, 20 February 1905, *Letters*, 4:1124; Richard D. Challener, *Admirals, Generals, and American Foreign Policy, 1898-1914*, p. 119; Embert Hendrickson, "Root's Watchful Waiting in the Venezuelan Controversy," *The Americas* 23 (October 1966): 115-29.

21. *Review of Reviews* 34 (November 1906): 529; Toth,

"Root," in Graebner, ed., *Uncertain Tradition,* p. 46; Elihu Root, *Speeches Incident to the Visit of Secretary Root to South America, July 4 to September 30, 1906,* pp. 12–13; Jessup, *Elihu Root,* 1:478–83, 485. In Root's words: "We really did have a wonderful journey, quite beyond belief. All South America went wild." Ibid., 1:489. According to the British ambassador in Argentina, Root's reception there was incredible; he was cheered every time he appeared in public in coach and four. W. Haggard to Grey, 20 August 1906, FO 115/1393, PRO. The British were equally impressed with the way Root was received in Brazil and seemed to think the United States had come to possess a special "moral authority" in Latin America. Francis Bertie to Grey, 3 October 1906, FO 115/1394, PRO; Foreign Office to Durand, [?] September 1906, FO 115/1393, PRO.

22. *Visita al Peru del Secretario de Estado de los Estados Unidos* (Lima, Peru: 1906), pp. i, 4, 7, 12–14, 16, 23, 26, 31, 36, 40, 54, 76–83, 116, 144, 147–48; C. Mallett to Lansdowne, 4 January 1904, FO 115/1307, PRO; George E. Welby to Lansdowne, 16 January 1905, FO 115/1351, PRO; Toth, "Root," in Graebner, ed., *Uncertain Tradition,* p. 46; Bemis, *Latin-American Policy,* p. 158. For additional Latin references to the Monroe Doctrine, see *Speeches Incident to the Visit of Secretary Root,* pp. 31, 36, 102, 130–31. Root also visited Mexico in 1907 with his wife and daughter and was received very cordially despite recurring reports of anti-American sentiment. Jessup, *Elihu Root,* 1:515–16; Reginald Tower to Grey, 8 and 22 October 1907, FO 414/195, PRO.

23. Robley D. Evans to Secretary of the Navy, 17 January 1908, Admiral Alfred Mahan Papers, Box 6, Library of Congress; Thomas A. Bailey, "The World Cruise of the American Battleship Fleet, 1907–1909," *Pacific Historical Review* 1 (September 1932): 404–405; Robert A. Hart, *The Great White Fleet,* pp. 105, 107, 118, 122, 132, 140–43.

24. *Outlook* 106 (1914): 485–86, 631, 636, 697. The name "Rio Roosevelt" was rejected because of the difficulty it posed for the Spanish style of pronunciation.

25. Ibid., 105 (1913): 837–38; 106: 304, 485–86, 636.

26. Ibid., 106: 183, 409, 411, 476, 632, 710, 802, 919–20; 107 (1914): 255.

27. Ibid., 106: 183, 361–62, 761; 107: 171.

28. Roosevelt's Instructions to Secretary of State Hay, 8 October 1901, *Letters,* 3:164–70.

29. Ibid.

30. Roosevelt to John Coit Spooner, 7 July 1905; Roosevelt to Alvey Adee, 24 August 1907, *Letters,* 4:1263–64; 5:772. See also Dana Munro, *The United States and the Caribbean Area,* chap. 5.

31. Roosevelt to Don Gonzalo de Quesada, 14 September 1906; Roosevelt to Taft, 25 September (two letters), 26 September, 2 and 10 October 1906, *Letters,* 5:412–13, 423–24, 437, 454; Howard C. Hill, *Roosevelt and the Caribbean,* pp. 100–104; David A. Lockmiller, *Magoon in Cuba: A History of the Second Intervention, 1906–1909,* pp. 43–44, 59, 65, 84–85.

32. William D. McCain, *The United States and the Republic of Panama,* p. 45. The treaty, which authorized arbitration of the Pious claims, was signed by the United States and Mexico on 22 May 1902. These claims, on behalf of the Catholic Church of California for trust funds held in Mexico under an old papal ruling, were to go before a panel consisting of two judges appointed by the United States, two by Mexico, and a fifth selected by mutual agreement from the Hague Tribunal list. *New York Tribune,* 23 May 1902.

33. Jessup, *Elihu Root,* 1:469, 516–17. When Root visited Panama, he was greeted as warmly as Taft had been; Consul General Shankin to Acting Secretary of State, 24 September 1906, *Foreign Relations* (1906), pt. 2, p. 1198. For a good description of Root's importance in Latin-American relations, see Roosevelt to Carnegie, 26 February 1909, *Letters,* 6:1539.

34. Roosevelt to Lodge, 27 September 1906, *Roosevelt-Lodge Correspondence,* 2:234; Beale, *Roosevelt,* pp. 156–60; Jean Jules Jusserand, *What Me Befell,* p. 217; Lansdowne to Balfour, 18 January 1905, Item 49729, Arthur James Balfour Papers, British Museum ("I should think Roosevelt would very likely agree that he would cooperate with us in defending Japan against a blow at her vitals"); Roosevelt to Kermit Roosevelt, 23 January 1909, Theodore Roosevelt Collection, Houghton Library, Harvard University; Durand to Lansdowne, 6 February 1905, FO 800/116, PRO ("U.S. Government will not allow understanding with Great Britain to be made too manifest"). One might be inclined to believe that Wilson in 1919 and FDR in 1945 enjoyed international esteem comparable to that of T.R. But Wilson's reputation plummeted within a matter of months, while the second Roosevelt was never as *universally* admired as his Oyster Bay cousin. Take, for example, those groups in Eastern Europe and the Orient who

held him responsible for the triumph of Communism. Nor is this to mention his image in the camp of Japan and the Axis powers.

35. Roosevelt to Joseph G. Cannon, 27 December 1904, *Letters,* 4:1080–81; Beale, *Roosevelt,* p. 210; Alexander E. Campbell, *Great Britain and the United States, 1895–1903,* p. 108. See also Roosevelt's *Autobiography,* p. 270, where he speaks of the "honor of the flag and of the nation." Admiral Evans wore only two stars on the world cruise, and Roosevelt tried in vain to have Congress raise his rank so that he would be equal, in terms of protocol, to his opposite numbers abroad. Hart, *Great White Fleet,* p. 45.

36. Roosevelt to Arthur Lee, 18 March 1901; Roosevelt to William Rockhill, 22 August 1905; Roosevelt to Trevelyan, 1 October 1911, *Letters,* 3:20; 4:1310; 7:352.

37. Abbott, *Impressions,* p. 196.

38. Roosevelt, *Benton,* in *Works,* ed., Hagedorn, 7:35; Warren I. Cohen, *America's Response to China,* p. 74; Roosevelt to Spring Rice, 13 August 1897; Roosevelt to St. Loe Strachey, 27 January 1900; Roosevelt to Frederick Selous, 7 February 1900; Roosevelt to Sternburg, 18 March 1901; Roosevelt to Arthur Lee, 25 September 1911, *Letters,* 1:645; 2:1144, 1176; 3:22; 7:346. T.R. once wrote to his sister Corinne (from his second honeymoon in Italy): "The Italians simply *can't* be as dirty as they would like to be, and as they are everywhere else—I have a nice, charitable feeling towards foreigners, you see; in fact one of my most charming and amiable characteristics is my gentle tolerance of moods of thought and habits of life that differ from my own." 8 February 1887, ibid., 1:121. One has the impression that he trained himself, over the years, to think as impartially as possible. See, for example, Roosevelt to Frederick Oliver, 22 July 1915 ("No nation acts properly all the time"); Roosevelt to William Wingate Sewall, 8 July 1899 ("If I am sure a thing is either right or wrong, why then I know how to act, but lots of times there is a little of both on each side and then it becomes mighty puzzling to know the exact course to follow"); ibid., 2:1031; 8:956. See also Roosevelt, *Cromwell,* in *Works,* ed. Hagedorn, 10:323 ("Mixed with the right there is invariably an element of what is wrong or foolish").

39. Roosevelt to Anna Roosevelt, 8 June 1884; Roosevelt to Peter Finley Dunne, 16 January 1900; Roosevelt to Frederick Oliver, 22 July 1915, *Letters,* 1:71; 2:1134; 8:956; David H. Burton, "Theodore Roosevelt and His English Correspondents: The Intellectual Roots of the Anglo-American Alliance," *Mid-America*

53 (January 1971): 24; Roosevelt, *Gouverneur Morris,* in *Works,*
ed. Hagedorn, 7:322. He demonstrated similar insight on the question of democracy in Germany: "Of course the Kaiser objects to
liberalism in his country. Liberalism has some great vices, and the
virtues which, in our opinion, outweight these vices, might not be
of weight in Germany." Roosevelt to Spring Rice, 13 August
1897, *Letters,* 1:646.

40. See, for example, Roosevelt to Henry White, 17 February
1904, Box 28, Henry White Papers, Library of Congress ("Hanna
was a very strong personality with many large and generous
traits"). Also, Theodore Roosevelt, Jr. to Arthur Lee, 23 July
1923, Arthur H. Lee Papers, Courtauld Institute, Portman
Square, London; Roosevelt, *Autobiography,* pp. 298, 302; Roosevelt to Josephine Shaw Lowell, 20 February 1900; Roosevelt to
Taft, 19 March 1903; Roosevelt to his son Theodore, Jr., 19
February 1904, *Letters,* 2:1193; 3:450; 4:732.

41. Roosevelt, *Autobiography,* p. 539; Roosevelt, *Works,* ed.
Hagedorn, 13:530–35; Roosevelt to St. Loe Strachey, 8 March
1901, 16 September 1904, 4 April 1907, John St. Loe Strachey
Papers, House of Lords Library, London; Roosevelt to Joseph B.
Bishop, 27 May 1903, Roosevelt Collection, Harvard University.
Typical of his approach is the following extract from a speech he
made in Canton, Ohio: "There is only one thing as important as
the discouragement of a feeling of envy and hostility toward
honest businessmen, toward honest men of means; that is, the discouragement of dishonest businessmen." The latter part of the
phrase was enthusiastically applauded, but not the first. So he
continued: "Wait a minute my friends, I don't want you to applaud this part unless you are willing to applaud also the part I
read first to which you listened in silence. . . . I will read a little
of it over again." This he did, with the crowd laughing and
applauding lustily. Jusserand, *What Me Befell,* p. 345.

42. Roosevelt was especially proud of his use of Canadian archives for his interpretation of the War of 1812. Roosevelt to
Charles Anderson Dana, 25 September 1889, *Letters,* 1:190. See
also Roosevelt, *Benton* and *Gouverneur Morris,* both in *Works,* ed.
Hagedorn, 7:13, 27–28, 37, 115–17, 186, 361. In *Gouverneur
Morris,* he not only points out that real good came of the French
Revolution, blood and chaos notwithstanding, but goes on to
berate Morris for allowing Napoleon's autocratic manners to blind
him to the real military genius of the man (pp. 393–94, 431). In his
Winning of the West, he emphasizes that the whites nearly always

outnumbered the Indians in battle and that whenever the two sides were equally armed and equally numerous, the Indians won. He also condemns white borderers as much as Indian renegades in assessing blame for frontier friction.

43. Roosevelt, *The Winning of the West,* in *Works,* ed. Hagedorn, 8:89-90; Roosevelt, *Benton* and *Gouverneur Morris,* in ibid., 7:13-15, 37, 78, 89, 183, 456; Roosevelt, *Cromwell,* in ibid., 10:319.

44. Roosevelt to George Harvey, 19 September 1904; Roosevelt to Arthur Lee, 19 November 1918; Roosevelt to Kipling, 23 November 1918, *Letters,* 4:947; 8:1396, 1406; Roosevelt, *Gouverneur Morris,* in *Works,* ed. Hagedorn, 7:421.

45. Theodore Roosevelt, *American Ideals and Other Essays,* pp. 21, 23, 24-25, 233, 242. He dismissed Henry James as an "undersized man of letters who flees his country," yet it was typical of him to argue the case for progressive income and inheritance taxes by citing the example of Britain, Germany, and France. Annual Address to Congress, *Foreign Relations* (1907), pt. 1, pp. xxi–xxii. See also, Roosevelt to Osborne Howes, 5 May 1892; Roosevelt to David Gray, 5 October 1911, *Letters,* 1:279; 7:406-407.

46. Roosevelt, *American Ideals,* pp. 17, 19; Roosevelt to Arthur Lee, 8 April 1908, Lee Papers, Courtauld Institute, Portman Square, London.

47. Roosevelt, *Autobiography,* pp. 15-16.

48. Kermit was commissioned in the British Air Corps, served in Mesopotamia, and later worked for both the Brazil Railway Company and the Anglo-Brazilian Iron Company. It might be noted that Elihu Root was also the first secretary of state to leave the country. For a description of Roosevelt's days in Dresden and the impressions he gained while there, see the *Autobiography,* pp. 24-26. The aunt and uncle who lived in Liverpool were Hattie and Irvine Bulloch.

49. See Appendix.

50. Abbott, *Impressions,* p. 187; Godfrey Benson, Lord Charnwood, *Theodore Roosevelt,* p. 164; Jusserand, *What Me Befell,* p. 277; Roosevelt to Kaneko, 23 April 1904, *Letters,* 4:777. One representative luncheon at Oyster Bay included the ministers of China and Norway, a sculptor, an author, a secretary of the navy, and two captains of the armed services. Howe, *Meyer,* p. 362.

51. Roosevelt's published letters to his children are wonder-

fully entertaining as well as eloquent testimony to the amount of time he devoted to his family. For a rare glimpse of the feeling he had for his wife, see his letter to Arthur Lee, 26 September 1899: "There is nothing in the world—no possible success, military or political which is worth weighing in the balance for one moment against the happiness that comes to those fortunate enough to make a real love match—a match in which lover and sweetheart will never be lost in husband and wife. I know what I am writing about, for I am just as much devoted to Mrs. Roosevelt now as ever I was." *Letters*, 2:1079.

52. Roosevelt to Lodge, 1 July 1891; Roosevelt to Anna Roosevelt, 31 December 1893, ibid., 1:256, 344; Sir Ian Malcolm, *Lord Balfour, A Memory,* p. 54; Lee, *Good Innings,* 1:523–24; 2:760; Lansdowne to Balfour, 13 January 1905, Item 49729, Balfour Papers, British Museum. One of the wedding gifts which Spring Rice received was a silver tea caddy with the inscription, "From Theodore Roosevelt with Love." Springy named his son Anthony Theodore, and his friendship with T.R. lasted until his death in 1918. One of the things that must have drawn the two together originally was the Englishman's cleverness as a writer of children's animal stories.

53. Jusserand, *What Me Befell,* p. 271.

54. In fairness to Adams, who was by far the most experienced diplomat ever to shape the course of American foreign relations, it must be noted that he began his apprenticeship with two visits to France under the watchful eye of his father. While stranded at Bilbao, he studied Spanish as well as French, then took up the history and language of the Netherlands when his father moved to Holland. Unlike Roosevelt, he enrolled at a foreign university (the university of Leyden). Soon after, at the age of fourteen, he became interpreter to the American envoy at St. Petersburg. En route to and from the Russian capital, he visited Berlin, spent an involuntary six weeks in Stockholm, and returned to the United States with an Italian friend of the family. The list of additional cities on his itinerary included Copenhagen, Kiel (again stranded), Hamburg, Bremen, and London. Most important of all, he served as American minister in four great capitals: the Hague, Berlin, St. Petersburg, and London. Finally, almost as if to make the picture complete, his wife was born and raised in England.

Appendix

IN the following excerpt from a letter to Nicholas Murray
Butler, dated 4 November 1903, Roosevelt lists the private
reading which he did during his first two years in the
White House. Better than anything else, it illustrates the
startling reach of a cosmopolitan mind.

You remember speaking to me about reading and especially
about the kind of books one ought to read. On my way back from
Oyster Bay on Election day I tried to jot down the books I have
been reading for the last two years, and they run as follows. Of
course I have forgotten a great many, especially ephemeral novels
which I have read before. These I did not read through, but simply
took out the parts I liked. Thus, in *Waverley,* I omitted all the
opening part; in *Pickwick* I skipped about, going through all my
favorite scenes. In Macaulay I read simply the essays that appealed to me, while in Keats and Browning, although I read again
and again many of the poems, I think that there must be at least
80 or 90 per cent of the old poetry of each, as far as bulk is concerned, which I have never succeeded in reading at all. The old
books I read were not necessarily my favorites; it was largely a
matter of chance. All the reading, of course, was purely for enjoyment and of most desultory character. With this preliminary explanation, here goes!

Parts of Herodotus; the first and seventh books of Thucydides; all of Polybius; a little of Plutarch; Aeschylus' Orestean
Trilogy; Sophocles' *Seven Against Thebes;* Euripides' *Hippolytus
and Bacchae;* and Aristophanes' *Frogs.* Parts of the *Politics* of
Aristotle; (all of these were in translation); Ridgeway's *Early Age
of Greece;* Wheeler's *Life of Alexander;* and some six volumes of
Mahaffey's *Studies of the Greek World*—of which I only read

chapters here and there; two of Maspero's volumes on the early
Syrian, Chaldean and Egyptian Civilizations—these I read super-
ficially. Several chapters of Froissart. The *Memoirs* of Marbot;
Bain's *Life of Charles the Twelfth;* Mahan's *Types of Naval Officers;* some of Macaulay's *Essays;* three or four volumes of Gibbon
and three or four chapters of Motley. The Life of Prince Eugene, of
Admiral de Ruyter, of Turenne, and of Sobieski (all in French). The
battles in Carlyle's *Frederick the Great;* Hay and Nicolay's *Lincoln,* and the two volumes of Lincoln's *Speeches and Writings*—
these I have not only read through, but have read parts of them
again and again; Bacon's *Essays*—curiously enough, I had never
really read these until this year; Mrs. Roosevelt has a volume
which belonged to her grandfather, which she always carries
around with her, and I got started reading this. *Macbeth; Twelfth
Night; Henry the Fourth; Henry the Fifth; Richard the Second;* the
first two Cantos of *Paradise Lost;* some of Michael Drayton's
Poems—there are only three or four I care for; portions of the
Nibelungenlied; portions of Carlyle's prose translation of Dante's
Inferno; Church's *Beowulf;* Morris' translation of the *Heims-
kringla,* and Dasent's translation of the sagas of Gisli and Burnt
Njal; Lady Gregory's and Miss Hull's *Cuchulain Saga* together
with *The Children of Lir, The Children of Turin,* the *Tale of
Deirdre,* etc.; *Les Précieuses Ridicules, Le Barbier de Séville;* most
of Jusserand's books—of which I was most interested in his
studies of the *Kingis Quhair;* Holmes' *Over the Teacups;* Louns-
bury's *Shakespeare and Voltaire;* various numbers of the *Edinburgh Review* from 1803 to 1850; Tolstoi's *Sebastopol* and *The
Cossacks;* Sienkiewicz's *Fire and Sword,* and parts of his other
volumes; *Guy Mannering; The Antiquary; Rob Roy; Waverley;
Quentin Durward;* parts of *Marmion* and the *Lay of the Last
Minstrel;* Cooper's *Pilot;* some of the earlier stories and some of
the poems of Bret Harte; Mark Twain's *Tom Sawyer; Pickwick
Papers; Nicholas Nickleby; Vanity Fair; Pendennis; The New-
comes; Adventures of Philip;* Conan Doyle's *White Company;*
Lever's *Charles O'Malley; Romances* of Brockden Brown (read
when I was confined to my room with a game leg, from motives of
curiosity and with no real enjoyment). An occasional half hour's
reading in Keats, Browning, Poe, Tennyson, Longfellow, Kipling,
Bliss Carmen; also in Poe's *Tales* and Lowell's *Essays;* some of
Stevenson's stories, and of Allingham's *British Ballads;* Wagner's
Simple Life. I have read aloud to the children, and often finished

afterwards to myself, *The Rose and the Ring;* Hans Andersen; some of Grimm; some Norse Folk Tales; and stories by Howard Pyle; *Uncle Remus* and the rest of Joel Chandler Harris's stories (incidentally, I would be willing to rest all that I have done in the South as regards the negro on his story "Free Joe"); two or three books by Jacob Riis; also Mrs. Van Vorst's *Woman Who Toils,* and one or two similar volumes; the nonsense verses of Carolyn Wells, first to the children, and afterwards for Mrs. Roosevelt and myself; Kenneth Grahame's *Golden Age;* those two delightful books by Somerville and Ross, *All on the Irish Shore* and *Experiences of an Irish M.P.;* Townsend's *Europe and Asia;* Conrad's *Youth; Phoenixiana;* Artemus Ward; Octave Thanet's stories, which I always like, especially when they deal with labor problems; various books on the Boer War, of which I liked best Viljoen's. Stevens', and studies by the writer signing himself Linesman; Pike's *Through the Subarctic Forest,* and Peer's *Cross Country with Horse and Hound,* together with a number of books on big-game hunting, mostly in Africa; several volumes on American outdoor life and natural history, including the rereading of much of John Burroughs; Swettenham's *Real Malay;* David Gray's *Gallops;* Miss Stewart's *Napoleon Jackson;* Janvier's *Passing of Thomas* and other stories; *The Benefactress;* the *People of the Whirlpool;* London's *Call of the Wild;* Fox's *Little Shepherd of Kingdom Come;* Hamlin Garland's *Captain of the Gray-horse Troop;* Tarkington's *Gentleman from Indiana;* Churchill's *Crisis;* Remington's *John Ermine of the Yellowstone;* Wister's *Virginian, Red Men and White, Philosophy Four, Lin McLean;* White's *Blazed Trail, Conjuror's House,* and *Claim Jumpers;* Trevelyan's *American Revolution.* Often I would read one book by chance, and it would suggest another.

There! that is the catalogue; about as interesting as Homer's Catalogue of the Ships, and with about as much method in it as there seems in a superficial glance to be in an Irish stew. The great comfort, old man, is that you need not read it and that you need not answer this! [*Letters,* 3:642–44]

Bibliography

PRIMARY SOURCES

Unpublished Official Records

National Archives, Washington, D.C.

General Records of the Department of the Navy (Record Group 80)
  Confidential Letters Sent
  General Records
    Copies of Letters Sent
    Translations of Ciphers
Naval Records and Library Collection of the Office of Naval Records and Library (Record Group 45)
Records of the Bureau of Naval Personnel (Record Group 24)
Records of the Chief of Naval Operations (Record Group 38)
  General Correspondence, 1903–1913
  Naval Correspondence
  Santo Domingo Correspondence
Records of the Department of State (Record Group 59)
  Confidential Letters Sent
  Despatches from China
  Despatches from the United States Minister to Germany
  Despatches from United States Ministers to Great Britain
  Despatches from United States Ministers to Japan
  Diplomatic Instructions from the Department of State to the United States Embassy in Berlin
  Miscellaneous Letters
  Notes from the German Embassy in the United States to the Department of State

Records of the Foreign Service (Record Group 84)
  Posts of the Department of State
    Records of the United States Embassy in Berlin
    Register of the United States Embassy in Berlin

Public Record Office, London

Admiralty Intelligence (ADM 116)
Cabinet Reports to the Monarch (CAB 41)
Confidential Print: North America (FO 414)
Confidential Print: Northern and Western Europe (FO 425)
Embassy and Consular Archives (FO 115)
General Correspondence: United States before 1906 (FO 5)
General Political Correspondence (FO 371)
General Treaty Correspondence (FO 372)
Guide to FO 5 (FO 566)
List of Confidential Prints, United States of America (FO 881)
Private Collections (FO 800)
Registers of Correspondence, 1823–1878 and 1900–1929 (FO 117)
Reports from Latin America (FO 55)

Auswärtiges Amt, Bonn

Abteilung A—Aktenzeichen Ver. Staaten von Amerika
Beziehungen der Vereinigten Staaten zu Venezeula (# 22)
Die Praesidenten und ihre Botschaften (# 11)
Die Presse Ver. St. (# 2)
Marine Angelegenheiten der Ver. St. (# 5a)
Staatsmaenner (# 6)
Vereinigten Staaten von Nordamerika (# 1)

Zentrales Archiv, Potsdam

Auswärtiges Amt—Abteilung IIS
  Die Bestimmungen über den Aufenthalt deutscher Kriegsschiffe
    in fremden Hafen und umgekehrt
Auswärtiges Amt—Handelspolitische Abteilung
  Fremder Handel
Auswärtiges Amt—Marine Akte, Jan. 1902–Okt. 1904
Auswärtiges Amt—Politische Abteilung
  Geschäftsgang
  Kassensachen
  Militaria

Reichskanzlei, 1900–1918
  Akten betreffend Ver. St. von Amerika
  Auswärtige Angelegenheiten
  Kriegsmarine, 1899–1918

Published Official Records

Lepsius, J.; Mendelssohn, Bartholdy; and Thimme, F., eds. *Die Grosse Politik der Europäischen Kabinette, 1871–1914.* 40 vols. Berlin, 1922–1927.

MacMurray, John V. A., ed. *Treaties and Agreements with and Concerning China, 1874–1919.* 2 vols. London: Oxford Press, 1921.

Miller, David Hunter, ed. *Treaties and Other International Acts of the United States of America.* Washington, D.C.: Government Printing Office, 1937.

Moore, John Bassett, ed. *Digest of International Law.* 8 vols. Washington, D.C.: Government Printing Office, 1906.

U. S. Congress, House of Representatives. *The Story of Panama: Hearings on the Rainey Resolution Before the Committee on Foreign Affairs of the House of Representatives.* Washington, D.C.: Government Printing Office, 1913.

U.S. Congress, Senate. *Diplomatic History of the Panama Canal.* 63rd Cong., 2nd sess., *Senate Documents,* vol. 15. Washington, D.C.: Government Printing Office, 1914.

U. S. Department of State. *Papers Relating to the Foreign Relations of the United States.* Washington, D.C.: Government Printing Office, 1901–1909.

Manuscript Collections

Auswärtiges Amt, Bonn
  Letters from the Kaiser to Theodore Roosevelt
Birmingham University Library, Birmingham, England
  Joseph Chamberlain Papers
Bodleian Library, Oxford University
  James Bryce Papers
  John Satterfield Sanders Papers
British Museum, London
  Arthur James Balfour Papers
Brown University Library, Providence, Rhode Island
  John Hay Miscellaneous Correspondence

Churchill College, Cambridge University
  Cecil Spring Rice Papers
Columbia University Library, New York
  Charlemagne Tower Papers
Connecticut State Library, Hartford
  Orville H. Platt Papers
Cornell University Library, Ithaca, New York
  Willard Straight Papers
Courtauld Institute, London
  Arthur H. Lee Papers
Georgetown University Library, Washington, D.C.
  Tomás Herrán Papers
Houghton Library, Harvard University, Cambridge, Massachu-
    setts
  William Woodville Rockhill Papers
  Theodore Roosevelt Collection
  William Roscoe Thayer Collection
House of Lords Library, London
  John St. Loe Strachey Papers
Library of Congress, Washington, D.C.
  Bunau-Varilla Papers
  Joseph Choate Papers
  George Dewey Papers
  Lloyd Griscom Papers
  John Hay Papers
  Stephen B. Luce Papers
  Admiral Alfred Mahan Papers
  George von Lengerke Meyer Diaries
  William Henry Moody Papers
  Horace Porter Papers
  Whitelaw Reid Papers
  George C. Remey Papers
  Theodore Roosevelt Papers and Diaries
  Elihu Root Papers
  George Smalley Papers
  Rear Admiral Charles S. Sperry Papers
  Cecil Spring Rice Correspondence with Theodore Roosevelt
  Oscar Straus Papers
  William Howard Taft Papers
  Henry Clay Taylor Papers
  Henry White Papers

General James H. Wilson Papers
Leonard Wood Papers
Massachusetts Historical Society, Boston
　　Adams Family Papers
　　Henry Cabot Lodge Papers
　　George von Lengerke Meyer Papers
Public Archives of Canada, Ottawa
　　Wilfrid Laurier Papers
　　Lord Minto Papers
　　Joseph Pope Papers
　　Clifford Sifton Papers
Public Record Office, London
　　Edward Grey Papers
　　Lord Lansdowne Papers
Royal Archives, Windsor Castle Library, Windsor
　　Personal Papers of Edward VII
Whittinghame, Scotland (via National Register of Archives, Edinburgh)
　　Arthur James Balfour Papers

Collected Works

Adams, Henry. *The Letters of Henry Adams, 1892-1918.* Edited by Worthington C. Ford. 2 vols. Boston: Houghton Mifflin Co., 1930-1938.
Bernstorff, Count Johann-Heinrich. *Memoirs of Count Bernstorff.* Translated by Eric Sutton. New York: Random House, 1936.
Bülow, Prince Bernhard von. *Letters of Prince von Bülow.* Translated by Frederic Whyte. London: Hutchinson and Co., n.d.
_____. *Memoirs of Prince von Bülow.* Translated by Fritz August Voigt. 4 vols. Boston: Little, Brown and Co., 1931-1932.
Butt, Archie. *The Letters of Archie Butt.* Edited by Lawrence F. Abbott. Garden City: Doubleday, 1924.
Clark, Alan, ed. *'A Good Innings': The Private Papers of Viscount Lee of Fareham.* London: J. Murray, 1974.
Dugdale, E. T. S., ed. *German Diplomatic Documents, 1871-1914.* 4 vols. London: Methuen and Co., 1928-1931.
Gooch, George P., and Temperley, Harold, eds. *British Documents on the Origin of the War, 1898-1914.* 11 vols. London, 1926-1938.

Hart, Albert Bushnell, and Ferleger, Herbert Ronald, eds. *Theodore Roosevelt Cyclopedia*. New York: Roosevelt Memorial Association, 1941.

Hay, John. *Letters of John Hay and Extracts from Diary*. Edited by Henry Adams and Clara Louise Stone. 3 vols. New York: Gordian Press, 1969.

_____. *Life and Letters of John Hay*. Edited by William R. Thayer. 2 vols. Boston: Houghton Mifflin Co., 1916.

Holstein, Friedrich von. *The Holstein Papers: The Memoirs, Diaries, and Correspondence of Friedrich von Holstein, 1837-1909*. Edited by Norman Rich and H. M. Fisher. 4 vols. Cambridge: Cambridge University Press, 1955-1963.

Hayashi, Count Tadasu. *The Secret Memoirs of Count Tadasu Hayashi*. Edited by Andrew M. Pooley. New York: G. P. Putnam's Sons, 1915.

Laurier, Sir Wilfrid. *Life and Letters of Sir Wilfrid Laurier*. Edited by Oscar Douglas Skelton. 2 vols. New York: Century Co., 1922.

Lee, Arthur H., 1st Viscount of Fareham, ed. *Letters That Remain (Friendly and Otherwise) from the Postbag of Arthur and Ruth Lee, 1891-1941*. London: privately printed, 1941.

Lodge, Henry Cabot, ed. *Selections from the Correspondence of Theodore Roosevelt and Henry Cabot Lodge, 1884-1918*. 2 vols. New York: Charles Scribner's Sons, 1925.

Long, John Davis. *The Papers of John Davis Long, 1897-1904*. Edited by Gardner W. Allen. Boston: Massachusetts Historical Society, 1939.

Mahan, Alfred Thayer. *Letters and Papers of Alfred Thayer Mahan*. Edited by Robert Seager II and Doris D. Maguire. 3 vols. Annapolis, Md.: Naval Institute Press, 1975.

Pope, Sir Joseph. *Public Servant: The Memoirs of Sir Joseph Pope*. Edited and completed by Maurice Pope. Toronto: Oxford University Press, 1960.

Roosevelt, Theodore. *Letters from Theodore Roosevelt to Anna Roosevelt, 1870-1918*. Edited by Anna Roosevelt Cowles. New York: Charles Scribner's Sons, 1924.

_____. *Letters of Theodore Roosevelt*. Edited by Elting E. Morison and John M. Blum. 8 vols. Cambridge: Harvard University Press, 1951-1954.

_____. *The Works of Theodore Roosevelt*. Edited by Hermann Hagedorn. 20 vols. National Edition. New York: Charles Scribner's Sons, 1926.

_____. *The Writings of Theodore Roosevelt.* Edited by William H. Harbaugh. Indianapolis: Bobbs-Merrill Co., 1967.

Root, Elihu. *Addresses on International Subjects by Elihu Root.* Edited by Robert Bacon and James Brown Scott. Cambridge: Harvard University Press, 1916.

_____. *Miscellaneous Addresses by Elihu Root.* Edited by Robert Bacon and James Brown Scott. Cambridge: Harvard University Press, 1917.

Schoen, Freiherr von. *The Memoirs of an Ambassador by Freiherr von Schoen.* Translated by Constance Vesey. London: G. Allen and Unwin, 1922.

Seltsam, William H., comp. *Metropolitan Opera Annals.* New York: H. W. Wilson and Co., 1947.

Spring Rice, Sir Cecil. *Letters and Friendships of Sir Cecil Spring Rice.* Edited by Stephen Gwynn. 2 vols. Boston: Houghton Mifflin Co., 1929.

White, Andrew D. *The Diaries of Andrew D. White.* Edited by Robert Morris Ogden. Ithaca: Cornell University Press, 1959.

Wilhelm II, Kaiser of Germany. *The Kaiser's Speeches.* Translated and edited by Wolf von Schierbrand. New York: Harper and Bros., 1903.

_____. *Letters from the Kaiser to the Czar.* Edited by Isaac Don Levine and N. F. Grant. London: Hodder and Stoughton, 1920.

Witte, Count Serge. *The Memoirs of Count Witte.* Translated and edited by A. Yarmolinsky. Garden City, New York: Doubleday and Co., 1921.

Memoirs and Other Works by Contemporaries

Abbott, Lawrence F. *Impressions of Theodore Roosevelt.* Garden City, New York: Doubleday, Page and Co., 1919.

Adams, Brooks. *America's Economic Supremacy.* New York: Macmillan Co., 1900.

_____. *The Law of Civilization and Decay.* New York: Macmillan Co., 1895.

Amos, James E. *Theodore Roosevelt: Hero to His Valet.* New York: John Day, 1927.

Barry, David. *Forty Years in Washington.* New York: Beekman Publishers, 1974.

Bernstorff, Johann Heinrich Andreas Hermann Albrecht. *My Three Years in America.* New York: Charles Scribner's Sons, 1920.

Beveridge, Albert J. *The Russian Advance*. New York: Harper and Bros., 1904.

Bowen, Herbert W. *Recollections Diplomatic and Undiplomatic*. New York: F. H. Hitchcock, 1926.

Bülow, Prince Bernhard von. *Imperial Germany*. London: Cassell and Co., 1914.

Bunau-Varilla, Philippe. *From Panama to Verdun: My Fight for France*. Philadelphia: Dorance and Co., 1940.

_____. *The Great Adventure of Panama*. New York: Doubleday, 1920.

_____. *Panama: The Creation, Destruction, and Resurrection*. New York: McBride, Nast and Co., 1914.

Carnegie, Andrew. *Triumphant Democracy; or, Fifty Years March of the Republic*. New York: Charles Scribner's Sons, 1886.

Cromer, Lord Evelyn Baring, 1st Earl of. *Ancient and Modern Imperialism*. New York: Longman's Green, 1910.

_____. *Modern Egypt*. New York: Macmillan Co., 1908.

Cullom, Shelby M. *Fifty Years of Public Service*. Chicago: A. C. McClurg and Co., 1911.

Davis, Oscar King. *Released for Publication*. Boston: Houghton Mifflin Co., 1925.

Dewey, George. *Autobiography of George Dewey, Admiral of the Navy*. New York: Charles Scribner's Sons, 1913.

Eckardstein, Baron Hermann von. *Ten Years at the Court of St. James's, 1895-1905*. London: T. Butterworth, 1921.

Evans, Robley D. *An Admiral's Log*. New York: D. Appleton and Co., 1911.

Foster, John W. *Diplomatic Memoirs*. 2 vols. Boston: Houghton Mifflin Co., 1909.

Grey, Sir Edward. *Twenty-Five Years, 1892-1916*. 2 vols. New York: Frederick A. Stokes Co., 1925.

Griscom, Lloyd. *Diplomatically Speaking*. Boston: Little, Brown and Co., 1940.

Hale, William Bayard. *A Week in the White House with Theodore Roosevelt*. New York: G. P. Putnam's Sons, 1908.

Huntington-Wilson, Francis M. *Memoirs of an Ex-Diplomat*. Boston: Humphries, 1945.

Jusserand, Jean Jules. *What Me Befell*. New York: Houghton Mifflin Co., 1933.

Leary, John J. *Talks with T.R.* Boston: Houghton Mifflin Co., 1920.

Lee, Arthur H., 1st Viscount of Fareham. *A Good Innings and A Great Parnership, Being The Life Story of Arthur and Ruth Lee.* 3 vols. London: privately printed, 1939.

Long, John Davis. *The New American Navy.* New York: Outlook Co., 1903.

Longworth, Alice Roosevelt. *Crowded Hours.* New York: Charles Scribner's Sons, 1933.

Mahan, Alfred Thayer. *Armaments and Arbitration: Of the Place of Force in International Relations of States.* New York: Harper and Bros., 1912.

_____. *The Influence of Sea Power on World History.* Boston: Little, Brown and Co., 1906.

_____. *The Interest of America in Sea Power, Present and Future.* Boston: Little, Brown and Co., 1898.

_____. *The Problem of Asia and Its Effect Upon International Policies.* Boston: Little, Brown and Co., 1900.

_____. *Some Neglected Aspects of War.* Boston: Little, Brown and Co., 1907.

_____. "The True Significance of the Pacific Cruise." *Scientific American* 97 (17 December 1907):407.

Marcosson, Isaac F. *Adventures in Interviewing.* New York: John Lane Co., 1919.

Matthews, Franklin. *With the Battle Fleet.* New York: Huebsch, 1908.

Nicolson, Sir Harold G. *Portrait of a Diplomatist.* Boston: Houghton Mifflin Co., 1930.

Paleologue, Maurice. *Three Critical Years.* New York: Robert Speller and Sons, 1957.

Perdicaris, Ion H. "In Raisuli's Hands: The Story of My Captivity and Deliverance, May 18 to June 26, 1904." *Leslie's Monthly Magazine* 58 (September 1904): 510-22.

Phillips, William. *Ventures in Diplomacy.* Boston: Beacon Press, 1953.

Riis, Jacob A. *Theodore Roosevelt, Citizen.* Washington, D.C.: Johnson, 1904.

Robinson, Corinne Roosevelt. *My Brother Theodore Roosevelt.* New York: Charles Scribner's Sons, 1929.

Roosevelt, Kermit. *The Happy Hunting Grounds.* London: Hodder and Stoughton, 1920.

Roosevelt, Nicholas. *Theodore Roosevelt: The Man as I Knew Him.* New York: Dodd, Mead and Co., 1967.

Roosevelt, Theodore. *American Ideas and Other Essays.* New York: AMS Press reprint ed., 1969.

_____. *An Autobiography.* New York: Macmillan Co., 1919.

_____. "Municipal Administration: The New York Police Force." *Atlantic Monthly* 80 (September 1897):289–300.

_____. Series of articles on Latin America for *Outlook* magazine 105 (1913):695–98, 800–802, 837–41; 106 (1914): 183–88, 266–67, 304–307, 360–63, 409–411, 475–86, 582–89, 631–37, 697–713, 759–61, 800–803, 844–48, 919–35; 107 (1915):171–85, 255–57, 306–309.

_____, and Lodge, Henry Cabot. *Hero Tales from American History.* New York: Century Co., 1902.

Roosevelt, Theodore, Jr. *All in the Family.* New York: G. P. Putnam's Sons, 1929.

Root, Elihu. "The Ethics of the Panama Question." In *The Panama Canal and Our Relations with Colombia, Senate Documents,* vol. 27, 63rd Cong., 2nd sess. Washington, D.C.: Government Printing Office, 1914.

_____. *Speeches Incident to the Visit of Secretary Root to South America, July 4 to September 30, 1906.* Washington, D.C.: Government Printing Office, 1906.

Rosen, Baron Roman. *Forty Years of Diplomacy.* 2 vols. New York: Alfred A. Knopf, 1922.

Stirling, Rear Admiral Yates, Jr., USN. *Sea Duty.* New York: Putnam, 1939.

Storer, Maria. *Roosevelt, The Child.* London: W. Straker, 1921.

Strachey, Amy Simpson. *St. Loe Strachey: His Life and His Paper.* New York: Brewer and Warren, 1930.

Strachey, John St. Loe. *The Adventure of Living: A Subjective Autobiography.* New York: G. P. Putnam's Sons, 1922.

Straus, Oscar. *Under Four Administrations: From Cleveland to Taft.* Boston: Houghton Mifflin Co., 1922.

Tirpitz, Alfred Peter Friedrich von. *My Memoirs.* 2 vols. New York: Dodd, Mead and Co., 1919.

Vigilans Sed Aequus [pseud. of William Thomas Arnold]. *German Ambitions as They Affect Britain and the United States of America.* London: Smith, Elder and Co., 1903.

White, Andrew Dixon. *Autobiography.* 2 vols. New York: Century Company, 1965.

Wilhelm II, Kaiser of Germany. *My Early Life.* New York: Doran, 1926.

_____. *My Memoirs, 1878-1918.* London: Cassell and Co., 1922.
Witte, Emil. *Revelations of a German Attaché.* New York: Doran, 1916.

Newspapers and Magazines

Atlantic Monthly
New York Evening Post
New York Herald
New York Times
New York Tribune
North American Review
Outlook
Review of Reviews
Yale Review

SECONDARY WORKS

Doctoral Dissertations

Blazsik, Gloria. "Theodore Roosevelt's Far Eastern Policy and the T'ang Shao-yi Mission." Georgetown University, 1969.
Favell, Thomas Royden. "The Antecedents of Panama's Separation From Colombia." Fletcher School of Law and Diplomacy, 1951.
Ferguson, John H. "American Diplomacy and the Boer War." University of Pennsylvania, 1939.
Fletcher, William G. "Canal Site Diplomacy: A Study in American Political Geography." Yale University, 1940.
Greenberg, Irving. "Theodore Roosevelt and Labor, 1900-1918." Harvard University, 1960.
Hussey, Lyman. "Anglo-Canadian Relations During the Roosevelt Era, 1901-1908." University of Georgia, 1969.
Sellen, Robert. "Roosevelt and Wilson as World Politicians." University of Chicago, 1959.

Articles

Ameringer, C. D. "The Panama Lobby of Philippe Buneau-Varilla." *American Historical Review* 68 (January 1963):346-63.

Andrews, Avery Delano. "Theodore Roosevelt as Police Commissioner." *New York Historical Society Quarterly* 42 (April 1958): 117–41.

Bailey, Thomas A. "The Root-Takahira Agreement of 1908." *Pacific Historical Review* 9 (March 1940):19–35.

_____. "Theodore Roosevelt and the Alaska Boundary Settlement." *Canadian Historical Review* 18 (June 1937):123–30.

_____. "The World Cruise of the American Battleship Fleet, 1907–1909." *Pacific Historical Review* 1 (September 1932):389–423.

Blake, Nelson M. "Ambassadors at the Court of Theodore Roosevelt." *Mississippi Valley Historical Review* 42 (September 1955):179–206.

Blum, John Morton. "The Presidential Leadership of Theodore Roosevelt." *Michigan Alumnus Quarterly Review* 65 (6 December 1958):1–9.

Braisted, William R. "The Philippine Naval Base Problem, 1898–1909." *Mississippi Valley Historical Review* 41 (June 1954): 21–40.

_____. "The United States Navy's Dilemma in the Pacific, 1906–1909." *Pacific Historical Review* 26 (August 1957):235–44.

Brooks, Sydney. "The Voyage of the American Fleet." *Fortnightly Review* [London], O.S. 89 (February 1908):201–15.

Buell, R. L. "The Development of the Anti-Japanese Agitation in the United States." *Political Science Quarterly* 37 (December 1922):605–38.

Burton, David H. "Theodore Roosevelt and Egyptian Nationalism." *Mid-America* 41 (April 1959):88–103.

_____. "Theodore Roosevelt and His English Correspondents: The Intellectual Roots of the Anglo-American Alliance." *Mid-America* 53 (January 1971):12–34.

_____. "Theodore Roosevelt and His Correspondents: A Special Relationship." *Transactions of the American Philosophical Society,* n.s., vol. 63, pt. 2, 1973.

_____. "T.R.: Confident Imperialist." *Review of Politics* 23 (July 1961):356–77.

Chamberlain, Leander T. "A Chapter of National Dishonor." *North American Review* 195 (February 1912):145–74.

Clifford, John Gary. "Admiral Dewey and the Germans, 1903: A New Perspective." *Mid-America* 49 (July 1967):214-20.

Clymer, Kenton J. "Humanitarian Imperialism: David Prescott Barrows and the White Man's Burden in the Philippines." *Pacific Historical Review* 45 (November 1976):495-517.

Collin, Richard H. "Henry Pringle's Theodore Roosevelt: A Study in Historical Revisionism." *New York History* 52 (April 1971): 151-68.

Collins, George W. "The Lure of Morocco: A Sidelight on United States Economic and Foreign Policy, 1904-1912." *North Dakota Quarterly* 37 (Autumn 1969):25-42.

Cummins, Lejeune. "The Formulation of the 'Platt' Amendment." *The Americas* 23 (April 1967):370-89.

Cunliffe-Owen, Fritz. "The New British Ambassador." *Munsey's Magazine* 30 (1903-1904):513-15.

Davis, Harold E. "The Citizenship of Jon Perdicaris." *Journal of Modern History* 13 (December 1941):517-26.

Dennis, A. L. P. "John Hay." In Samuel Flagg Bemis, ed., *The American Secretaries of State and Their Diplomacy*, vol. 9, pp. 115-89. New York: Alfred A. Knopf, 1927-1929.

Dulles, Foster Rhea. "John Hay." In Norman Graebner, ed., *An Uncertain Tradition: American Secretaries of State in the Twentieth Century*, chap. 2. New York: McGraw Hill, 1961.

Eastman, Anthony F. "The Algeciras Conference, 1906." *The Southern Quarterly* 7 (January 1969):185-205.

Esthus, Raymond. "The Changing Concept of the Open Door, 1899-1910." *Mississippi Valley Historical Review* 46 (December 1959):435-54.

_____. "The Taft-Katsura Agreement: Reality or Myth." *Journal of Modern History* 31 (March 1959):46-51.

Etzold, Thomas H. "Protection or Politics? 'Perdicaris Alive or Raisuli Dead.'" *The Historian* 37 (February 1975):297-305.

Eyre, James K., Jr. "Russia and the American Acquisition of the Philippines," *Mississippi Valley Historical Review* 28 (March 1942):539-62.

Friedlander, Robert A. "A Reassessment of Roosevelt's Role in the Panamanian Revolution of 1903." *Western Political Quarterly* 14 (June 1961):535-43.

Garraty, John A. "Henry Cabot Lodge and the Alaskan Boundary Tribunal." *New England Quarterly* 24 (December 1951):469-94.

Godwin, Robert K. "Russia and the Portsmouth Peace Conference." *American Slavic and East European Review* 9 (December 1950):279–91.

Gordon, Donald C. "Roosevelt's 'Smart Yankee Trick.'" *Pacific Historical Review* 30 (November 1961):351–58.

Gow, Douglas R. "How Did the Roosevelt Corollary Become Linked to the Dominican Republic?" *Mid-America* 58 (October 1976):159–65.

Grantham, Dewey W., Jr. "Theodore Roosevelt in American Historical Writing, 1945–1960." *Mid-America* 43 (January 1961):3–35.

Greene, Fred. "The Military View of American National Policy, 1904–1940." *American Historical Review* 66 (January 1961):354–77.

Grenville, J. A. S. "Diplomacy and War Plans in the United States, 1890–1917." *Transactions of the Royal Historical Society,* series 5, vol. 11. pp. 1–21. London, 1961.

———. "Great Britain and the Isthmian Canal, 1898–1901." *American Historical Review* 61 (October 1955):48–69.

Hall, Luella J. "The Abortive German-American-Chinese Entente of 1907–1908." *Journal of Modern History* 1 (June 1929): 219–35.

———. "A Partnership in Peacemaking: Theodore Roosevelt and William II." *Pacific Historical Review* 13 (December 1944):390–411.

Hendrickson, Embert. "Root's Watchful Waiting in the Venezuelan Controversy." *The Americas* 23 (October 1966):115–29.

Hitchman, James H. "The Platt Amendment Revisited: A Bibliographical Survey." *The Americas* 23 (April 1967):343–69.

Holbo, Paul S. "Perilous Obscurity: Public Diplomacy and the Press in the Venezuelan Crisis, 1902–1903." *The Historian* 32 (May 1970):428–48.

———. "Perspectives on American Foreign Policy, 1890–1916: Expansion and World Power." *Social Studies* 58 (November 1967):246–56.

Johnson, Arthur M. "Theodore Roosevelt and the Navy." *United States Naval Institute Proceedings* 84 (October 1958):76–82.

Johnson, Rear Admiral Lucius W. "When T.R. Streamlined the Officers." *United States Naval Institute Proceedings* 78 (December 1952):1310–13.

Leuchtenburg, William E. "Progressivism and Imperialism: The Progressive Movement and American Foreign Policy,

1898-1916." *Mississippi Valley Historical Review* 39 (December 1952):483-504.

Lewis, Thomas T. "Franco-American Relations During the First Moroccan Crisis." *Mid-America* 55 (January 1973):21-36.

Livermore, Seward Wright. "American Naval Base Policy in the Far East, 1850-1914." *Pacific Historical Review* 13 (March 1944):113-35.

_____. "The American Navy as a Factor in World Politics, 1903-1913." *American Historical Review* 63 (July 1958): 863-79.

_____. "Battleship Diplomacy in South America, 1905-1925." *Journal of Modern History* 16 (March 1944):31-48.

_____. "Theodore Roosevelt, the American Navy, and the Venezuelan Crisis of 1902-1903." *American Historical Review* 51 (April 1946):452-71.

Luce, Clare Boothe. "Ever Hear of Homer Lea?" *Saturday Evening Post* 214 (7 and 14 March 1942).

Mallan, John P. "Roosevelt, Brooks Adams, and Lea: The Warrior Critique of the Business Civilization." *American Quarterly* 8 (Fall 1956):216-30.

Markowitz, Gerald E. "Progressivism and Imperialism: A Return to First Principles." *The Historian* 37 (February 1975):257-75.

May, Ernest R. "The Far Eastern Policy of the United States in the Period of the Russo-Japanese War: A Russian View." *American Historical Review* 62 (January 1957):345-51.

Miller, Jessie Ashworth. "The United States and Chinese Territorial Integrity, 1908." In Dwight E. Lee and George E. McReynolds, eds., *Essays in History and International Relations in Honor of George Hubbard Blakeslee*, pp. 233-56. Worcester, Mass.: Clark University Press, 1949.

Miller, Raymond C. "Theodore Roosevelt, Historian." In James Lea Cate and Eugene Anderson, eds., *Medieval and Historiographical Essays in Honor of James Westfall Thompson.* Chicago: University of Chicago Press, 1938.

Minger, R. E. "Taft's Missions to Japan: A Study in Personal Diplomacy." *Pacific Historical Review* 30 (August 1961): 279-94.

_____. "William H. Taft and the United States Intervention in Cuba in 1906." *Hispanic American Historical Review* 41 (February 1961):75-89.

Moore, John Bassett. "Santo Domingo and the United States." *Review of Reviews* 31 (March 1905):293-98.

Morton, Louis. "Army and Marines on the China Station: A Study in Military and Political Rivalry." *Pacific Historical Review* 29 (February 1960):51–73.

_____. "Military and Naval Preparations for Defense of the Philippines during the War Scare of 1907." *Military Affairs* 13 (Summer 1949):95–104.

Neu, Charles. "Theodore Roosevelt and American Involvement in the Far East." *Pacific Historical Review* 35 (November 1966):433–49.

Parks, E. Taylor, and Rippy, J. Fred. "The Galápagos Islands: A Neglected Phase of American Strategy and Diplomacy." *Pacific Historical Review* 9 (March 1940):37–45.

Parsons, Edward B. "The German-American Crisis of 1902–1903." *The Historian* 33 (May 1971):436–52.

_____. "Roosevelt's Containment of the Russo-Japanese War." *Pacific Historical Review* 38 (February 1969):21–43.

Patterson, John. "Latin-American Reactions to the Panama Revolution of 1903." *Hispanic American Historical Review* 24 (May 1944):342–51.

Penfield, W. L. "Anglo-German Intervention in Venezuela." *North American Review* 177 (July 1903):86–96.

Platt, D. C. M. "The Allied Coercion of Venezuela, 1902." *Inter-American Economic Affairs* 15 (Spring 1962):3–28.

Raat, William Dirk. "The Diplomacy of Suppression: Los Revoltosos, Mexico, and the United States, 1906–1911." *Hispanic American Historical Review* 56 (November 1976):529–50.

Rippy, J. Fred. "Antecedents of the Roosevelt Corollary." *Pacific Historical Review* 9 (September 1940):267–79.

_____. "British Bondholders and the Roosevelt Corollary of the Monroe Doctrine." *Political Science Quarterly* 49 (June 1934): 195–206.

_____. "The Initiation of the Customs Receivership in the Dominican Republic." *Hispanic American Historical Review* 17 (November 1937):419–57.

Robinson, Elwyn B. "Theodore Roosevelt: Amateur Historian." *North Dakota History* 25 (January 1958):5–13.

Schiff, Warren. "German Military Penetration into Mexico during the Late Diaz Period." *Hispanic American Historical Review* 39 (November 1959):568–79.

Scott, James Brown. "Elihu Root." In Samuel Flagg Bemis, ed., *The American Secretaries of State and Their Diplomacy*, vol. 9, pp. 193–282. New York: Alfred A. Knopf, 1927–1929.

Seed, Geoffrey. "British Reactions to American Imperialism Reflected in Journals of Opinion, 1898-1900." *Political Science Quarterly* 73 (June 1958):254-72.

_____. "British Views of American Policy in the Philippines Reflected in Journals of Opinion, 1898-1907." *Journal of American Studies* 2 (April 1968):49-64.

Sellen, Robert W. "Theodore Roosevelt: Historian with a Moral." *Mid-America* 41 (October 1959):223-40.

Snowbarger, W. E. "Pearl Harbor in Pacific Strategy, 1898-1908." *The Historian* 19 (May 1957):361-84.

Sontag, Raymond. "German Foreign Policy, 1904-1906." *American Historical Review* 33 (January 1928):278-301.

Spector, Ronald. "Roosevelt, the Navy, and the Venezuela Controversy: 1902-1903." *American Neptune* 32 (October 1972): 257-63.

Stein, Harry H. "Theodore Roosevelt and the Press: Lincoln Steffens." *Mid-America* 54 (April 1972):94-107.

Steinberg, Jonathan. "Germany and the Russo-Japanese War." *American Historical Review* 75 (December 1970):1965-86.

Steiner, Zara S. "Great Britain and the Creation of the Anglo-Japanese Alliance." *Journal of Modern History* 31 (March 1959):27-36.

Thornton, Harrison John. "Theodore Roosevelt." In William T. Hutchinson, ed., *The Marcus W. Jernegan Essays in American Historiography,* pp. 227-51. Chicago: University of Chicago Press, 1937.

Thorson, W. B. "American Public Opinion and the Portsmouth Peace Conference." *American Historical Review* 53 (April 1948):439-64.

_____. "Pacific Northwest Opinion on the Russo-Japanese War of 1904-1905." *Pacific Northwest Quarterly* 35 (October 1944):305-322.

Toth, Charles W. "Elihu Root." In Norman Graebner, ed., *An Uncertain Tradition: American Secretaries of State in the Twentieth Century,* chap. 3. New York: McGraw Hill, 1961.

Tuchman, Barbara W. "Perdicaris Alive or Raisuli Dead." *American Heritage* 10 (August 1959):18-21, 98-101.

Vagts, Alfred. "Hopes and Fears of an American-German War, 1870-1915." *Political Science Quarterly* 54 (December 1939):525-32.

Van Norman, Louis E. "Latin American Views of Panama and the Canal." *Review of Reviews* 29 (March 1904):334-37.

———. "President Roosevelt as Europe Sees Him." *Review of Reviews* 30 (September 1904):299–305.

Varg, Paul A. "The Myth of the China Market, 1890–1914." *American Historical Review* 73 (February 1968):742–58.

Vevier, Charles. "The Open Door, An Idea in Action, 1906–1913." *Pacific Historical Review* 24 (February 1955):49–62.

Washburn, Charles G., ed. "Memoir of Henry Cabot Lodge." *Proceedings of the Massachusetts Historical Society* (April 1925):324–76.

Williams, William A. "Brooks Adams and American Expansion." *New England Quarterly* 25 (June 1952):217–32.

Wright, T. P., Jr. "United States Electoral Intervention in Cuba." *Inter-American Economic Affairs* 13 (Winter 1959):50–71.

Books

Akagi, Roy Hidemichi. *Japan's Foreign Relations.* Tokyo: Hokuseido Press, 1936.

Alfonso, Oscar. *Theodore Roosevelt and the Philippines.* Quezon City: University of the Philippines Press, 1970.

Allen, H. C. *Great Britain and the United States.* New York: St. Martin's Press, 1955.

Amery, Julian S. *The Life of Joseph Chamberlain.* 4 vols. London: Macmillan and Co., 1932–1951.

Anderson, Eugene N. *The First Moroccan Crisis, 1904–1906.* Chicago: University of Chicago Press, 1930.

Andrew, Christopher. *Théophile Delcassé and the Making of the Entente Cordiale.* New York: St. Martin's Press, 1968.

Bailey, Thomas A. *America Faces Russia.* Reprint. Gloucester, Mass.: Peter Smith, 1964.

———. *The Art of Diplomacy.* New York: Appleton-Century-Crofts, 1968.

———. *A Diplomatic History of the American People.* Englewood Cliffs, N.J.: Prentice-Hall, 1974.

———. *Presidential Greatness.* New York: Appleton-Century-Crofts, 1966.

———. *Theodore Roosevelt and the Japanese-American Crises.* Reprint. Gloucester, Mass.: Peter Smith, 1964.

Barker, J. Ellis. *Modern Germany.* New York: Dutton, 1905.

Beale, Howard K. *Theodore Roosevelt and the Rise of America to World Power.* Baltimore: Johns Hopkins University Press, 1956.

Beisner, Robert L. *Twelve against Empire*. New York: McGraw Hill, 1968.

Beloff, Max. *The Great Powers*. London: George Allen and Unwin, 1959.

Bemis, Samuel Flagg, ed. *The American Secretaries of State and their Diplomacy, 1776-1925*. 18 vols. New York: Alfred A. Knopf, 1927-1929.

_____. *A Diplomatic History of the United States*. New York: Holt, 1936.

_____. *The Latin-American Policy of the United States*. New York: Norton, 1967.

Beringause, Arthur F. *Brooks Adams: A Biography*. New York: Alfred A. Knopf, 1955.

Bishop, Joseph B. *Charles Joseph Bonaparte*. New York: Charles Scribner's Sons, 1922.

_____. *The Panama Gateway*. New York: Charles Scribner's Sons, 1913.

_____. *Theodore Roosevelt and His Time Shown in His Letters*. 2 vols. New York: Charles Scribner's Sons, 1920.

Blum, John Morton. *The Republican Roosevelt*. New York: Atheneum, 1967.

Bourne, Kenneth. *Britain and the Balance of Power in North America, 1815-1908*. Berkeley: University of California Press, 1967.

Braisted, William R. *The United States Navy in the Pacific, 1897-1909*. Austin: University of Texas Press, 1958.

Brandenburg, Erich. *From Bismarck to the World War: A History of German Foreign Policy, 1870-1914*. Translated by Annie Elizabeth Adams. London: Oxford University Press, 1927.

Burns, E. Bradford. *The Unwritten Alliance*. New York: Columbia University Press, 1966.

Burton, David H. *Theodore Roosevelt*. New York: Twayne, 1972.

_____. *Theodore Roosevelt: Confident Imperialist*. Philadelphia: University of Pennsylvania Press, 1968.

Callcott, Wilfrid H. *The Caribbean Policy of the United States, 1890-1920*. Baltimore: Johns Hopkins Press, 1942.

Campbell, Alexander E. *Great Britain and the United States, 1895-1903*. London: Longmans, 1960.

Campbell, Charles S., Jr. *Anglo-American Understanding, 1898-1903*. Baltimore: Johns Hopkins Press, 1957.

Challener, Richard D. *Admirals, Generals, and American Foreign Policy, 1898-1914*. Princeton: Princeton University Press, 1973.

Chapman, Charles E. *A History of the Cuban Republic.* New York: Macmillan Co., 1927.

Charnwood, Lord Godfrey Rathbone Bensen, 1st Baron of. *Theodore Roosevelt.* Boston: Atlantic Monthly Press, 1922.

Chessman, G. Wallace. *Governor Theodore Roosevelt.* Cambridge: Harvard University Press, 1965.

_____. *Theodore Roosevelt and the Politics of Power.* Boston: Little, Brown and Co., paperback ed., 1969.

Chung, Han-Kyung. *The Oriental Policy of the United States.* New York: Fleming H. Revell Co., 1919.

Clinard, Outten J. *Japan's Influence on American Naval Power, 1897–1917.* Berkeley: University of California Press, 1947.

Clyde, Paul H. *International Rivalries in Manchuria, 1689–1922.* Columbus: Ohio State University Press, 1928.

Clymer, Kenton J. *John Hay: The Gentleman as Diplomat.* Ann Arbor: University of Michigan Press, 1975.

Cohen, Warren I. *America's Response to China.* New York: John Wiley and Sons, 1971.

Cornwell, Elmer. *Presidential Leadership of Public Opinon.* Bloomington: Indiana University Press, 1965.

Cortissoz, Royal. *Life of Whitelaw Reid.* 2 vols. New York: Charles Scribner's Sons, 1921.

Croly, Herbert. *Willard Straight.* New York: Macmillan Co., 1925.

Curti, Merle. *The Growth of American Thought.* 3rd ed. New York: Harper and Row, 1964.

Davis, Calvin DeArmond. *The United States and the Second Hague Peace Conference.* Durham, N.C.: Duke University Press, 1976.

Davis, Kenneth. *FDR: The Beckoning of Destiny.* New York: G. P. Putnam's Sons, 1972.

DeConde, Alexander, and Rapaport, Armin, eds. *Essays Diplomatic and Undiplomatic of Thomas A. Bailey.* New York: Appleton-Century-Crofts, 1969.

Defoe, John W. *Clifford Sifton in Relation to His Times.* Toronto: Macmillan Co., 1931.

Dennett, Tyler. *Americans in Eastern Asia.* New York: Macmillan Co., 1922.

_____. *John Hay: From Poetry to Politics.* New York: Dodd, Mead and Co., 1934.

_____. *Roosevelt and the Russo-Japanese War.* Reprint. Gloucester, Mass.: Peter Smith, 1959.

Dennis, A. L. P. *Adventures in American Diplomacy.* New York: E. P. Dutton and Co., 1928.

Digby, Kenelm. *The Broadstone of Honour.* 5 vols. London: B. Quartich, 1876–1877.

Dugdale, Blanche Elizabeth Campbell. *Arthur James Balfour, First Earl of Balfour.* 2 vols. New York: G. P. Putnam's Sons, 1937.

Dulles, Foster Rhea. *America's Rise to World Power.* New York: Harper and Row, paperback ed., 1955.

Duncan, Bingham. *Whitelaw Reid.* Athens, Ga.: University of Georgia Press, 1975.

Duval, Miles P. *Cadiz to Cathay.* Palo Alto: Stanford University Press, 1940.

Einstein, Lewis. *Roosevelt: His Mind in Action.* Boston: Houghton Mifflin Co., 1930.

Ekirch, Arthur A., Jr. *The Civilian and the Military: A History of the American Antimilitarist Tradition.* Colorado Springs, Colo.: Ralph Myles, paperback ed., 1972.

_____. *Ideas, Ideals, and American Diplomacy.* New York: Appleton-Century-Crofts, paperback ed., 1966.

Esthus, Raymond A. *Theodore Roosevelt and the International Rivalries.* Waltham, Mass.: Ginn-Blaisdell, paperback ed., 1970.

_____. *Theodore Roosevelt and Japan.* Seattle: University of Washington Press, 1967.

Falk, Edwin A. *Fighting Bob Evans.* New York: J. Cape and H. Smith, 1931.

Fisher, H. A. L. *James Bryce.* 2 vols. New York: Macmillan Co., 1927.

Fitzgibbon, Russell H. *Cuba and the United States, 1900–1935.* Menasha, Wis.: George Banta Publishing Co., 1935.

Garraty, John A. *Henry Cabot Lodge.* New York: Alfred A. Knopf, 1953.

Gatewood, Willard B., Jr. *Theodore Roosevelt and the Art of Controversy.* Baton Rouge: Louisiana State University Press, 1970.

Gauss, Christian. *The German Emperor as Shown in His Public Utterances.* New York: Charles Scribner's Sons, 1915.

Gelber, Lionel M. *The Rise of Anglo-American Friendship: A Study in World Politics, 1898–1906.* London: Oxford University Press, 1938.

Graber, Doris Appel. *Crisis Diplomacy: A History of United States Intervention Policy.* Washington, D.C.: Public Affairs Press, 1959.

Graebner, Norman A., ed. *An Uncertain Tradition: American Secretaries of State in the Twentieth Century.* New York: McGraw Hill, 1961.

Graybar, Lloyd J. *Albert Shaw of the Review of Reviews: An Intellectual Biography.* Lexington: University of Kentucky Press, 1974.

Grenville, John A. S. *Lord Salisbury and Foreign Policy: The Close of the Nineteenth Century.* London: University of London Press, 1964.

_____, and Young, George Berkeley. *Politics, Strategy, and American Diplomacy.* New Haven: Yale University Press, 1966.

Griswold, A. Whitney. *The Far Eastern Policy of the United States.* New Haven: Yale University Press, 1938.

Grunder, Garel A., and Livezey, William E. *The Philippines and the United States.* Norman: University of Oklahoma Press, 1951.

Hagedorn, Hermann. *Leonard Wood.* New York: Harper and Bros., 1931.

_____. *The Life of Theodore Roosevelt.* London: Harrap, 1919.

Hale, Oron James. *Germany and the Diplomatic Revolution, 1904-1906.* Philadelphia: University of Pennsylvania Press, 1931.

_____. *Publicity and Diplomacy, with Special Reference to England and Germany, 1890-1914.* New York: Appleton-Century-Crofts Co., 1940.

Hall, Luella J. *The United States and Morocco, 1776-1956.* Metuchen, N.J.: Scarecrow Press, 1971.

Halle, Louis J. *Dream and Reality.* New York: Harper and Row, 1958.

Harbaugh, William H. *The Life and Times of Theodore Roosevelt.* New York: Collier, paperback ed., 1967.

Harrington, F. H. *God, Mammon, and the Japanese: Dr. Horace N. Allen and Korean-American Relations, 1884-1905.* Madison: University of Wisconsin Press, 1944.

Hart, Robert A. *The Great White Fleet.* Boston: Little, Brown and Co., 1965.

Healey, David F. *The United States in Cuba, 1898-1902.* Madison: University of Wisconsin Press, 1963.

Heindel, Richard H. *The American Impact on Great Britain, 1898-1914.* Philadelphia: University of Pennsylvania Press, 1940.

Herwig, Holger. *Politics of Frustration: The United States in Ger-*

man Naval Planning, 1889-1941. Boston: Little, Brown and Co., 1976.

Hill, Howard C. *Roosevelt and the Caribbean*. Reprint. New York: Russell and Russell, 1965.

Hishida, Seiji. *Japan among the Great Powers*. London: Longmans, Green and Co., 1940.

Hofstadter, Richard. *The American Political Tradition*. New York: Random House, Vintage Books, 1948.

_____. *Social Darwinism in American Thought, 1860-1915*. Philadelphia: University of Pennsylvania Press, 1944.

Houghton, Walter. *The Victorian Frame of Mind, 1830-1870*. New Haven: Yale University Press, 1957.

Howe, Mark A. DeWolfe. *George von Lengerke Meyer, His Life and Public Services*. New York: Dodd, Mead and Co., 1920.

Hunt, Michael H. *Frontier Defense and the Open Door: Manchuria in Chinese-American Relations, 1895-1911*. New Haven: Yale University Press, 1973.

Hurwitz, Howard. *Theodore Roosevelt and Labor in New York State, 1880-1900*. New York: Columbia University Press, 1943.

Iriye, Akira. *Pacific Estrangement: Japanese and American Expansion, 1879-1911*. Cambridge: Harvard University Press, 1972.

Jessup, Philip C. *Elihu Root*. 2 vols. New York: Dodd, Mead, and Co., 1938.

Johnson, Willis Fletcher. *Four Centuries of the Panama Canal*. New York: Henry Holt and Co., 1906.

Jones, Chester L. *The Caribbean Since 1900*. New York: Prentice Hall, 1936.

Kawakami, Kiyoshi K. *American-Japanese Relations*. New York: Fleming H. Revell Co., 1912.

Kneer, Warren G. *Great Britain and the Caribbean, 1901-1913: A Study in Anglo-American Relations*. East Lansing: Michigan State University Press, 1975.

Knight, Melvin M. *The Americans in Santo Domingo*. New York: Vanguard Press, 1928.

Knox, Dudley W. *A History of the United States Navy*. New York: G. P. Putnam's Sons, 1936.

LaFeber, Walter. *The Panama Canal*. New York: Oxford University Press, 1977.

Langley, Lester D. *The Struggle for the American Mediterranean: United States-European Rivalry in the Gulf-Caribbean, 1776-1904*. Athens: University of Georgia Press, 1975.

Lee, Sir Sidney. *King Edward VII.* 2 vols. New York: Macmillan Co., 1925–1927.

Leopold, Richard W. *Elihu Root and the Conservative Tradition.* Boston: Little, Brown and Co., 1954.

Livezey, William E. *Mahan on Sea Power.* Norman: University of Oklahoma Press, 1947.

Lockmiller, David A. *Magoon in Cuba: A History of the Second Intervention, 1906–1909.* Chapel Hill: University of North Carolina Press, 1938.

McCain, William D. *The United States and the Republic of Panama.* Durham, N.C.: Duke University Press, 1937.

McCullough, David. *Path between the Seas: The Creation of the Panama Canal, 1870–1914.* New York: Simon and Schuster, 1977.

Mack, Gerstle. *The Land Divided.* New York: Alfred A. Knopf, 1944.

McKee, Delber L. *Chinese Exclusion versus the Open Door Policy, 1900–1906: Clashes over China Policy in the Roosevelt Era.* Detroit: Wayne State University Press, 1977.

Malcolm, Sir Ian. *Lord Balfour, A Memory.* London: Macmillan and Co., 1930.

Marder, Arthur J. *The Anatomy of British Sea Power: A History of British Naval Policy in the Pre-Dreadnought Era, 1880–1905.* New York: Alfred A. Knopf, 1940.

―――. *Fear God and Dread Nought.* 3 vols. Cambridge: Harvard University Press, 1952–.

―――. *From the Dreadnought to Scapa Flow: The Royal Navy in the Fisher Era, 1904–1919.* 5 vols. New York: Oxford Press, 1961–1970.

Martin, Edward S. *The Life of Joseph Hodges Choate.* 2 vols. New York: Charles Scribner's Sons, 1920.

Matthews, Joseph J. *George W. Smalley.* Chapel Hill: University of North Carolina Press, 1973.

May, Ernest R. *American Imperialism: A Speculative Essay.* New York: Atheneum, 1968.

―――. *Imperial Democracy: The Emergence of America as a Great Power.* New York: Harcourt, Brace and World, 1961.

Millett, Allan Reed. *The Politics of Intervention: The Military Occupation of Cuba, 1906–1909.* Columbus: Ohio State University Press, 1968.

Miner, Dwight C. *The Fight for the Panama Route.* New York: Columbia University Press, 1940.

Monger, George W. *The End of Isolation: British Foreign Policy, 1900-1907.* London: T. Nelson, 1963.

Morison, Elting E. *Admiral Sims and the Modern American Navy.* Boston: Houghton Mifflin Co., 1942.

Mott, Frank Luther. *A History of American Magazines, 1885-1905.* 5 vols. Cambridge: Harvard University Press, 1957.

Mowry, George W. *The Era of Theodore Roosevelt.* New York: Harper and Row, paperback ed.: 1962.

Munro, Dana. *Intervention and Dollar Diplomacy in the Caribbean, 1900-1921.* Princeton: Princeton University Press, 1964.

_____. *The United States and the Caribbean Area.* Boston: World Peace Foundation, 1934.

Neu, Charles. *An Uncertain Friendship: Theodore Roosevelt and Japan, 1906-1909.* Cambridge: Harvard University Press, 1967.

Nevins, Allan. *Henry White: Thirty Years of American Diplomacy.* New York: Harper and Bros., 1930.

Newton, Lord Thomas. *Lord Lansdowne: A Biography.* London: Macmillan and Co., 1929.

Nish, Ian H. *The Anglo-Japanese Alliance: The Diplomacy of Two Island Empires, 1894-1907.* London: Athlone Press, 1966.

O'Gara, Gordon C. *Theodore Roosevelt and the Rise of the Modern Navy.* Princeton: Princeton University Press, 1943.

Osgood, Robert Endicott. *Ideals and Self-Interest in America's Foreign Relations.* Chicago: University of Chicago Press, Phoenix Books, 1965.

Parks, E. Taylor. *Colombia and the United States, 1765-1934.* Durham: Duke University Press, 1935.

Perkins, Bradford. *The Great Rapprochement.* New York: Atheneum, 1968.

Perkins, Dexter. *A History of the Monroe Doctrine.* Boston: Little, Brown, and Co., paperback ed., 1963.

_____. *The Monroe Doctrine, 1867-1907.* Reprint. Gloucester, Mass.: Peter Smith, 1966.

_____. *The United States and the Caribbean.* Cambridge: Harvard University Press, 1947.

_____. *Yield of the Years.* Boston: Little, Brown and Co., 1969.

Perris, George Herbert. *Germany and the German Emperor.* New York: Henry Holt and Co., 1912.

Peterson, Harold E. *Diplomat of the Americas: A Biography of William L. Buchanan, 1852-1909.* Albany: State University of New York Press, 1976.

Pollard, James E. *The Presidents and the Press.* New York: Macmillan Co., 1947.

Porter, Charles W. *The Career of Théophile Delcassé.* Philadelphia: University of Pennsylvania Press, 1936.

Pratt, Fletcher. *A Compact History of the United States Navy.* New York: Hawthorn Books, Inc., 1962.

Pringle, Henry. *Theodore Roosevelt.* New York: Harcourt, Brace and World, paperback ed., 1956.

Puleston, William D. *The Life and Work of Alfred Thayer Mahan.* New Haven: Yale University Press, 1939.

Putnam, Carleton. *Theodore Roosevelt: The Formative Years, 1858-1886.* New York: Charles Scribner's Sons, 1958.

Rappaport, Armin. *The Navy League of the United States.* Detroit: Wayne State University Press, 1962.

Rhodes, James Ford. *The McKinley and Roosevelt Administrations, 1897-1909.* New York: Macmillan Co., 1922.

Rich, Bennett Milton. *The Presidents and Civil Disorder.* Washington, D.C.: Brookings Institute, 1941.

Rich, Norman R. *Friedrich von Holstein.* 2 vols. Cambridge: Cambridge University Press, 1965.

Rippy, J. Fred. *The Caribbean Danger Zone.* New York: G. P. Putnam's Sons, 1940.

Romanov, Boris A. *Russia in Manchuria, 1892-1906.* Ann Arbor: University of Michigan Press, 1952.

Schieber, Clara E. *The Transformation of American Sentiment toward Germany, 1870-1914.* Reprint. New York: Russell and Russell, 1973.

Schriftgiesser, Karl. *The Gentleman from Massachusetts: Henry Cabot Lodge.* Boston: Little, Brown and Co., 1944.

Scott, James B. *Robert Bacon, Life and Letters.* Garden City, N.Y.: Doubleday, Page and Co., 1923.

Spector, Ronald. *Admiral of the New Empire: The Life and Career of George Dewey.* Baton Rouge: Lousiana State University Press, 1974.

Sprout, Harold, and Sprout, Margaret. *The Rise of American Naval Power.* Princeton: Princeton University Press, 1936.

Stevenson, Elizabeth. *Henry Adams.* New York: Macmillan Co., 1955.

Street, Julian. *The Most Interesting American.* New York: Century Co., 1915.

Sykes, Sir Percey M. *The Right Honourable Sir Mortimer Durand.* London: Cassell and Co., 1926.

Tansill, Charles C. *Canadian-American Relations, 1875-1911*. New Haven: Yale University Press, 1943.

Thayer, William R. *Theodore Roosevelt*. Boston: Grosset and Dunlap, 1919.

Tompkins, Pauline. *American-Russian Relations in the Far East*. New York: Macmillan Co., 1949.

Trani, Eugene. *The Treaty of Portsmouth: An Adventure in American Diplomacy*. Lexington: University of Kentucky Press, 1969.

Treat, Payson J. *Diplomatic Relations between the United States and Japan, 1895-1905*. Palo Alto: Stanford University Press, 1938.

Trevelyan, George M. *Grey of Fallodon: The Life and Letters of Sir Edward Grey, Afterwards Viscount Grey of Fallodon*. Boston: Houghton Mifflin Co., 1937.

Uribe, Antonio José. *Colombia y los Estados Unidos de América*. Bogotá: Impreta nacional, 1931.

Usher, Roland G. *Pan-Germanism*. New York: Grosset and Dunlap, 1914.

Vagts, Alfred. *Deutschland und die Vereinigten Staaten in der Weltpolitik*. 2 vols. New York: Macmillan Co., 1935.

Varg, Paul A. *The Making of a Myth*. East Lansing: Michigan State University Press, 1968.

_____. *Missionaries, Chinese and Diplomats*. Princeton: Princeton University Press, 1958.

_____. *Open Door Diplomat: The Life of W. W. Rockhill*. Urbana: University of Illinois Press, 1952.

Vevier, Charles. *The United States and China, 1906-1913*. New Brunswick, N.J.: Rutgers University Press, 1955.

Wagenknecht, Edward C. *The Seven Worlds of Theodore Roosevelt*. New York: Longmans, Green and Co., 1958.

Weber, Ralph E. *As Others See Us*. New York: Holt, Rinehart and Winston, 1972.

Weinberg, Albert K. *Manifest Destiny*. Chicago: Encounter, paperback ed., 1963.

Welles, Sumner. *Naboth's Vineyard: The Dominican Republic, 1844-1924*. New York: Payson and Clarke, 1928.

White, John A. *The Diplomacy of the Russo-Japanese War*. Princeton: Princeton University Press, 1964.

Wile, Frederic W. *Men around the Kaiser*. Philadelphia: Lippincott, 1913.

Williamson, Samuel R., Jr. *The Politics of Grand Strategy: Britain and France Prepare for War, 1904-1914.* Cambridge: Harvard University Press, 1969.

Young, Kenneth. *Arthur James Balfour: The Happy Life of the Politician, Prime Minister, Statesman, and Philosopher, 1848-1930.* London: G. Bell and Sons, 1963.

Zabriskie, Edward. *American-Russian Rivalry in the Far East, 1895-1914: A Study in Diplomacy and Power Politics.* Philadelphia: University of Pennsylvania Press, 1946.

Index

DATE DUE

APR 6 '89			